CHURCH

IN THE MAKING

Alan K. Scotland

ISBN-13: 978-1514858059

ISBN-10: 1514858053

Part One:

The Legacy of the Old Testament

Part Two:

The Church of The New Testament

INTRODUCTION

THE AUTHENTIC CHURCH:

WHATEVER THE GENERATION

The progressive revelation of the Church is discernible throughout the scriptures. Unfortunately, in the name of modernism, and humanity's constant desire to formulize everything, we are in danger of blurring the true concept of Church. It does not hold true that any attempt to trace the meaning of Church is an attempt to shrink back into primitiveness. God, in His revealed intention, is committed to the continuation of His purpose. He is true to His Word and ethical in His dealings with His creation. Contrary to some beliefs, there is sufficient evidence in the Word of God for us to see His purposes for all generations.

Christendom today is challenged by the constant pressure to have updated programs and "business strategies," to manufacture what is believed to be "The Twenty-First Century Church." This fundamentally reflects a partial and inadequate revelation of Church as revealed in the Bible.

God has made clear His intention and He remains committed to the continuation of His purpose. The basis of His dealings with mankind is relational; He is a God of Covenant. The legacy of the Old Testament is rich in revelation about God's covenantal relationship with His people. Too often leaders are quick to move forward with their own human endeavors to "manufacture" a contemporary Church. It is essential that any attempt in leading and teaching in the Church ought not to neglect divine revelation from God's Word about His intended covenantal strategy for His people. Leadership must also seek empowerment through the Holy Spirit to equip for the task, not just for today, but for generations to come.

This book seeks to navigate believers and students of the Word through the heritage of the Church as revealed in the scriptures. It is designed to be a practical tool to engage students and challenge leadership teams as they study the true meaning of Church and God's divine strategy for His people. My hope is to encourage readers to delve deeper into God's unchanging covenant purposes for their lives and for the Church today.

This book is divided into two parts. The first part maps out the Old Testament legacy of the Church, and illustrates the covenant relationship between God and His people: His persistence and perseverance, coupled with His atoning sacrifice in Jesus, culminating in the New Covenant. Part two looks more closely at the New Testament, in particular the book of Acts, aligning God's Word with the empowerment of His Holy Spirit's strategy for the Church.

CHAPTER ONE

THE ECCLESIA:
THE "CALLED OUT" PEOPLE OF GOD

The word *ecclesia*, the most common word used to denote "Church" in the New Testament, expresses a distinctive characteristic about God's people. It is derived from the combination of two other words: *ek* (out) and *kalleo* (to call).[1] God's people are a people who have been called out or set apart for both covenant relationship with Him and responsibility towards others. The word "covenant" means a binding agreement made between two parties. In a biblical context, God draws up the terms of agreement with His people Israel – the new covenant being the summation of all the covenants in the Old Testament. Peter used this description of God's people when he expressed the nature of the call of God in the life of the believing community: "But you are a chosen people, a royal priesthood, a holy nation, a people belonging to God, that you may declare the praises of him who called you out of darkness into his wonderful light".[2] This sense of being called out and set apart is essential to the Hebrew and biblical understanding of what it is to be God's holy people.

---

[1] The word *ecclesia* derives from the Septuagint (the Greek translation of the Old Testament), although it is also regularly used in classical Greek. There are two words used in the Hebrew (original) Old Testament: *ēdhāh* (congregation) and *qāhāl* (assembly). These two words are distinct, yet they would be used together in the phrase 'the assembly of the congregation' (Exodus. 12:6; Num. 14:5; Jeremiah. 26:17). In the following example, the Greek (Septuagint) translation of the Old Testament retains this sense:

"I was almost in utter ruin. In the midst of the assembly and congregation."

After the return of God's people from the Babylonian and Greek exile, the word for "assembly" came to be used to embrace "the assembled congregations," especially for Greek speaking Jews, hence the dominant usage of the Greek word *ecclesia*.

[2] 1 Peter 2:9

Paul uses the same phrase as Peter in 1 Corinthians 1:9, adding that the calling *out* is simultaneously a calling *into* fellowship (*koinōnia*) with his Son, Jesus Christ. It follows, then, that believers are also called into fellowship with those who bear His name, to serve them and to bless them.

Another connotation of the Greek *koinōnia* carries the meaning that believers are called out to "participate" or "take part in" God's plan for His people. So, although joined with Christ as individuals, through baptism in water and in the Spirit, Christians are also incorporated; that is, made part of the body of Christ which is the Church. The most profound expression of this togetherness is our participation in the Lord's Supper, Holy Communion, or the Eucharist (thanksgiving). Here believers gather together to celebrate their new life in Christ, a corporate unity represented by the one loaf of bread. The reference to the 'body' is metaphorical and not literal. It is picture language that is used to establish truth. The Apostle Paul takes this up in 1 Corinthians 12:27-31 when he equates the Church to a body with different members. This is an attempt to establish commitment to Christ, coupled with responsibility to one another. All too easily this significance is missed.

Community is the context in which believers are to "work out their salvation" as God works in them to His good purpose. Caring for God's people is not only the responsibility of pastors,[3] but of all God's people.[4] Paul taught that the Church are members of one another,[5] who are to care for one another,[6] being devoted to one another in love,[7] just as Jesus had

---

[3] Acts 20:28

[4] Galatians 6:10

[5] Romans 12:5; Ephesians 4:25

[6] 1 Corinthians 12:25

[7] Romans 12:10

commanded His disciples.[8]

The Church is called out for:
Covenant relationship with God
And responsibility towards others

This other-centeredness is to be *the* defining characteristic of the Church, both in attitudes towards one another and in attitudes toward the rest of the world. As William Temple[9] so aptly expressed it, "The Church is the only club that exists for the sake of its non-members". Yet if the Church cannot care for one another, what does it have to offer the world? It is precisely for this reason that the bible stresses the importance of caring first for the Church. The Church is to show proper respect for everyone, but especially the brotherhood of believers,[10] and to do good to all people, but especially to those who belong to the family of believers.[11] Christians do not have the choice to opt out of fellowship or the subsequent responsibility.

An Ethical Stance: A People of the Covenant

The reason for this lack of choice is that believers are *covenanted* in baptism to follow through on a commitment to Christ and to His Church. God's love is freely and graciously given – as Graham Buxton puts it, "He neither negotiates a deal with us, nor is there any 'small print' at the bottom of the page".[12] God's commitment to mankind is absolute and His promise

---

[8] John 15:9 -17
[9] William Temple (1881-1944) was the 98th Archbishop of Canterbury.
[10] 1 Peter 2:17
[11] Galatians 6:10
[12] G. Buxton, *Dancing in the Dark: The Privilege of Participating in the Ministry of Christ* (Carlisle, Paternoster, 2001), p. 50.

irrevocable. A gift of grace is made effectual by faith alone, and the expression and authenticating mark of that faith is obedience. This is the essential argument of the Epistle of James. The absolute and unqualified nature of God's commitment to mankind, and its supremely incarnational manifestation in Christ, demands a correspondingly committed response. Being covenanted to God, means that the believer has bound him or herself to a life of obedience in the fellowship of the Spirit.

In the contemporary Western situation, the Church suffers greatly for its confusion over the nature of this commitment. An overemphasis on the freedom of grace and the offer of a ready pardon for sins has cheapened discipleship. Dietrich Bonheoffer exposed these tendencies in his devastating critique of the Church, *The Cost of Discipleship*. Prevailing twentieth-century evangelical understandings of salvation, with their anti-nominal[13] stress on conversion without the need for baptism or any other "works"[14] have further obscured the importance of Church commitment. There is no such thing as an independent Christian who has no need of fellowship; the identity of the Christian is inextricably tied to the Church. Gordon Fee, in his book *Paul, The Spirit and The People of God*, remarks: "the third-century Church father, Cyprian, had it right: there is no salvation outside the Church, because God is saving a people for His name, not a miscellaneous, unconnected set of individuals."[15] Just as humans are born into and raised within families, so it is with the new birth and adoption into God's family. God has indicated that it is as part of a community that He intends mankind to be saved.

---

[13] Free from law approach, Anti = against, Nominal = law

[14] See D. Willard's *The Divine Conspiracy* (Harper Collins, 1998) where he states that the most telling thing about the contemporary Christian is that he or she has no compelling sense that the understanding of, and conformity with the clear teachings of Christ is of any vital importance to their life, and certainly not that it is essential.

[15] G. Fee, *Paul, the Spirit and the People of God* (Peabody, Hendrickson Publishers, 1996), p. 64.

The natural and proper place for the expression of the covenantal commitment is, of course, the local Church; this is what the New Testament would seem to suggest. The most common use of the word *ecclesia* is in reference to local gatherings of believers.[16] However, in the twenty-first century, many technological advances have increased mobility and offered greater choice, which has led to a cultural trend of non-commitment. In many mainline Churches today, the figures for weekly attendance are thought to give a more accurate picture of a congregation's commitment than those figures for baptisms. Many believers are more comfortable seeing themselves as part of a diverse, but nonetheless unified, movement or as part of a tradition or broader fellowship, allowing for greater confessional mobility than the average denominational Church. A developing of Christian programming in the media becomes an added enticement for some to see themselves as part of an electronic or digital Church. However, the modern means of communication ought to supplement the existence of local Church mentality and not encourage an allegiance to a program at the cost of responsible engagement in the Church as a whole.

In contrast, the biblical picture is of a people who, although grievously unfaithful to their calling, are clear about the terms of the covenant and the nature of the commitment expected of them. The concept of covenant is so basic to the Hebrew worldview that in many of the key texts the actual word[17] hardly seems to need explicit mention. E.P. Sanders ventures to say that it is "the fundamental nature of the covenant conception which largely accounts for the relative scarcity of appearances of the term 'covenant' in rabbinic literature."[18]

---

[16] See 1 Corinthians 1:2; Galatians 1:2; 2 Thessalonians 1:1

[17] *Berith* in Hebrew

[18] E. P. Sanders, *Paul and Palestinian Judaism* (London, SCM Press, 1977), p. 420.

A Special Legacy not to be Forgotten

The basis of the covenant was, of course, the promise to the Patriarchs: Abraham, Isaac and Jacob. It was extended to Joseph and his sons (Ephraim and Manasseh), and to Moses, with a promise of grace and of blessing, which saw its initial fulfillment in the deliverance of their descendants out of the slavery of Egypt.[19] Yahweh later added attendant responsibilities in the form of a large body of statutes and laws to be observed.[20] For subsequent generations, the Torah came to be understood as the covenant document, which was, as N.T. Wright explains, "grounded upon the faithfulness of Israel's God, provided for His people the way of life by which they should express their unswerving fidelity to Him."[21]

The drama that is Israel's history can indeed be rightly understood only when this essential concept is grasped. In the book of Deuteronomy, the last words of Moses, as the people stood on the threshold of the Promised Land, are a series of addresses: two poems and a song.[22] These are a celebration of God's faithfulness as a covenant-keeping God. The central part of the book is a rehearsal of the people's obligation to live a life of obedience and faith. This book of the covenant proved to be of seminal importance for the Deuteronomic histories: to Jeremiah, as he laments Israel's unfaithfulness; and to Hosea, whose savage prophecies of judgment are mitigated only by his portrayal of a gracious and compassionate God who has bound Himself by covenant:

---

[19] Exodus 2:24

[20] Exodus 18:16

[21] *The New Testament and the People of God* (London: SPCK, 1997), p. 261.

[22] For poems, see the structure of Deuteronomy Chapters 12:13-19; - written on an ABC: CBA pattern. "Frequently used by authors and editors of antiquity to structure diverse materials." (Page 392 *The Jewish Study Bible*, Oxford Press, 2004.) The Song of Moses reference to poem 32:1-27; 32:44; 33:1-29: - More clearly outlined in the Septuagint as a poem. (p. 444)

How can I give you up, Ephraim?

　　How can I hand you over, Israel?

How can I treat you like Admah?

　　How can I make you like Zeboiim?

My heart is changed within me;

　　all my compassion is aroused.

I will not carry out my fierce anger,

　　nor will I turn and devastate Ephraim.

For I am God, and not man –

　　the Holy One among you.[23]

God's commitment to His covenant and His love for the people of the covenant, according to its provisions, cause Him to repent of the anger that had been kindled against them. This is *hesed*, God's covenantal love - a Hebrew word that conveys a steadfast loyalty and a true and heartfelt concern.

This is in spite of, or perhaps even because of, Israel's propensity to sin. Significantly, Moses knows from the outset that Israel will experience the curse as well as the blessing. The inevitability of disobedience and exile[24] is offset, however, by Moses' prophetic conviction that their return to the Lord will once more bring prosperity, a return from exile to the Promised Land, the renewal of the covenant, circumcision of the heart, and a deeper obedience to the law.[25]

The prophets of the exile take up this theme of forgiveness and restoration, but when the return is complete, in the light of the glorious prophecies of Isaiah,[26] Jeremiah[27] and Ezekiel,[28] it seems something of an

---

[23] Hosea 11:8–9

[24] Deuteronomy 28:15-68; 29:16-28; 31:16-21, 27, 29

[25] Deuteronomy 30: 1-10

[26] Isaiah 40:1-2

anticlimax. Israel was still under foreign rule and the glory of the Lord had not returned to the temple. The Jews of the second-temple period concluded that though they had returned to the land, these themes of forgiveness and restoration were still, in every sense, what mattered. It was never seriously doubted that the Lord would one day decisively deliver Israel from its alienation. This conviction was an assumed part of Israel's worldview – but just how this would come about was now open to question.

A wrestling with the meaning of the covenant characterizes the apocryphal writings of the second-temple period. Covenant theology was, as N.T. Wright puts it, "the air breathed by the Judaism of this period".[29] It is hardly surprising that the first Christians interpreted the coming of Christ from the standpoint of the covenant. The letter to the Hebrews could not be more explicit that the blood that He shed atoned for sin fully, perfectly and sufficiently – once for all[30] – thus inaugurating a New Covenant and a new and living way to God. For the author of the letter to the Hebrews, this New Covenant both fulfils and supersedes the covenant with Abraham, as spoken of by the prophet Jeremiah:

"The time is coming," declares the Lord,
    "when I will make a new covenant
with the house of Israel
    and with the house of Judah.
It will not be like the covenant
    I made with their forefathers

---

[27] Jeremiah 31:31, 34, 38, 40
[28] Ezekiel 36:24-25, 28
[29] ibid. p. 262.
[30] Hebrews 7:27; 10:2

when I took them by the hand

to lead them out of Egypt,

because they did not remain faithful to my covenant,

And I turned away from them,

declares the Lord.

This is the covenant I will make with the house of Israel

after that time, declares the Lord.

I will put my laws in their minds

and write them on their hearts.

I will be their God,

and they will be my people.

No longer will a man teach his neighbour,

or a man his brother, saying, 'Know the Lord,'

because they will all know me,

from the least of them to the greatest.

For I will forgive their wickedness

and will remember their sins no more." [31]

Further Study

1   *Why did God assemble a nation, rather than call out individuals?*

2   *Why do you think we in the West have emphasized individual experience and not the corporate nature of Church life?*

---

[31] Hebrews 8:8-12 and Jeremiah 31:31-34

CHAPTER TWO

THE CRAFTING OF THE CHURCH

Believers do have to be careful in handling such a legacy of information, revelation and functional commitment on God's part. Every generation needs to recognize and understand the basis on which God operates. He is committed to establish a people of every generation, whose faith is informed and whose commitment is in line with His ultimate intentions for the world.

The biblical narrative, which is largely retrospective, provides the backdrop of the shaping of a society within the paradigm of family. Such a theme comes through in the story of the patriarchs; Abraham himself was considered the father of a nation.

The Covenant with the Patriarchs

It was always God's purpose to prepare for Himself a people for His name, for His own possession and glory among the nations. This can be seen in the promise to the patriarchs. The essence of the promise was that Abram's offspring would one day become a great nation,[1] that the blessing of God upon them would make them a blessing to all the peoples of the earth,[2]

---

[1] Genesis 12:2

[2] Genesis 12:3

and that God would lead them to a new land.[3] When this nation, mightily delivered from the bondage of Egypt, is finally assembled and given their trust before the mountain in the desert, it is in accordance to this covenant with Abraham. They are a people called out and set apart for covenant relationship with God and responsibility for others.

The search for the meaning of the Church can be traced as far back as Genesis. Ellicott put it so well when referring to such records as being of the highest interest "…not only because it is probably the oldest writing in the world, but also because it is the foundation upon which the whole bible is built. The Jewish, as well as the Christian traditions, have their roots in this book, and there is no doctrine of Christianity, however advanced, which is not to be found, at least in outline therein".[4] As Baxter states, "Genesis is the seed plot of the whole Bible".[5]

The Covenant with Adam and Eve and the Fall from Grace

The covenant with the patriarchs, which provides the framework for understanding *ecclesia,* the people of the covenant, cannot be understood without reference to the covenant God makes with Adam, to Adam and Eve's betrayal, and to the curse that follows.

God had intended that Adam and Eve should be fruitful and that their progeny should always enjoy His benevolent presence and provision. Adam is blessed with a charge[6] that is addressed both to him personally and to his descendants: "Be fruitful and increase in number; fill the earth and subdue it." As bearer of the image, he who is Lord of all creation; it is

---

[3] Genesis 12:7

[4] D. D. Ellicott, *A Bible Commentary for English Readers, vol.1* (UK, Cassell and Co, 1897).

[5] S. Baxter, *Explore the Book* (Grand Rapids, Zondervan Publishing Hourse)

[6] Genesis 1:28

---

given in trust and in perpetuity for his good use, for his stewardship, as both gift and responsibility. As later scripture details, it is God's will that man should multiply and fill the earth. He envisaged a human society that is both diverse and unified, inclusive of all, truly universal, and whose relationships are characterized by a loving mutuality.[7] "The chief end of man is to glorify God and to enjoy Him forever and *together*."[8] Human beings are made to be together, for the worship and enjoyment of God.

All the essential elements of the later covenants are present in the covenant with Adam. There is the promise of blessing, the stipulation of covenant responsibility, and the condition for obtaining the blessing.[9] God was present with Adam and Eve in the garden[10] and held forth the promise of eternal life, of deep and unending fellowship with Him, signified by the tree of life in the midst of the garden.[11] The commandment given in the garden is spoken of later by Paul as that "which promised eternal life."[12]

Adam and Eve are given the garden as a gift and its fruits are theirs to enjoy. But Adam breaks covenant with God, and he and his offspring are cursed. They choose instead to eat of the one tree that was forbidden them, and in the transgression of the commandment, they know evil. God's curses rain down upon them; the very ground beneath their feet is cursed and they are at enmity.

Even as His curse comes down upon them, He gives a glimmer of hope to keep them from despair. In the words to the serpent He speaks of a

---

[7] See especially Revelation 5:9; 7:9-10; 19:6-9; 21:1-7

[8] The Shorter Westminster Catechism answer number 1: "Man's chief and highest end is to glorify God, and fully to enjoy him forever." (The shorter Westminster Catechism is composed of 107 questions written in the 1640s by English and Scottish divines.)

[9] Genesis 1:28

[10] Genesis 3:8

[11] Genesis 2:9

[12] Romans 7:10

future deliverance: in the fullness of time God will raise up a deliverer from their offspring who shall crush the head of the serpent.[13]

The Covenant with Noah

By the time of Noah, God is overcome with grief and "regrets" the creation of man.

> "The Lord saw how great man's wickedness on the earth had become, and that every inclination of the thoughts of his heart was only evil all the time. The Lord was grieved that He had made man on the earth, and His heart was filled with pain. So the Lord said, 'I will wipe mankind, whom I have created, from the face of the earth – men and animals, and creatures that move along the ground, and birds of the air – for I am grieved that I have made them'."[14]

It is at this point that the work of redemption begins. It is the "gathering out" of the world a remnant for the sake of the world's salvation. Only Noah is righteous. "Blameless among the people of his time,"[15] he alone walks with God. God determines to destroy every living thing under the heavens, sparing only Noah and his offspring, with whom He promises to re-establish His covenant. Two of every kind of animal are chosen and enter the ark of salvation. As the waters of the deluge of God's wrath subside, creation is renewed. As in baptism, the old is washed clean away and a new creation emerges. God reaffirms His covenant with Adam, and Noah and his sons and daughters inherit the procreation and

---

[13] Genesis 3:15

[14] Genesis 6:5-7

[15] Noah was a "type" of Christ! His name means "rest", "comfort". Noah was considered righteous before God (2 Peter 2:5).

ruling role of Adam and Eve.

But sin is not eradicated; its degenerative effect has merely been slowed. As the descendants of Noah move eastward, they come to the plains of Shinar and there determine to build a tower reaching to the heavens as a monument to the great achievement of their civilization. They seek a name for themselves, forgetting the name of the Lord. And so they are scattered over the face of the whole earth, their speech confused, the fellowship of the human race broken.[16]

The Covenant with Abraham

Out of the migrations that followed the dispersion of Babel, a nomadic family from Ur of the Chaldeans finally comes to settle in Haran in the north of Canaan. From this undistinguished, unknown family, God calls Abraham to be the father of all who believe:

> "The LORD had said to Abram, 'Leave your country, your people and your father's household and go to the land I will show you.
> I will make you into a great nation
>   and I will bless you;
> I will make your name great,
>   and you will be a blessing.
> I will bless those who bless you,
>   and whoever curses you I will curse;
> and all peoples on earth
>   will be blessed through you'."[17]

---

[16] Genesis 11:6-9
[17] Genesis 12:1-3

God promises to lead Abram to a new land, a land that he and his offspring would come to see as their God-given home. He vows to bless Abram and his "seed" and promises that they will be a blessing to all the nations. Abram must only believe God: "Leave . . . I will show you."[18]

Abram and his family journey to the land of Canaan where the patriarch builds altars to the Lord – first at the great tree of Moreh[19] and then between Bethel and Ai,[20] where he calls on the name of the Lord, the God of the covenant.

Subsequent chapters show that even this great patriarch of faith is human. In the land God has promised him, he finds only wasted crops and famine and is forced to take refuge in Egypt.[21] In fear of Pharaoh, his faith fails and he abandons Sarai to the Pharaoh's harem. He shows great promise by allowing Lot the best of the land promised to his own descendants, and is encouraged by a reaffirmation of the Lord's promise.[22] He steps up again in his bold confession of faith before the king of Sodom,[23] but when he looks at his own aging and his apparently barren wife, his faith fails, turning instead first to adoption as a way beyond this impasse[24] and then to a concubine.[25] After thirteen years, Abram appears penitent: the Lord appears to him again and Abram falls face down, humbled by God Almighty's faithfulness.[26] In spite of Abram's lack of faith, the covenant is reaffirmed again and again as the Lord impresses

---

[18] Genesis 12:1

[19] Genesis 12:6-7

[20] Genesis 12:8

[21] Genesis 12:10-20

[22] Genesis 13

[23] Genesis 14, especially verses 22-24

[24] Genesis 15:3

[25] Genesis 16

[26] Genesis 17

upon him the irrevocable nature of His promise.[27] The Lord gives Abram and Sarai new names: Abraham, the father of many, and Sarah, the mother of nations.

The Significance of Circumcision

The sign and seal of this covenant of faith is circumcision. Thereafter, circumcision would symbolize inclusion into the covenant community, established by the initiative of God's grace. In circumcision Abraham and his sons are humbled in their flesh as their manhood is brought under authority. The people of God were to be meek – their strength restrained, their drives harnessed – that they might be a great nation with a great name among the nations. All this was for the furtherance of God's Kingdom in which strength is made perfect in weakness. Significantly, Jesus' interpretation of who the true sons of Abraham are reveals that it is the meek who inherit the earth.[28]

Circumcision was to be an outward sign of an inward grace. Although "made with hands," circumcision represented a heart of deep obedience. Moses clearly understands that this is what is meant by the rite when he admonishes the people of Israel in the plains of Moab, and calls for them to circumcise their hearts and to be hardened against God no more.[29] Elsewhere he appears to have been given prophetic intuition into the future consummation of the promise inherent in the rite: "The Lord your God will circumcise your hearts and the hearts of your descendants, so that you may love Him with all your heart and with all your soul, and

---

[27] Genesis 13:14-17; 15:1, 5, 7, 18-21; 17:4-8; 18:18-19; 22:17-18
[28] Matthew 5:5
[29] Deuteronomy 10:16

live."[30] This hope is taken up again by Jeremiah,[31] and appears to be what he envisaged under the covenant of consummation.[32] Paul concludes that a "man is not a Jew if he is only one outwardly, nor is circumcision merely outward and physical. No, a man is a Jew if he is one inwardly; and circumcision is circumcision of the heart, by the Spirit."[33]

Further Study

Read John 8:31–41

1   *Who, according to Jesus, are the true sons of Abraham?*

2   *Do you think that the Jews understood the covenant of circumcision? How would you describe their attitude?*

The Faith of Abraham

In the matter of circumcision Abraham proves himself true, but he is soon tested again.   This time, fearing danger, he allows Sarah to enter Abimelech's harem.[34] Once more, in spite of Abraham's weakness, God is faithful to His promise and Sarah is protected.

At last Isaac is born. Abraham and Sarah have waited for many years. With the birth of the child, Abraham's faith has come to maturity. When God demands the child's life, Abraham is meek and submissive in his

---

[30] Deuteronomy 30:6
[31] Jeremiah 4:4
[32] Jeremiah 31:33
[33] Romans 2:28-9
[34] Genesis 20

obedience. He has witnessed wonders and is past doubting.[35] Abraham believes God and it is "credited to him as righteousness."[36] Ultimately, it is faith that seals the covenant. This is how Abraham comes to be called the father of the faithful: not by blood, but by faith expressing itself in obedience.[37]

For Paul, the justification of the Gentiles by faith and the consummation of the covenants in Jesus Christ, are implicit in the promise to Abraham: "All the nations will be blessed through you."[38] Indeed, Jesus came under the judgment of God for this purpose, "in order that the blessing given to Abraham might come to the Gentiles through Jesus Christ, so that by faith we might receive the promise of the Spirit."[39]

Further Study

Jesus clearly intends that the blessing of Abraham should be extended to all the peoples of the earth. Read Matthew 28:16–20. Here Jesus gathers the disciples for the great commission. In the light of Jesus' earlier rebuke to the unbelieving Jews who protested that Abraham was their father (John 8:39), identify one of the defining marks of the true Church.

What does this passage tell us about the continuity of God's purpose for the people of the covenant?

---

[35] Genesis 22:1-18

[36] Genesis 15:6; 22; cf. also Romans 4:3

[37] John 8:31-41; cf. also James 2:20-24

[38] Galatians 3:8

[39] Galatians 3:14

Continuity of Purpose – the Reaffirmation of the Covenant

The covenant, or promise, with Abraham is reaffirmed with each succeeding generation, so that first Isaac[40] and then Jacob[41] likewise become fathers of the nation of Israel. By the time the story of Joseph's trial in the land of Egypt is told, the covenant with the fathers looms larger than ever. When Joseph makes himself known to his desperate brothers, he uses the following words: "God sent me ahead of you to preserve for you a remnant on earth and to save your lives by a great deliverance. So then, it was not you who sent me here, but God."[42] The Creator God has found a way of redeeming His creation: He has chosen, and called out, a people, in the line of this very family, through whom He is acting and will act, even as He has promised. As Joseph explains later in the story, when his brothers grow fearful of him upon the death of their father, God's good purpose cannot be thwarted. "Do not be afraid. Am I in the place of God?" he says. "You intended to harm me, but God intended it for good to accomplish what is now being done, the saving of many lives."[43] Nothing falls without the providence of God, who "works all things for the good of those who love Him and who have been called according to His good purpose."[44]

The promised clan is delivered from the famine of Canaan and, for a time at least, enjoys the favor of Egypt. With their father's blessing, they inherit the promise to the patriarchs[45] and, in spite of the hardship that lies before them, they multiply until, in God's time, they are poised to become the promised nation.

---

[40] Genesis 26:2-5, 24
[41] Genesis 28:10-15 and 35:11-13
[42] Genesis 45:7-8
[43] Genesis 50:19-20
[44] Romans 8:28
[45] Genesis 48

What makes the covenant with Abraham so important in understanding what it is to be part of the people of God?

CHAPTER THREE

THE SHAPING OF A NATION:
THE COVENANT WITH MOSES

The pattern of salvation is discernible in the narratives of Noah, Abraham, Jacob and Joseph, and that of being "called out" is most strikingly evident here in the story of the Exodus. It is through the Exodus and the Mosaic Covenant that the nature of Israel's responsibility becomes clearer. This event, God's greatest act of salvation in the Old Testament, coupled with the giving of the Law, shaped Israel's understanding of itself as God's chosen people more than any other, and is also paradigmatic for believers today. The Israelites are delivered from the bondage of Egypt, they pass through the (proto-baptismal) waters of the Red Sea,[1] and they are gathered before the mountain of the Lord. Now, by law and statute, they are set apart as a people for His name to enjoy the blessing and favor of God, and for covenant responsibility toward others.

The Exodus

In the midst of their great suffering, at the moment when many would have given up hope of deliverance, when the persecution had reached the

---

[1] Exodus 14:23; Hebrews 11:29

terrible depths of infanticide,[2] God remembers His covenant with Abraham and determines that now is the time for the gathering of His people. "The Israelites groaned in their slavery and cried out, and their cry for help because of their slavery went up to God. God heard their groaning and He remembered His covenant with Abraham, with Isaac and with Jacob".[3]

From among the people, He raises up a deliverer, Moses, revealing Himself to him as the God of his fathers – of Abraham, Isaac and Jacob – and reaffirming the covenant He had made with them.[4]

Moses falters, knowing that he is inadequate to the task before him, but is reassured that the Lord will be with him by God revealing Himself as Yahweh, the present one, in accordance with the promise to the patriarchs. Reminiscent of His promise to Abram, the Lord says to Moses, "Go . . . and I will be with you." It is by faith that believers take hold of the promise and by obedience discover its truth.[5]

Although Moses is obedient in carrying the Lord's word to Pharaoh, he is spurned: "Who is the Lord that I should obey Him and let Israel go? I do not know the Lord and I will not let Israel go".[6] Pharaoh's denial of the Lord is simultaneously a denial of the covenant and a refusal to recognize Israel as a nation. In the plagues that follow, the Lord enacts His judgments upon the gods of Egypt and proves that He alone is Lord of all the earth.[7] The Nile River, sacred for its associations with the gods Khnum, Hapi and Osiris, is turned to blood.[8] The goddess Heqt, represented by a

---

[2] Exodus 1:15
[3] Exodus 2:23-4
[4] Exodus 3:6-10
[5] John 8:31-2
[6] Exodus 5:2
[7] Exodus 9:29; 12:12
[8] Exodus 7:14-24

frog, is humiliated when Pharaoh is forced to set the time for Moses to pray an end to the revolting plague.[9] The sky god, Nut, is impotent to intervene when the hail comes crashing down upon them.[10] Isis and Seth, gods of the harvest, are overwhelmed.[11] The sun god, Re, can do nothing to lift the heavy blanket of darkness that covers all Egypt for three days.[12] Yet, in all the places where the Israelites lived, there is light.[13] As Paul was later to express it, speaking of the holy calling of the Church: "What fellowship can light have with darkness?"[14]

The Israelites are clearly differentiated from the Egyptians, most significantly in God's final judgment: the killing of the firstborn of all Egypt on the night of the Passover.[15] The children of Israel are spared; the blood of the sacrifice, God's gracious provision for their deliverance, daubed upon their doorframes as a sign of the promise, shields them from the wrath of the Lord. As a people, they are once again set apart for covenant relationship with God. Not one of them is lost. They leave in haste, with the Egyptians urging them on for fear of the great calamity that had befallen them.[16]

The Lord keeps vigil over Israel "to bring them out of Egypt" and all the tribes are brought safely to Succoth.[17] On the day of their deliverance the sons of all Israel are consecrated to the Lord.[18] As one people they cross

---

[9] Exodus 8:1-15, especially verses 8-11

[10] Exodus 9:13-35

[11] Exodus 10:12-15

[12] Exodus 10:21-9. Also see J. Davis, *Moses and the Gods of Egypt* (Grand Rapids, Baker, 1971)

[13] Exodus 10:23

[14] 2 Corinthians 6:14

[15] Exodus 11:1 – 12:30

[16] Exodus 12:31-6

[17] Exodus 12:37-42, especially verses 40-42

[18] Exodus 13:1-16

the sea "with a wall of water on their right and on their left."[19] Together they witness the drowning of an army.

> "And when the Israelites saw the great power the Lord displayed against the Egyptians, the people [together] feared the Lord and put their trust in Him and in Moses His servant."[20]

A People of God's Word, Possessing a Polemic - The Law

God delivers Israel out of the bondage of Egypt for covenant relationship with Him.[21] At Sinai He gathers His people to Himself on "the day of the *qähäl* (assembly)."[22] With the giving of the Law, He impresses upon them the responsibilities of belonging to God, and so they become a nation. "Now if you obey me fully and keep my covenant, then out of all nations you will be my treasured possession."[23]

Israel is to be set apart and defined by its adherence to this covenant. The nation of Israel exists only as a people in covenant with the Lord – the covenant is what gives the nation its very identity – and breaking covenant with God will thus lead to the paradox of Israel being no longer Israel, as defined by biblical parameters.

---

[19] Exodus 14:23
[20] Exodus 14:31; brackets and contents mine
[21] Exodus 19:3-6
[22] cf. Acts 7:38
[23] Exodus 19:5

The Nature of God's Covenant Commitment

Comparisons with other ancient Near Eastern treaties give a better understanding of the nature of this covenant. Some such treaties were unilateral and involved a reward for loyalty being given by the king virtually without condition.[24] Others, such as the Hittite king-vassal treaties, as Albert Baylis describes them, "always started with an *identification of the king* who was extending the covenant. This was followed by a listing of the *gracious actions and provisions* that the king had given in the past. This, of course, would call for a response of gratitude and loyalty. The *requirements* that follow are those that the covenant names as the appropriate, grateful response."[25]

Although this latter form would seem to resemble more closely the pattern of Exodus 20, the covenant established with Israel differs from both of these in one important aspect: Israel's covenant is a covenant with Yahweh. So, although this covenant has a conditional aspect, "the purpose of God to redeem a people to Him makes it certain that these conditions shall be met"[26], the history of Israel proves that, ultimately, the promise is neither a reward for loyalty nor dependent upon it for its continuing validity. But this certainty does not relieve Israel of its obligations, since the covenant surely required the loving commitment of both parties.[27] Although Yahweh expects loyalty from Israel, He has bound Himself to the people in such a way as to obligate Himself to the keeping of the covenant regardless of their obedience. Only disowning their inheritance, a

---

[24] See Ancient Near East treaties and contracts. Akkadian – Hittite treaty – version: Kub, III, 14.

[25] *From Creation to the Cross* (Grand Rapids, Zondervan, 1996), p. 123. Baylis cites G. E. Mendenhall as the first to recognize this parallel and cites K. A. Kitchen's *The Bible in Its World* (Downers Grove, Intervarsity, 1977), pp. 79–85, as a good introduction to the subject.

[26] O. Palmer Robertson, *The Christ of the Covenants* (Phillipsburg, Presbyterian and Reformed Publishing Co., 1980), p. 247.

[27] Exodus 6:5;

complete denial of the covenant-God's existence, could provoke His abandonment of them. This distinction is given profound expression in the trustworthy saying of oral tradition, quoted by Paul in his second letter to Timothy: "... if we endure, we will also reign with Him. If we disown Him, He will also disown us; if we are faithless, He will remain faithful, for He cannot disown Himself."[28] Such a saying could only originate with a people whose worldview was pregnant with the idea of covenant. More than this, in the sovereignty of God, given the nature of His commitment, it would have been almost impossible for the Jews of this period to conceive of His disowning His chosen people. Although there are hints of the possibility in Jesus' rhetoric to the Jews in John 8:37-59, for Paul "God's gifts and His call are irrevocable."[29]

A People Set Apart

At Sinai, Yahweh makes His dwelling in the midst of Israel, giving them the command that they must now "be holy, for I am holy."[30] In Leviticus 20:26, Yahweh's purpose is clear: "You are to be holy to Me because I, Yahweh, am holy, and I have set you apart from the nations to be My own." Israel is to act in accordance with its special status, or election. "Although the whole earth is mine, you will be for me a Kingdom of priests and a holy nation."[31] They are a people called out and set apart for covenant relationship with God and responsibility for others.

The Law is given in ever-widening circles. The Ten Commandments

---

[28] 2 Timothy 2:12-13
[29] Romans 11:29
[30] Leviticus 11:44-45; 19:2; 20:7
[31] Exodus 19:5-6

come first[32] and summarize the rest of the decrees, statutes and ordinances that make up the remainder of the nation's body of law. The contours of Yahweh's vision of a just society are drawn in what is referred to as The Book of the Covenant.[33] The Israelites are to be a People of the Book. These statutes are revealed as all the more remarkable when set beside other law codes of the Ancient Near East.[34] Next are the laws pertaining to tabernacle worship,[35] and, finally, the regulations concerned with maintaining Israel's separate and distinct identity as God's chosen people.[36] [37]

The essential message of the Ten Commandments, the principles that are expanded upon in the remainder of the Pentateuch, is that Israel is first to be faithful to God, and then to be faithful to one another.[38] Jesus, however, emphasizes more profoundly that to be faithful, one must first love: "If you love me, you will obey what I command."[39] Thus the most important of the commandments for Jesus is the love of God and neighbor.[40]

A People in Need of Grace

Jesus knows that outward obedience is short-lived, and, as such, love quickly grows cold. Just as Peter, who, although confident of his own

---

[32] Exodus 20:1-17

[33] Exodus 20:22 – 23:19

[34] A term used of Christians by Muslim people and Jews. In Arabic it is "Followers of the Holy books" Quran 5:15

[35] Exodus 25–40; continued in Leviticus 1–10

[36] Leviticus 11 to the end; Numbers 5–8, 15, 19, 28–30

[37] Baylis, *From Creation to the Cross* (Grand Rapids, Zondervan, 1996) pp. 124–130.

[38] Exodus 20:1-17

[39] John 14:15

[40] Mark 12:28-31; cf. Deuteronomy 6:4-5 and Leviticus 19:18

loyalty,[41] discovers his own need for the strengthening intercession of Christ, so the other disciples will also need that intercession.[42] Intercession makes up for what is lacking in the flesh or because of sin, and allows an unholy people to enjoy the presence and favor of God.

For the Israelites and, as discussed later in a different way for Christians, this is the purpose of priesthood. The priests stand in the gap, bridging the divide between holy Yahweh and His unclean people. Thus the book of Leviticus contains explicit and special provision for how they are to maintain ritual purity.[43]

The means of this grace is sacrifice. The sacrifices prescribed in the Old Testament[44] function sacramentally, as windows on the divine, enabling the worshiper to grasp something of the holiness, the moral otherness, of God. The performance of these rituals effects a transformation in the life of the believing community. The primary function of the system of sacrifices was to provide a means of restoring the covenant relationship when the fellowship between God and His people had been broken as a result of sin. The sacrifice is a gift, freely offered by the worshiper as an indication of his or her commitment to the covenant, but also as a necessary expiation for sin if communion is to be restored.[45]

The Substitution for Sin

When the covenant relationship was broken because of a transgression, the

---

[41] John 13:34-8 and Luke 22:24-34, especially verses 31-34

[42] John 14:15-17

[43] See Leviticus, especially chapters 21–22

[44] Detailed in the book of Leviticus, especially chapters 1–7

[45] R. B. Dillard and T. Longman III, *An Introduction to the Old Testament* (Leicester, Apollos, 1995), p. 77. See also G. Wenham's *The Book of Leviticus, New International Commentary on the Old Testament* (Grand Rapids, Eerdmans, 1979), pp. 25–6.

penitent could offer a substitution; a sacrifice would take the punishment on his behalf. The stated purpose of sacrifice in Hebrews – that without the shedding of blood there can be no forgiveness[46] – is difficult for the modern mind to fathom, but it is fundamentally about justice. There can be no forgiveness without justice, and for justice to be done a price must be paid by the transgressor that fits the crime. It is evident that one cannot keep the covenant as a whole without obeying its parts, and so to be guilty of transgression in part is to hold the whole in contempt. Yahweh would have been just in instituting one punishment for all sins, but instead He provided a means of atonement. The essential idea is enshrined for us in the principle of "life for life." Truly, but for priestly intercession, "the wages of sin is death."[47]

Essential to the expiatory[48] shedding of blood then is the concept of cost. Although, in a sense, Yahweh provides the sacrifice, it is nonetheless costly for the worshiper who must give up the animal to ritual slaughter and consumption by the priests, except in the case of the special grace of the fellowship offering.[49] This sacrifice and the burning of that which remained conveyed the idea that the blessing of Yahweh is worth far more than the benefit to be had from the care or butchery of this animal. Of course, it hardly needs to be added that the attempt at adequacy or parity ultimately only serves to highlight God's grace; nothing can adequately express the gratitude of the believer who has been spared a death sentence.

---

[46] Hebrews 9:22

[47] Romans 6:23

[48] Atoning

[49] Leviticus 23:19, 7:11-34; sometimes referred to as "peace offering."

A Holy God Dwelling in the Midst of Israel

The sacrificial system centered on the tabernacle or "tent of meeting." The purity laws, often of special relevance to the priests but generally for all Israel,[50] functioned to remind Israel of the holiness of God and of the privilege of His dwelling in their midst. When the glory of the Lord fills the tabernacle,[51] it is in fulfillment of the promise to Moses; indeed their deliverance was for this very purpose, "that I might dwell among them."[52]

In Deuteronomy, God's presence is often expressed through His Name (Deut 12:11), which functions to remind the people of His ownership and dominion. Dillard and Longman comment that this usage functions to "affirm the very real presence of God in the fullness of His character and covenantal commitment to those on whom He had set that name."[53]

The Church in the Desert

God was already showing great patience with Israel. While Moses is on the mountain receiving instruction on how the tabernacle is to be constructed and ornamented, the people make themselves an idol and an orgy of pagan revelry ensues. "They made an idol in the form of a calf. They brought sacrifices to it and held a celebration in honor of what their hands had made."[54] God threatens to withdraw from Israel; they may enter the land promised to them but He will not go with them.[55] Moses knows that without His presence among them, they will be just as the other nations:

---

[50] See Leviticus 11–17

[51] Exodus 40:34-5

[52] Exodus 29:45-46

[53] R. B. Dillard and T. Longman III, *An Introduction to the Old Testament* (Leicester, Apollos, 1995), p. 103.

[54] Acts 7:41

[55] Exodus 33:3

"If your Presence does not go with us, do not send us up from here. How will anyone know that you are pleased with me and with your people unless you go with us? What else will distinguish me and your people from all the other people on the face of the earth?"[56] The Lord relents but determines that before Israel may come into its inheritance, the people must learn to follow His presence, trusting themselves to their God and to the mediator of the covenant.

It is forty years before God deems that Israel is ready to take possession of the Promised Land. Forty years of bitterness and anger, of chastisement and rebuke, before they have begun to understand the faithfulness of the Lord and what is required of them by the covenant. An entire generation perishes in the wilderness and are denied the promised rest because of their disobedience and unbelief.[57]

The people are rebellious and slow to learn, but God does not abandon them. Israel inherits the land as a gift of grace and stewardship from the Lord.[58] God is faithful to His promise to their forefathers.

Further Study

Read Numbers 11

In the wilderness, God tests the heart of Israel and Israel is repeatedly found to be stubborn, "stiff-necked" and wayward. Israel "murmurs" against Moses and Aaron, but the Lord treats this as rebellion against Himself. Nothing is more destructive for a community and its leadership than gossip. Gossip undermines trust, the building of which is the purpose of testing.

---

[56] Exodus 33:15-16
[57] Numbers 14:20-24; Deuteronomy 1:29-36; Hebrews 3:15-19
[58] Deuteronomy 4:21; 12:9; 15:4; 19:10

The Pattern of Exodus in the New Testament

The Exodus tells the story of the fulfillment of God's covenant with the Patriarchs, of how Israel was called out from Egypt for covenant relationship with God and to be the bearer of the promise of universal blessing to the world. As such, it provides a pattern for understanding God's present and future endeavors to bring about the redemption and restoration of humankind.

Jesus inaugurates the New Covenant by a deliberate and self-conscious re-enactment of the story of the Exodus:

- In analogy with the Exodus experience, baptism in the Jordan at the hands of John is Jesus' Red Sea crossing.[59]
- After He is baptized, Jesus is led by the Spirit, just as the Israelites were led by the pillar of cloud and fire, into the wilderness.[60]
- Here Jesus undergoes temptations, relating to those confronted by Israel in the desert, to which He replies to the devil, quoting Moses' rebuke of Israel.[61]
- Jesus calls out His disciples[62] and soon afterwards climbs the mountain[63] to give His "Sermon on the Mount." This new law to be written in the minds and on the hearts of His followers was also spoken of by the prophet Jeremiah.

---

[59] Mark 1:9-11
[60] Matthew 4:1-11
[61] Deuteronomy 6:13; 6:16; 8:3
[62] Matthew 4:18-22
[63] Matthew 5:1

41

- On the cross, where the New Covenant is inaugurated and this deeper obedience made possible, Jesus becomes the Passover lamb, sacrificed for the sin of the world.[64]

---

[64] Matthew 26:19; 1 Corinthians 5:7

CHAPTER FOUR

THE PROMISED LAND: ISRAEL'S INHERITANCE

The final element of the promise to the patriarchs, which had been reaffirmed in the covenant with Moses, was, as yet, unfulfilled. This was the inheritance of the land given on oath by Yahweh.[1]

God's blessing and favor is integral to His people's enjoyment of the covenant relationship. Part of what it means to enjoy the blessing of God is to enjoy His Sabbath rest.[2] Entry into the land promised to Abraham offers that possibility.[3] In accordance with the covenant made under Moses, they were to keep the Sabbath as a sign of their devotion to Yahweh, much like the sign of circumcision under Abraham.[4] If Israel is obedient in the land Yahweh is giving them, the result will be "rest."[5]

Joshua and the Promised Rest

Joshua is faithful to the covenant and is careful to obey all the laws given under Moses. The book of Joshua tells the story of this generation's

---

[1] Joshua 1:3-5

[2] Exodus 31:16-17; Hebrews 4:3-11; Matthew 11:28-30

[3] Joshua 1:6

[4] Exodus 31:12-17

[5] Exodus 33:14; Joshua 21:44-45

"baptism" in the Jordan, recalling aspects of the Red Sea crossing,[6] circumcision,[7] commemoration of the Passover,[8] the subsequent conquest of the land[9] and its distribution among the tribes.[10] Israel does indeed enter into a time of rest, but that rest is only temporary. Joshua warns Israel that without the people's continuing obedience, the promise is forfeited: "If you violate the covenant . . . you will quickly perish from the good land He has given you."[11]

With this warning, Joshua assembles the tribes of Israel at Shechem for a renewal of the covenant.[12] Through Joshua, the Lord recounts the history of Israel's salvation. Abraham is *taken* from the land beyond the River, *led* throughout Canaan and *given* many descendants as his offspring.[13] Similarly, Moses is *sent* and Israel is *brought out*,[14] and, in time, when their testing in the desert is over, they are *brought* to the land of the Amorites east of the Jordan to *take possession* of their land.[15] God has acted in sovereign strength to raise up a people for His name, for His glory among the nations.

Joshua summons the people to serve the Lord with all faithfulness[16] but insists that the choice is theirs, for the Lord is a holy God and a jealous God and He requires their total commitment.[17] Israel responds with a resounding affirmation of the covenant, which Joshua commemorates with

---

[6] Joshua 3-4
[7] Joshua 5:1-9
[8] Joshua 5:10
[9] Joshua 5:13 – 12:24
[10] Joshua 13-22
[11] Joshua 23:16
[12] Joshua 24
[13] Joshua 24:3
[14] Joshua 24:5
[15] Joshua 24:8
[16] Joshua 24:14
[17] Joshua 24:15-24

a memorial stone under the oak near the holy place of the Lord.[18]

Israel is faithful throughout the lifetime of Joshua and his generation, and yet the promise of "rest" is only partially fulfilled. This is indicated by the fact that only part of the Promised Land has been possessed, and by the short-lived nature of that rest before the turmoil and conflict resume during the period of the judges. Later fulfillments are likewise incomplete.[19] The full and everlasting rest that was promised to Abraham[20] was never experienced in Israel and now functions as the eschatological hope of the new Israel: "There remains, then, a Sabbath-rest for the people of God."[21] We look for a heavenly country, as indeed did the Patriarchs.[22]

Decline and Corruption

The book of Judges continues the story of the relationship between Israel and its covenant God. The narrator frequently returns to the conundrum presented by the tension between God's gracious promises and the disobedience of Israel before the righteous requirements of the Law. The question of how God will redeem His people under these conditions preoccupies the reader throughout.

Joshua's generation is gathered to their fathers and another generation grows up "who knew neither the Lord nor what He had done for Israel," and does evil in the sight of the Lord.[23] They forsake Him for the idols of the land and provoke His just anger.[24] They cease to discern the difference

---

[18] Joshua 24:26

[19] 2 Samuel 7:1; 1 Kings 5:4

[20] 2 Samuel 7:10-11

[21] Hebrews 4:9

[22] Hebrews 11:15-16

[23] Judges 2:10-11

[24] Judges 2:12-13

between Yahweh and the "various gods of the peoples around them."[25] Yahweh withdraws from Israel, so they must fight their enemies in their own strength. Worse, they are now under the curse sworn to them by Moses and the hand of the Lord is turned against them to defeat them.[26]

But the Lord does not abandon them. Again and again He has compassion on His people in their oppression and He raises up judges to save them.[27] As each of these deliverers dies, the people return to "ways even more corrupt than those of their fathers,"[28] and are given over to their enemies once more. Finally, Yahweh determines that the nations shall not be driven from the land promised to Israel, but instead shall be allowed to remain: "I will use them to test Israel and see whether they will keep the way of the Lord and walk in it as their forefathers did."[29] Love always hopes and perseveres through every disappointment.

With the death of Samson, for whom God had great plans, and of whom so much was expected,[30] God ceases the appointment of judges in Israel. In the absence of godly judges, one would have expected the priesthood to stand in the gap for Israel. Instead, the book ends with two shocking stories: Firstly Micah, who stole silver from his own mother and for its honest return, receives from her an idol cast out of the stolen coins.[31] Secondly, a man of the priestly tribe allows his concubine to be raped and abused while he sleeps, and later decides to use the act as a pretext for war.[32] There is none that is righteous; each one does as he sees fit. How can God save Israel if Israel will show no regard for the covenant?

---

[25] Judges 2:12
[26] Judges 2:15; Deuteronomy 28:25
[27] Judges 2:18
[28] Judges 2:19
[29] Judges 2:22
[30] Judges 13
[31] Judges 17:1-6
[32] Judges 19-20

At the time there was no definite resolution of this tension between the unconditional and conditional dimensions of the promise – to this question of how God will redeem His people under these conditions – neither here nor in the rest of the Deuteronomic History.[33] However, there was a clearly emerging and increasingly articulate conviction that a righteous king will bring about the needed reconciliation and secure the promise. The ambiguous refrain, "There was no king in Israel; everyone did as he saw fit,"[34] suggests that the author, writing at some point after the beginning of the monarchy, saw this problem of leadership as at the heart of the cultural malaise of the period.

The Promise of Redemption

Against this background of decline and corruption, the story of Israel's redemption continues in the book of Ruth. This is a heart-warming, behind-the-scenes story of the tender mercy of God and the faithful obedience of a true servant. The veil that so often hides the outworking of God's providence from view is, for a moment, drawn aside as we witness God's grace in the lives of ordinary people.

In seeking to escape the ravages of famine in the land (which may be reflective of God's judgment during this period of Israel's history[35]), Elimelech and his wife Naomi have made their dwelling in Moab,[36] and their two sons have married Moabite women.[37] (The Moabites were related to Israel through Lot, though were nonetheless foreign.) First

---

[33] Joshua – Kings
[34] Judges 17:6; 18:1; 19:1; 21:25
[35] Leviticus 26:3-5, 18-20
[36] Ruth 1:2
[37] Ruth 1:4

Elimelech dies, leaving the family in financial strain. Then his sons, whose wives bore them no sons after ten years of marriage, also die, leaving the women alone and without name or future. When Naomi resolves to return to her people, Ruth insists that she accompany her in spite of her mother-in-law's protestations. Ruth is determined that Naomi's people will become her own and that Israel's God will become hers too.[38] Ruth takes refuge in Yahweh and, in her loyalty to Naomi, she is welcomed by the God of Israel.[39] Upon their return in the providence of God, she finds herself working in the fields of Elimelech's clansman, Boaz, one of their kinsman-redeemers.[40]

After a beautiful courtship,[41] Boaz redeems Ruth and receives the blessing of the town's elders:

> "May the Lord make the woman who is coming into your home like Rachel and Leah, who together built up the house of Israel. May you have standing in Ephrathah and be famous in Bethlehem. Through the offspring the Lord gives you by this young woman, may your family be like that of Perez, whom Tamar bore to Judah."[42]

With this blessing, the reader is reminded of the covenant with the patriarchs. Yahweh is called upon to make Ruth like Rachel and Leah, the mothers of all Israel; and Boaz's family is likened to that of Perez, whose Canaanite mother, Tamar, had "bore to Judah" after her ploy to win a

---

[38] Ruth 1:16

[39] Ruth 2:11-12

[40] Ruth 2:3. Kinsman redeemer: the principle of a close kin legally able to buy back that which was lost; ransom (Ruth 2:20; 4:4)

[41] Ruth 3

[42] Ruth 4:11-12

---

levirate marriage[43] failed.[44] If God could bless such a line, how much more might He bless the line of the faithful Moabitess and her kinsman-redeemer!

By the end of the book of Judges, God appeared to have abandoned His people, but in Ruth Yahweh's steadfast love is shown, expressed in His inclusion of the Moabite in the genealogy of redemption.[45] It is significant that the same Hebrew word, *hesed*, used to describe that steadfast love, is also used for the love that is between Boaz and Ruth. These were faithful "Israelites" who learned the true nature of that love and whose marriage so beautifully and fully gave expression to it. God sought out these faithful hearts and in them He reaffirmed His promise never to forsake His people. Ruth had been so deeply influenced by her first husband's family that covenant commitment characterized her every thought and action. Boaz too, mindful of the covenant nature of his relationship with God and of his responsibility for others and his regard for the Law of Israel, stood out against the backdrop of the failings of the judges. Boaz and Ruth's obedience would have saving ramifications for all Israel. It is in the ordinary, everyday incidents of life that God weaves the divine tapestry of His Kingdom purpose. God is indeed the ultimate choreographer, determining every step and every move in order to fulfill the dance of His redemption in human history.

---

[43] Jeremiah 31:11; Leviticus 25:25: A levirate marriage is the marriage of a woman to her husband's brothers after his death, in the hope of producing an heir for that brother. This was only the case when there was no son from the previous marriage.

[44] Genesis 38:1-26

[45] Ruth 4:17-22; cf. Matthew 1:1-17, especially 5–6

Further Study

1   This pattern of sin and deliverance is clearly demonstrated in the career of the first judge, Othniel. Read Judges 2:10-3:11 and see if you can trace this pattern yourself.

As has been noted, there is also deterioration in the quality of the leadership, which is indicative of the state of the nation, so that the history of Israel follows something of a downward spiral. Much attention is given in the narrative to the personal flaws of the major judges of this period. Whilst Othniel (3:7-11) functions as a model of what a judge should be (and the account of his rule is correspondingly brief), the others show increasing signs of self-interest and indulgence.

2   Compare the stories of Ehud (3:12-30), Deborah (4:1-5:31), Gideon (6:1-9:56), Jephthah (10:6-12:6), and Samson (13:1-16:31) with that of Othniel and see if you can trace this downward spiral in the fortunes of Israel.

CHAPTER FIVE

THE COVENANT WITH DAVID

Looking to the Leader

In the last chapter, in the repeated refrain of the writer of the book of Judges, the issue of leadership, which came to be regarded as the heart of the cultural malaise of Israel, was discussed. The establishment of a kingdom was seen as the only way forward out of the impasse created by Israel's disobedience. There is a sense in which the people were both right and wrong in their conviction that a king needed to be appointed/crowned.

That Israel should one day be ruled by a king and that this was part of God's saving purpose for the nation is evident in the Deuteronomic provision.[1] This was also implicit in Jacob's prophecy of the fulfillment of obedience under a kingly messiah from the house of Judah.[2] However, the people were wrong to think that the establishment of a dynasty would give them safety from foreign invasion and that they could thus secure the blessing of the land without the necessity of obedience.[3] They wanted to be like the other nations by having a king to rule over them, giving the nation stability. Israel's failure to trust in Him alone as their King is what incurred

---

[1] Deuteronomy 17:14-20
[2] Genesis 49:10
[3] Deuteronomy 8

Yahweh's displeasure.[4] Samuel's sons, having proved poor judges, did not want to wait until the next invasion for a deliverer to arise. The elders of Israel had, in effect, rejected God's chastisement. The people were seeking blessing without responsibility; it is in this sense that their faith in a monarchy was misplaced. Rather, they were to be a people called out and set apart for covenant relationship with God and responsibility for others, for *His* glory among the nations. Blessing without responsibility is the delusion for so many of God's people – seeking out a blessing, preoccupation with their own interests, unable to see that there is a greater blessing for those who serve the purposes of God in their generation.

It is in this spirit of rebellion that Saul rules the nation. Contrary to the Law's specific stipulation,[5] Saul believed that he was above the law and that his authority was absolute. He does not wait for the prophet Samuel before offering his sacrifices at Gilgal (1 Samuel 13), nor does he attend to God's word regarding the Amalekites, whom he was commanded to utterly destroy (1 Samuel 15). It is because of his disobedience that the kingdom does not pass to his sons and, eventually, it costs him his right to rule. Eugene Peterson sums up the derailment of Saul's reign when he writes:

> "...King Saul's ideas of God and religion were thoroughly twisted and completely self-serving..."[6]

The Kingdom of David

David's kingdom was established along very different lines. Yahweh

---

[4] 1 Samuel 8:6-8

[5] Deuteronomy 17:18-20

[6] E. Peterson, *Leap Over the Wall* (Harper Collins, 1997) p.67

holds forth the promise of blessing once more. He makes it plain from the outset that the expansion of the covenant is also a renewal of the terms of the previous covenants with the patriarchs and with Moses. Not only does David discern Yahweh's hand in his becoming king,[7] but he also sees it in the establishment of the kingdom from Jerusalem,[8] in his defeat of the Philistines,[9] and in the bringing of the Ark of the Covenant back to the city of God.[10] The Lord shows His pleasure with David's obedience by giving him rest from all his enemies.[11] This pattern of events is intentionally reminiscent of Joshua's leadership. Joshua reiterated the promise of "rest" to Israel in Joshua 1:13 that Moses had promised to the nation in Deuteronomy 3:20. David has regard for the covenant and God responds by renewing the old promise and making it even better.[12]

Further Study

1   *Compare David's covenant renewal with that of Joshua (Joshua 24).*

2   *Throughout David's prayer (2 Samuel 7) the new king uses a surprising word to describe who he is before God. What does this choice say about David's understanding of himself, and of the nature and terms of the covenant?*

The promise to David includes all the major elements of the previous covenants.[13] The continuity of the promises is important to grasp because it

---

[7] 2 Samuel 5:12
[8] 2 Samuel 5:9-10
[9] 2 Samuel 5:17-25
[10] 2 Samuel 6:12-19
[11] 2 Samuel 7:1
[12] 2 Samuel 7:8-16
[13] 2 Samuel 7:8-11

is these promises that constitute the identity of the people of God. There is the concept of the people being sovereignly called out by God and set apart from other nations, and of them being blessed with a name for their posterity, led to a land of their own and given rest from their enemies. In reaffirming these aspects of the promises to the patriarchs and to Moses, Yahweh is also underscoring that the essential condition of the promise still applies: Israel is blessed in order to be a blessing.

Whilst a superficial reading might conclude that this covenant is unconditional, the reaffirmation of previous covenants leaves David with no doubt that God has given these great promises for the sake of His Word.[14]

The distinctive aspect of the covenant with David is the promise of the kingdom. The promise of an enduring house, throne and kingdom is added to these already wonderful promises, and although God seeks the heart obedience of the whole people, special importance is attached to the righteousness of the king. A king mediates the covenant between God and the people: David,[15] Josiah[16] and Zedekiah[17] understand that their authority to rule is given only insofar as they do so according to the terms of the covenant. The king rules by vice-regency,[18] as the "son" of God, and by divine right. As such, his exemplary obedience is of paramount importance.[19]

The conditional nature of the covenant, requiring the obedience of Israel and its king, is further emphasized in the way that God responds to the disobedience that follows. God had warned that disobedience would

---

[14] 2 Samuel 7:21
[15] 2 Samuel 5:3
[16] 2 Kings 23:1-3
[17] Jeremiah 34:8
[18] One who acts as a regent; comes from the Latin word *regens* ("who reigns")
[19] 2 Samuel 7:14

be punished.[20] When David commits adultery with Bathsheba and has Uriah the Hittite put to death, taking his wife for his own, he brings down God's curse upon him and his house: "Now, therefore, the sword shall never depart from your house."[21] First his own son, Absalom, revolts,[22] and then, led astray by Solomon, the kingdom is finally torn asunder after his death.[23]

In the remainder of the Deuteronomic history, taking the covenant detailed therein as the interpretive framework for the narrative, the reader can trace the outworking of the curses that follow first David's, and then his sons' disobedience[24]: disease,[25] drought,[26] cannibalism,[27] exile and defeat.[28] With Manasseh's great idolatry,[29] the Lord's anger against Judah will not be assuaged and he passes a chilling judgment upon them:

> "I am going to bring such disaster on Jerusalem and Judah that the ears of everyone who hears of it will tingle. . . . I will wipe out Jerusalem as one wipes out a dish, wiping it and turning it upside-down. I will forsake the remnant of my inheritance and hand them over to their enemies. They will be looted and plundered by all their foes, because they have done evil in my eyes and have provoked me to anger from the day their forefathers came out of Egypt until this day."[30]

---

[20] 2 Samuel 7:14
[21] 2 Samuel 12:10
[22] 2 Samuel 13 – 19
[23] 1 Kings 12, especially vv. 16-19
[24] Deuteronomy 28:15-68
[25] 2 Samuel 24
[26] 1 Kings 17–18
[27] 2 Kings 6:24-30
[28] 2 Kings 17:24-32; 25:18-24
[29] 2 Kings 21:1-18
[30] 2 Kings 21:12-15

The covenant is renewed under Josiah, whose reforms are far-reaching[31] and whose zeal in repentance is second to none; but his obedience is not enough to turn the heat of the Lord's fierce anger from Judah.[32] Sadly, Josiah's good work is undone by his successors. The last days of Judah are characterized by incompetence and desperation as the last three kings – Jehoiakim, Jehoiachin and Zedekiah – seek alliances first with Egypt and then with Babylon in order to delay the inevitable. The irreversible nature of God's judgment upon Judah for the sin of Manasseh[33] appears to suggest that grace had ceased for the chosen people. The dynasty had endured for four hundred years and had outlasted even the most long-lived in Egypt and Mesopotamia, but it nevertheless stopped short of the promise.

An Eternal Kingdom?

Again the reader is presented with the conundrum of how God can achieve the redemption of the nation of Israel without Israel's obedience. Yahweh had promised that the throne of David would endure forever and that his kingdom would be without end. Yet although the author of Kings articulates the waywardness of the leaders and of the people, the author ultimately wants the reader to know that the promise is not forgotten: Jehoiachin is released from prison, spoken kindly to and given a seat of honor at the Babylonian king's table.[34] Even in exile God has not forgotten David's descendants.

The question of the "remainder" of the prophetic promise, which was

---

[31] 2 Kings 22 – 23
[32] 2 Kings 23:25-27
[33] 2 Kings 21:3-9; 2 Chronicles 33:10
[34] 2 Kings 25:27-30

left implicit and apparently unfulfilled, perplexed Israel throughout the exile and even into the period of the second temple. During this time, Israel remained under foreign rule, never seeing the restoration of the monarchy for which the people had so long hoped. As far as the writer of the histories is concerned, whatever else might be said, Yahweh remains Israel's covenant God and Israel remains the people of the covenant. Just how Yahweh will redeem His people is still a mystery to the writer at this point. But He will.

To the eyes of faith it is evident that the messianic hope, which is implicit in the promise of an eternal Kingdom, provides the key. This hope is developed in the kingly Psalms[35] and in Isaiah.[36] These and other Old Testament texts look forward to a king of Davidic descent whose Kingdom would be without end. Paul, in Romans 1:3, said of Jesus that He "was born of a descendant of David according to the flesh," and Jesus Himself also hinted, albeit cryptically, at His divine origin: "How is it that the teachers of the law say that the Christ is the son of David? David himself, speaking by the Holy Spirit, declared: 'The Lord said to my Lord: Sit at My right hand until I put Your enemies under Your feet'".[37] Jesus is not practicing deliberate obfuscation; there is no rational answer to His question. As Ladd puts it, "How can the Messiah be David's Son if he is also David's Lord?"[38] It is not that He denies His Davidic son-ship, but that His being David's Lord is of weightier importance. Like so much of Jesus' speech, His sayings and parables, the truth is counter-intuitive, so that it must be expressed as paradox.

This said, it must be noted that this theme in the prophetic writings

---

[35] Psalm 2; 45:6; 89:1-4, 19-29; 132:11-12

[36] Isaiah 9:6-7; 11

[37] Mark 12:35-6

[38] G. E. Ladd, *A Theology of the New Testament* (Grand Rapids, Wm B Eerdmans, 1993) p. 142.

and in the Psalms only finds prominence in the New Testament apostolic interpretation. The many references to a messianic figure in the Old Testament, although read with diligence, may not have been as shaping of Jewish expectation in this period as were some of the more immediate political and revolutionary writings of the time. In Jewish tradition, for the most part, this idea lay dormant for many centuries until its resuscitation by the early Christians.

Nevertheless, these and other texts[39] suggest the hope of an end-time reconciliation of all things in Christ. The promise to David hinged on Israel's fulfillment of covenant obligations, but the demands of the law were such that the people could not hope to meet them. Furthermore, the sacrificial system was such that it could never suffice for atonement. In words that look forward to the obedience of Christ, David prays, "You do not delight in sacrifice, or I would bring it; you do not take pleasure in burnt offerings. The sacrifices of God are[40] a broken spirit; a broken and contrite heart, O God, You will not despise."[41]

So it was that David's rule, indeed its very imperfection, anticipated the beneficent reign of the coming Messiah, for "from Him and through Him and to Him are all things."[42] It is this covenant of consummation in Christ that the people of God are looking forward to during the period of the exile and the second temple. David so eloquently provides the reader with the words that help to understand the magnificence of God's commitment toward His people.

---

[39] "Qumran literature provides a picture of 1st Century Judaism. The Qumran community treasured teaching on apocalypses...This is proved by the fact that fragments of their books have been found. This includes ten manuscripts of Jubilees, four of the five parts of Enoch, etc..." see Ladd's *The Presence of the Future* 1996. P.78

[40] Or *My sacrifice, O God, is...*

[41] Psalm 51:16-17; cf. Philippians 2:5-8

[42] Romans 11:36

"The David story anticipates the Jesus story... There are several strands that make up the answer, but prominent amongst them is David's earthiness. He's emphatically human... If we are going to get the most of Jesus' story, we'll want first to soak our imaginations in the David story."[43]

David embodies the heart of a devoted worshiper, a provocation to all believers throughout the centuries. The Church today cannot help but be challenged and not merely observe. She must participate in what God is doing.

---

[43] E. Peterson, *Leap Over the Wall* (Harper Collins, 1997) p.9

CHAPTER SIX

EXILE AND RETURN

The note of hope upon which the bible's historical books end is the hope that sustains God's covenant people through the exile. Whilst the prophets of the pre-exilic period consistently spoke the word of judgment, the hope of salvation predominates during the exile and beyond. Israel had broken covenant with Yahweh and had experienced the horror of "not being" (what they were meant to be was "an obedient people"), cast from His presence and the land that He had given them. Yet the promise is sure[1]: "The Israelites will be like the sand on the seashore, which cannot be measured or counted. In the place where it was said to them, 'You are not my people,' they will be called 'sons of the living God'."[2]

In the place of God's judgment, Israel experiences a profound spiritual renewal as penitent hearts search for meaning in the history of the people of God.[3] Repentance is held forth by the writer of Kings as the hope of Israel.[4] Though alienated from Him, He will not abandon them in their exile.

---

[1] See Jeremiah 31:15-25

[2] Hosea 1:10

[3] Many scholars have come to the conclusion that it was precisely this fervency of prayer and repentance that gave rise to the first scriptures, as the oral tradition is exhaustively pored over and preliminary editions of the Pentateuch, the Histories and the Prophets are completed.

[4] 1 Kings 8:47-50

Times of Renewal and Restoration: Ezra-Nehemiah

After seventy years of ignominy among the nations, Cyrus, King of Persia, "in order to fulfill the word of the Lord spoken by Jeremiah,[5] is moved to make a proclamation throughout his realm, inviting the descendants of the people of God who were carried off to Babylon and Egypt to go up to Jerusalem and rebuild the temple. A remnant is called forth first to rebuild the temple[6] and then the city itself.[7]

When the work of rebuilding is complete, the people are "assembled as one man"[8] before Ezra the priest for a renewal of the covenant. Ezra reads from the book of the law and the people grieve for their sins and the sins of their fathers. This would seem the appropriate response, but apparently the people have missed the point and should be celebrating rather than grieving. The Levites move among them to comfort them. Nehemiah tells them not to weep but to take heart and be joyful. Their restoration, the rebuilding and their rediscovery of the books of the law ought to give them cause for great celebration, for Yahweh was welcoming them home and they would once again be the recipients of His grace and favor in the land promised to their forefathers. On the second day of the seventh month, as if to confirm the word of their leaders, they discover that the Feast of Booths, the festival commemorating the exodus, will soon be upon them and they disperse with great joy to gather the branches to make the booths.[9] They return to celebrate the festival with great gladness and the scriptures tell us that, "from the days of Joshua son of Nun until that day, the Israelites had not celebrated it like this. And their joy was

---

[5] Ezra 1:1; cf. Isaiah 44:28 - 45:1
[6] Ezra 1-6
[7] Nehemiah 1-6
[8] Nehemiah 8:1
[9] Nehemiah 8:14-15

very great."[10] There is no question that God is a God of intervention. Religion or life without God is a pale reflection of what it is meant to be. Significant moments such as these are a part of the journey and the enrichment of the life of God's people throughout the generations.

When the festival is over they gather together once more to repent and to conclude the renewal of the covenant with a formal agreement. Yahweh is vindicated as faithful to His covenant of love and just in His judgment: "In all that has happened to us, you have been just; you have acted faithfully, while we did wrong."[11] In view of the compassion and mercy of God, the people make a binding agreement "with a curse and an oath to follow the Law of God given through Moses the servant of God and to obey carefully all the commands, regulations and decrees of the Lord our Lord."[12]

The remnant of Israel has once again become a holy people, called out and set apart for covenant relationship with God and responsibility for others. They are a holy people in a holy city. But, as the woeful lament that concludes the prayer of confession cannot but bewail, they remain as slaves in the land given to their forefathers; its abundant harvest gathered by the kings Yahweh has placed over them. "They rule over our bodies and our cattle as they please. We are in great distress."[13]

---

[10] Nehemiah 8:17
[11] Nehemiah 9:33
[12] Nehemiah10:29
[13] Nehemiah 9:36-37

1   *Compare Ezra's renewal of the covenant (Nehemiah 8) with Joshua's (Joshua 24) and David's (2 Samuel 5:1 – 7:16).*

2   *What reoccurring words or phrases in the people's agreement with Yahweh (Nehemiah 10:30–39) indicate that they have understood the nature of their covenant obligation?*

For Discussion

In particular, the people pledge that they will avoid intermarriage and keep the Sabbath, and not neglect the service of the house of their God or the duty of offering first fruits and tithes (Nehemiah10:30-39).

What important distinctive of God's people do these practices express?

An Awkward Conclusion

The book of Nehemiah thus reaches an awkward conclusion. Israel's restoration is only in part. Still uncertain of their inheritance, the people falter. Faced with a series of compromises, the thirteenth chapter of Nehemiah narrates his final reforms. While Nehemiah is away, Eliashib the priest allows one of the temple storerooms to be taken over for secular use.[14] Tobiah moves in, bringing his household gods with him, and Nehemiah is appalled. He also discovers that in his absence the Levites have not received their portion of the offerings, their food by which they are strengthened for service, and the singers have returned to the fields.[15] Nehemiah orders that the storehouse should be filled once more and that

---

[14] Nehemiah 13:4-9
[15] Nehemiah 13:10-12

those in the service of the sanctuary should return to their ministries. How quickly the people turned back on their promises! The Sabbath is ignored by farmer and tradesman alike and Nehemiah is forced to station guards upon the wall for the express purpose of deterring the merchants camped outside.[16] Men of Judah take women from Ashdod, Ammon and Moab and are assimilated into their culture such that they forget their native language![17] Nehemiah rebukes them and curses them, recalling Solomon's downfall for the very same sin. He beats them, tearing out their hair in his fury. His grief is such that he pleads with Yahweh that they not go unpunished. As Dillard and Longman point out, the mention of Solomon is significant. "The question is, will Israel survive only to repeat the sins of the past? Intermarriage dragged Solomon and the entire nation into a vortex of doom that led to the Exile. Will the postexilic generation go the same way?"[18]

When the Jews were marched off into Exile, Jeremiah had held forth the promise of return and rest.[19] Rachel wept then and refused to be comforted, but the Lord had promised that her children, who were "no more", who had become "not my people", would return to their own land and enjoy the favor of God once more. Now the Jews have returned to their land, but they remain as slaves under Gentile rulers. Rachel will not be comforted, but she hopes on against hope, looking for the fulfillment of the promise.

---

[16] Nehemiah 13:15-22

[17] Nehemiah 13:23-24

[18] R. B. Dillard and T. Longman III, *An Introduction to the Old Testament* (Leicester, Apollos, 1995) p. 187.

[19] Jeremiah 31:15-25

Perplexity in the Inter-Testament Period

The apocryphal literature of the second-temple period is characterized by this same perplexity. Faith in the covenant was alive, but as N. T. Wright has shown, expectations as regards its fulfillment soon diverged. Several different trains of thought emerged:

> "The Maccabaean crisis was all about covenant. The setting up of the Essene communities took place in the belief that Israel's god had renewed his covenant at last (but secretly, with them alone). The book of *Jubilees* celebrated the special status of Israel in virtue of the covenant. The later wisdom literature, for all its borrowings of ideas and idioms from Israel's neighbours, stressed the Jewish covenant if anything more strongly than the biblical wisdom tradition had done. The apocalyptic writings looked in eager expectation for their god to fulfil his covenant, and thus to vindicate Israel. The later rabbis examined ever more carefully the obligations through which Israel was to act out her part in the divine covenant. It was the covenant which meant that Israel's oppression was seen as a theological as well as a practical problem, and which determined the shape which solutions to that problem would have to take. It was the covenant that drove some to 'zeal' for the Torah, others to military action, others to monastic style piety. The covenant raised, and helped to answer, the question of who really belonged to Israel."[20]

---

[20] N. T. Wright, *The New Testament and the People of God* (London, SPCK, 1995) pp. 261–262.

It seems that many of these groups had begun to wonder whether God was about to call out from among them a new Israel, a faithful remnant who would constitute the new ecclesia in the new age.[21]

The Hope of Israel

This new hope gave focus to some in a cluster of related texts bearing on the promise of a new covenant in Jeremiah,[22] which held forth the promise of a return to the land, of blessing, healing of the nation's divisions, forgiveness of sins, of rest and of a deeper enablement in the doing of God's will. In another cluster, centered particularly on the messianic "son of man" figure of Daniel 2, 7 and especially 9 (the influence of which text is discernible in similarly apocalyptic writings of the inter-testamental period[23] and in several of the various messianic movements that preceded the coming of Christ[24]), it is evident that the dawn of this new age was closely associated in people's minds with a divine deliverer.

But when the Messiah comes, He is not at all like these groups think He will be: Jesus subverts the thinking of scribe, Pharisee, Essene and zealot alike. Although the people yearn for the coming Kingdom, and the fulfillment of the promises in a new and better covenant, the hopes of many in Israel are misplaced.

---

[21] The period of about 400 years between Malachi (397 BC) and the book of Matthew; the socio/political regimes being Persian, Greek, Egyptian, Syrian Maccabean and Roman. In the religious domain several zealous groups emerged after the time of Malachi: the Pharisees, the Sadducees and the Herodians. Also new organizations with significant influence rose up, such as the Scribes, the Sanhedrin, and the establishment of synagogues.

[22] Jeremiah 31:31-34. Cf. also Jeremiah 32:27-44; 50:4; Ezekiel 37:15-28; and Isaiah 55:1-5 and 61:1-9, which make similar reference to an "everlasting covenant."

[23] See especially 1 Enoch 37-41

[24] N. T. Wright, *The New Testament and the People of God* (London, SPCK, 1995) pp. 307-320

CHAPTER SEVEN

THE COVENANT OF CONSUMMATION

The expulsion of the people of God from the land of their inheritance was an ordeal that impressed on Israel their massive and inescapable failure to keep faith with the God of the covenant. Although the generation in exile is not abandoned, and a remnant is called out to go up and possess the land once more, they soon understand that their restoration is only partial. Given the persistence of sin in their midst, they will remain forever insecure regarding the promise.

In the period of the second temple[1] many within Israel are seen to be "grasping at straws" as they seek a better salvation than that which is theirs according to the covenant, as seen in the Maccabean period of political unrest and foreign rule. Others, as careful study of the Apocryphal literature and the history of the period shows, had begun to place their hope in a messianic deliverer. In chapter four it was noted how those who read the scriptures carefully were looking forward to a kingly messiah in the line of David, who, at an unspecified time in the future, would establish the Kingdom once more, this time on a surer foundation and for all eternity. In chapter 5 another strand of messianic thinking was added to the weave: the "son of man" figure of Daniel and 1 Enoch. Jesus' implicit claim to be a kingly messiah, as well as the cryptic suggestion of

---

[1] Ezra 5:2- Ezra led the people back to work. The second temple was completed in 515BC.

divine nature and origin,[2] and the "messianic secret" of Jesus' true identity, is given greater emphasis in His own use of this related title, the Son of Man, as a way of describing Himself. In Daniel the "son of man" is more clearly a heavenly and eschatological figure who brings the Kingdom to His afflicted people.[3] Jesus takes up this title and pours into it the content of the suffering servant passages of Isaiah,[4] showing how the Son of Man must first take on the flesh of man and be together with humanity in all its frailty and sufferings, before He is revealed in glory.[5] This deliberate reinterpretation can be traced most easily in the Gospel of Mark.[6]

To complete the picture, the Gospel writers use a third title for Jesus that brings His identity into still sharper focus: the Son of God. This is not a title that Jesus used of Himself, but one that the Gospel writers note others frequently used of Him. The voice from heaven speaks of Him in this way at both his baptism[7] and transfiguration[8] and, significantly, He is also recognized as such by demons, as well as by men.[9] The promises to David emphasize this paternity strongly, but the title never seems to have become familiar in later Judaism. Nevertheless, it appears not to have needed any explanation; its implications are all too clear. Jesus seems to have preferred the former title as it left him some room for maneuver in the face of the hostility of the Pharisees. Careful use of the Davidic title and reinterpretation of Daniel's "son of man" typology would allow Him to keep His identity a closely guarded secret. In the early Church the Son of

---

[2] Mark 2:10; 16:16-17- Mark emphasises the Messianic nature of Christ; John 8:58; 10:30; Matthew 26:63-64

[3] Daniel 7:13-14

[4] Especially chapter 53

[5] See G. E. Ladd, *A Theology of the New Testament* (Grand Rapids, Wm B Eerdmans, 1993) Chapter 11

[6] Emphasis in Mark is on "servanthood"; Mark 2:10; 14:62; 10:45

[7] Mark 1:11

[8] Mark 9:7

[9] Mark 5:6-8

God could be used without restraint to indicate his incarnate supremacy.[10]

The Gospel of the Kingdom - The Messianic Mission

Jesus' mission was to manifest and then establish the Kingdom in the midst of Israel. In His person He confronts the people with its reality and the realities of death and judgment in order to bring on a crisis of decision for or against God's rule.[11] Those who repent are delivered from the powers of evil and from slavery to sin so that they might experience an inner righteousness that is entirely the work of the Spirit by the grace of God.

With this objective in mind, it is not surprising that Jesus found Himself from early on in His ministry locked in to a conflict from which, ultimately, He would not emerge until after His death. The tumultuous events of Jesus' life culminate in the cross, where a new covenant in His blood is inaugurated for all who will receive Him and believe in His name.[12] This covenant, the covenant of consummation, is what makes believers children born of God, established in Christ, and as the people of God today.

The New Covenant in the Blood of Christ

The New Covenant consummates successive Old Testament covenants. As such, it can only be rightly understood in the context of the promises to the

---

[10] See G. E. Ladd, *A Theology of the New Testament* (Grand Rapids, Wm B Eerdmans, 1993) Chapter 12

[11] Matthew 5:6

[12] John 1:12

patriarchs, the Mosaic Law, and Israel's history of violating the previous covenants before and after David.

The way that God set apart the priesthood for the work of intercession and the special burden laid on them to maintain their ritual purity for the sake of the worship of Israel has already been discussed. The nation must be holy before Yahweh for the promise to hold true, and given the continuing presence of sin, sacrifice was necessary to make that worship acceptable to Him. The priests offered sacrifices continually "first for their own sins, and then for the sins of the people".[13] On the Day of Atonement the High Priest would enter the Holy of Holies within the sanctuary to offer further sacrifice for the cleansing of all Israel.[14] On this day alone, and for this man alone, there was access to the most holy presence of God.

Yahweh had come near, but He desired to be nearer still.[15] To do so He needed to raise up a priest of a different order, like Melchizedek, whose intercession would be effective neither on the basis of his ancestry, nor the meticulous observance of the prescribed ritual, but solely because of His righteousness.[16] Such a one full of grace and truth was indestructible, exercising a permanent priesthood to save and to preserve all those who come to God through Him.[17]

> "Such a high priest meets our need – one who is holy, blameless, pure, set apart from sinners, exalted above the heavens. Unlike the other high priests, He does not need to offer sacrifices day after day, first for His own sins, and then

---

[13] Hebrews 7:27
[14] Leviticus 16, especially verse 30
[15] Hebrews 7:19
[16] Hebrews 7:16
[17] Hebrews 7:23-25

for the sins of the people. He sacrificed for their sins once for all when He offered Himself."[18]

Only such a sacrifice could satisfy the demand of God. Under the old covenant, the nature of the sacrifice meant that it had to be perpetual: there was always sin that remained for which atonement must be made. God's justice could not ultimately be satisfied according to its terms.[19] Only a priceless sacrifice would suffice. And so God gave His only Son.

Christ obeys the law perfectly,[20] committing no sin[21] so that there is no need for Him to sacrifice for His own sins. In fulfilling the law in this way[22] on behalf of Israel, and making this ultimate sacrifice, He does away with the need for legal obedience and of the sacrificial system designed to compensate for covenant violation.

This has implications, too, for the Kingdom. By His obedience, the Son of David secures for Israel its everlasting inheritance. Palmer Robertson explains that:

"David's covenant hinged conditionally on the responsible fulfillment of covenant obligations by Jesus Christ, the seed of David. He satisfied in Himself all the obligations of the covenant. Not only did He maintain perfectly every statute and ordinance of the Mosaic Law as required of David. He also bore in Himself the chastening judgments deserved by David's seed through their covenant violations."[23]

---

[18] Hebrews 7:26-27

[19] Hebrews 10:11-12

[20] Romans 5:18-19

[21] 1 Peter 2:22

[22] Matthew 5:17

[23] O. P. Robertson, *The Christ of the Covenants* (Phillipsburg, Presbyterian and Reformed Publishing Co., 1980), p. 248

Hereafter, God's holy people are accepted as such because of His righteousness.[24]

Christ's atoning sacrifice is full (withholding nothing and thus redeeming humanity in every part), perfect (absolute and without defect, thus the best and most costly of sacrifices conceivable), and sufficient (in no way deficient, thus needing no further sacrifice or supplementary good work), and it is offered once and for all – as a final atonement that is potentially efficacious for all of humankind. How unlike the trespass is the gift! "For," as Paul writes to the Romans, "if the many died by the trespass of the one man [Adam], how much more did God's grace and the gift that came by the grace of the one man, Jesus Christ, overflow to the many!"[25]

In His sacrifice there is abundant grace for all who will receive it as their own. "If we [die] with Christ, we believe that we will also live with Him. For we know that since Christ was raised from the dead, He cannot die again; death no longer has mastery over Him. The death He died, He died to sin once for all; but the life He lives, He lives to God."[26] "In the same way," Paul writes, "count yourselves dead to sin but alive to God in Christ Jesus."[27] It is this dying and raising that is recalled and dramatized in the sacrament of the Eucharist, or thanksgiving, an "outward and visible sign" in the form of a ritual, the performance of which effects a transformation in the life of the believing community with the imparting of an "inward and spiritual grace."

"For Christ, our Passover lamb, has been sacrificed. Therefore let us keep the Festival, not with the old yeast, the yeast of malice and wickedness, but with bread without yeast, the bread of sincerity and

---

[24] 1 Peter 3:18
[25] Romans 5:15
[26] Romans 6:8-10
[27] Romans 6:11

truth."[28] The "Paschal lamb" now substituted for my sin. What can be offered in thanksgiving? As one hymn writer cries in wonder, "What can I give Him, poor as I am?"[29] In view of God's great mercy, Paul replies that we must offer what we have, our bodies, as he puts it, ourselves, all that we are, "as living sacrifices, holy and pleasing to God"; this, says Paul, is our "spiritual act of worship".[30] Come out from the world, says Paul, conform no longer to its pattern, "but be transformed by the renewing of your mind. Then you will be able to test and approve what God's will is – His good, pleasing and perfect will."[31] Paul's thinking here shows clear parallels with the already quoted passage from Jeremiah,[32] which also appears at this point in the argument of the epistle to the Hebrews and is highly suggestive of the indwelling of the Spirit.

The epistle to the Hebrews is concerned with the transformation of the Christian believers' worship in the tabernacle[33] and the eternal priesthood of Christ in the heavenly tabernacle.[34] This is much more fully developed elsewhere in Paul's writings. He uses the imagery of the temple in particular to convey this sense of the Spirit's dwelling in the midst of the people. This is expressed both corporately, in keeping with its Old Testament precedents,[35] and in believers as individuals.[36] This empowering presence of the Spirit in the heart of the believer is, for Paul, the defining mark of the new covenant faith.

It is adherence to this new covenant in continuity with the old that

---

[28] 1 Corinthians 5:7b-8

[29] C Rossetti *In the Bleak Midwinter* (1872)

[30] Romans 12:1; cf. also Hebrews 13:15-16

[31] Romans 12:2

[32] Jeremiah 31:31-34

[33] Hebrews 10:22

[34] Hebrews 10:19-22

[35] 1 Corinthians 3:16-17; 2 Corinthians 6:16; Ephesians 2:22

[36] 1 Corinthians 6:19-20

brings such fulfillment. It is more wonderful, offering a better justice and, consequently, a better hope of a more intimate relationship and an eternal inheritance. This marks the people of God today, a people called out and set apart for covenant relationship with God and responsibility for others.

CHAPTER EIGHT

THE KINGDOM — A PROPHETIC REALITY

John the Baptist

> "It is written in Isaiah the prophet:
>> 'I will send My messenger ahead of You, who will prepare Your way' –
>> 'a voice of one calling in the desert, "Prepare the way for the Lord, Make straight paths for Him."'[1]
>
> And so John came…"[2]

John's significance in salvation history is often missed. It is possible that the drama of his appearance is lost without the background of apocryphal confusion. For centuries the living voice of prophecy has been silent. Israel's return from exile is frustrated and there is no one to interpret the reason for the continuing Gentile oppression. The scribes enjoin a more scrupulous obedience to the Law and the hopes of the apocalyptists grow ever more eschatological. Qumran sectarians withdraw from the mainstream of society. Frustrated militants increasingly take up arms in the cause of national liberation as if they could force God's hand and usher in the Kingdom by military means. Meanwhile the majority look on in

---

[1] Mark 1:2-3

[2] Mark 1:4

bewilderment.

And then a voice cries out in the wilderness.

John's appearance and his message leave the crowds who flock to him in little doubt that there is a prophet among them. "The Kingdom of God is at hand,"[3] is his startling cry. God is about to act in all the splendor of His majesty. The atmosphere in the country is electric and news of the prophet's message spreads like wildfire throughout the region.

John urges the people to repent and be baptized for the forgiveness of their sins.[4] Rejecting all nationalistic and legalistic ideas of righteousness, John insists on nothing less than full conversion, *metanoia*, the turning of the whole person to God. Neither being a descendent of Abraham, nor hair-splitting obedience to the law will do; such is the righteousness of God that salvation is only possible by grace.[5]

Situating himself beyond the Jordan in the wilderness,[6] John consciously draws on Old Testament typology as he enacts a new exodus. The people are *called out* from Jerusalem, against whose temple cult John stands in marked opposition, as is evident in his reference to Jesus as the Lamb of God, whose (implied) sacrifice alone will take away the sin of the world.[7] In baptism they pass through the waters of the Jordan and from thence into the wilderness beyond to await the consummation of their hopes in the coming of Christ.

As Moses leads Israel to the mountain, John leads the chosen of God to the Christ, the fulfillment of the law. He prophesies a baptism with the

---

[3] Mark 1:5

[4] Mark 1:4

[5] Sola Gratia = by grace alone. Salvation cannot be earned: it is a gift from God. Ephesians 1:7-10; Grace undeserved; free love of God in action on the behalf of humanity.

[6] John 1:28

[7] John 1:29

Holy Spirit by One far greater, in accordance with the prophecies of the Old Testament. Here the believer is led to expect that the Spirit will impart a life-giving power to the descendants of Jacob,[8] effecting a resurrection of the nation[9] and enabling a deeper obedience to God's will.[10]

There is no doubt that John heralds the dawn of a new age, that he expects the coming of the Kingdom in all its fullness, and that he anticipates the inauguration of a new covenant. It is hard to say what implications he envisages this will have for the people of God. What is evident when looking at Jesus, however, is that the Messiah came to Israel expecting to be received as Messiah; His mission was to proclaim to *Israel* that God was now acting to fulfill His promises and to bring *Israel* to its true destiny.[11]

Jesus and Israel - New For Old

Jesus comes as a Jew to the Jewish people. From the time of His birth, His parents have been careful to "fulfill all righteousness"[12] and there is no reason to suppose that He Himself was not fully observant in the keeping of the Torah. Luke notes that it was Jesus' custom as a young man to attend the synagogue[13] so that He is completely at home when He returns from the wilderness to the synagogues of Galilee and, eventually, to His own in the town of Nazareth.[14] His understanding of the scriptures is

---

[8] Isaiah 44:3-5

[9] Ezekiel 37:14

[10] Ezekiel 36:27

[11] G. E. Ladd, *A Theology of the New Testament Revealed* (Grand Rapids, Wm B Eerdmans, 1974), p. 105.

[12] Luke 2:21-24; 2:41

[13] Luke 4:16

[14] Luke 4:14-16

profound even as a boy[15] and they are remarkably present to mind through the period of temptation.[16]

In continuity with the purpose of Israel's calling from among the nations, Jesus comes to Israel, for the glory of Israel, in order that He might also be a light for revelation to the Gentiles.[17] Although He journeys occasionally beyond the borders, His priority is clearly "the lost sheep of Israel,"[18] to whom He sends His disciples and to whom He remains first of all committed in spite of the interruptions from faithful Gentiles.

Despite Jesus' obvious desire that Israel should embrace the hope to which they have been called, the people, as a whole, reject His messianic claims. His proclamation of the Kingdom is, in the end, silenced. But God's plan for the redemption of humankind is not to be thwarted. Although the people initially reject Him, a remnant does indeed respond to Him and to His message. Those who received His message, most fully expressed in His person, become the true Israel. The concept of the remnant is present in His referring to His disciples as His "little flock," the sheep of God's pasture,[19] to whom Jesus came as a shepherd to seek and to save.[20] They were sheep not of a separate fold, but nonetheless "lost." Significant also is Jesus' calling of twelve disciples; as the nucleus of a new Israel, the twelve are to sit on the twelve thrones judging the twelve tribes of Israel.[21]

In agreement with this dual emphasis on the continuity and discontinuity in the Old Testament *ecclesia* regarding discipleship, is Jesus'

---

[15] Luke 2:42-51

[16] Luke 4:1-13

[17] Luke 2:32

[18] Matthew 10:5-6; 15:24

[19] Luke 12:32

[20] Luke 19:10

[21] Matthew 19:28; Luke 22:30

proclamation that He will build His *ecclesia* upon the confessed faith of the disciples, of whom Peter is the representative.[22] Jesus takes up Old Testament terminology and concepts. His teaching and preaching remain very much within the context of Israel's system of beliefs. But He adds a distinctive: He describes the *ecclesia* as "My *ecclesia*". "The true Israel now finds its specific identity in its relationship to Jesus."[23]

Thus, there is the combined idea that what God is doing is in continuity with His saving purposes for Israel (i.e. prior to a New Testament Church) and that the development of something new is in process. At its beginning, the Church only exists in incipient form as part of the Jewish community; it has not yet taken the distinctive and coherent form of the Pauline epistles. The Church as we know it, called out and set apart as the new Israel, is a later development.

Further Study

Read the story of the healing of the centurion's servant (Mat 8:5-13).

What does Jesus' reference to the patriarchs Abraham, Isaac and Jacob suggest about God's plan for the Gentiles?

The Kingdom and the Church

If Jesus did not come to establish the Church, what then was His purpose? Jesus' message is that the promised eternal Kingdom of the kingly Psalms[24] and of Isaiah[25] has come. It is such that "in His very person and mission

---

[22] Matthew16:18-20

[23] G. E. Ladd, *A Theology of the New Testament Revealed* (Grand Rapids, Wm B Eerdmans, 1974), p. 108.

[24] Psalm 2; 45:6; 89:1-4, 19-29; 132:11-12

[25] Isaiah 9:6-7; 11, and elsewhere

God has invaded human history" and will triumph over evil in His resurrection from the dead and through His death-defying sacrifice, even though the final deliverance will not occur until the end of the age.[26] God has acted to establish His Kingdom, which is "above the heavens" and "over all,"[27] among men. The Kingdom of God refers to the reign and rule of God, His sovereignty and proportionately, the sphere in which that rule is experienced.[28]

Ladd expounds this relationship under five points.[29] The first is that *the Kingdom is not the Church.* If one was to substitute "Church" for "Kingdom" in the context of the preaching of the early missionaries[30] this would distort the gospel. The Kingdom offers a brighter hope than the Church! Jesus broadened the believer's point of reference beyond a congregational constituency. The call to the believer was to be an obedient citizen of God's Kingdom. The Church is the servant of the Kingdom of God, the Harbinger.

The second is that *the Kingdom creates the Church.* Jesus announces the Kingdom, but what comes into being is the Church. In the parable of the dragnet,[31] all sorts of conditions of men are caught. In the Church, which results from the preaching of the Kingdom, these must coexist until the judgment. Here are found the people of the Kingdom, but also many who are not true sons and daughters of the king.

The third point to consider under the nature of this relationship is that *the Church witnesses to the Kingdom.* This is reflected in the commissioning

---

[26] G. E. Ladd, *A Theology of the New Testament Revealed* (Grand Rapids, Wm B Eerdmans, 1974) p. 65.

[27] Psalm 103:19

[28] G. E. Ladd, *A Theology of the New Testament Revealed* (Grand Rapids, Wm B Eerdmans, 1974), p. 109.

[29] Ibid. pp. 109-117.

[30] Acts 8:12; 19:8; 20:25; 28:23, 31

[31] Matthew 13:47-50

of the twelve[32] and of the seventy-two,[33] in the proclamation of the apostles throughout the book of Acts, and in the corporate display of Kingdom life. In all this the Church bears witness not to itself, but to the Kingdom.

Furthermore, *the Church is the instrument of the Kingdom.* The apostles did not only bear witness to the Kingdom but, because of their faith, they became instruments of the Kingdom, as the works of the Kingdom were performed through them in the power of the Holy Spirit. They healed the sick and cast out demons,[34] and even exercised power over death; even the gates of Hades shall not prevail against them.[35]

Finally, *the Church is the custodian of the Kingdom.* According to the rabbis, Israel was the custodian of the Kingdom because the law, through which the rule of God is experienced, was entrusted to Israel alone. When the nation as a whole rejected Jesus and His gospel, Jesus' disciples became the new custodians of the Kingdom. Thus Jesus gives to his *ecclesia* the keys of the Kingdom of heaven with power to bind and loose for all eternity.[36] These keys, the keys of knowledge it appears, are taken from the Pharisees[37] and entrusted to the disciples on the basis of their spiritual insight, for which Jesus commends Peter in Matthew 16:19.

Jesus announces that the Kingdom is both a present reality and a future reality; it is both "now" and "not yet." The Kingdom has come in His life and person and it is experienced in the life of the Church. But, more profoundly, it will be known in all its fullness as the new age reaches its consummation and "heaven descends to earth and lifts historical

---

[32] Matthew 10
[33] Luke 10
[34] Matthew 10:8; Luke 10:17
[35] Matthew 16:18
[36] Matthew 16:19
[37] Luke 11:52; Matthew 23:13

existence to a new level of redeemed life."[38] It is to this climactic event in the history of God's salvation that the Church is looking forward.

In the coming Kingdom all the promises of successive covenants find their ultimate fulfillment. The new Jerusalem (the Holy City wherein dwell the resurrected righteous of every age, tribe and nation[39]), which symbolizes the harmonious society of the perfected *ecclesia*, comes down out of heaven to enjoy the blessing and favor of God's presence,[40] His rest,[41] and His refreshment.[42]

A People of Witness – The Primitive Church

It seems, then, that the Church ought not to be defined as the consummate hope for humankind. Rather it is the (human) witness "between the times" to a greater, future realization of God's purpose in calling out and setting apart a people for covenant relationship with Himself and responsibility for others. Jesus preached the Kingdom, but historically what came into being was the Church. He hoped for Israel and remained dedicated to God's chosen people to the end, but nevertheless recognizes the stubbornness and intransigence of the people from early on in His ministry. Preparing for this eventuality, He gathers to Himself a remnant – the nucleus of the true Israel – so that at the ascension, the Church, already in incipient form, is not a separate synagogue but is distinguished certainly by discipleship.

---

[38] G. E. Ladd, *A Theology of the New Testament Revealed* (Grand Rapids, Wm B Eerdmans, 1974) p. 67; See also, Revelation 21:2-3

[39] Revelation 5:9

[40] Revelation 21:3

[41] Revelation 21:4

[42] Revelation 21:6

The Day of Pentecost

Jesus had told the disciples to remain in Jerusalem and await the baptism of the Spirit prophesied by John.[43] Not yet understanding His meaning, the disciples had asked whether this was the moment they had all been waiting for: the restoration of the Kingdom to Israel.[44] But Jesus is evasive; God alone is sovereign in the unfolding of His purposes for their redemption. While they worry over Israel's election, He promises the empowering presence of the Holy Spirit to enable their witness not only in Jerusalem, but in all Judea and Samaria, and to the ends of the earth.[45]

On the day of Pentecost the disciples are gathered together in one place, when suddenly there is the sound of an almighty wind blowing out of heaven. They see what appear to be tongues of fire dividing and resting on each one of them, and they speak, intelligibly, in all kinds of languages.[46] God-fearing Jews "from every nation under heaven"[47] hear the wonders of God told to them in their own dialects. These phenomena are suggestive of unity and diversity: the *ecclesia* is to be characterized both by its oneness and its universality of scope.[48] Peter proclaims to the wondering crowds that what they are witnessing is the fulfillment of the prophecy of Joel: "In the last days, God says, I will pour out my Spirit on *all flesh.*"[49] God is restoring the fellowship of the human race, so hopelessly spoiled when the language of men is confused at Babel. He is gathering

---

[43] Acts 1:4

[44] Acts 1:6

[45] Acts 1:8

[46] Acts 2:1-4

[47] Acts 2:5

[48] G. E. Ladd, *A Theology of the New Testament Revealed* (Grand Rapids, Wm B Eerdmans, 1974) p. 385.

[49] Joel 2:28–32; Acts 2:17

from every nation, tribe and tongue a Kingdom of priests to serve God.[50]

The Life of the Primitive Church

Although it is some time before the mission to the Gentiles really gets underway, the primitive Church nevertheless bears the distinctive hallmarks of unity and diversity that will later be the building blocks for Paul's theology of the Church. At Pentecost, the New Testament *ecclesia* had come into being as a creation of God through the Holy Spirit. G. E. Ladd explains that this baptism of the Spirit constituted the individuals present as members of the body of Christ. "It is therefore impossible to be a believer and not be in the *ecclesia*, for when one believes, he or she is baptized with all other believers into the body of Christ."[51] Reflecting this corporate identity in Christ, the first believers "devoted themselves to the apostles' teaching and to the fellowship, to the breaking of bread and to prayer."[52] Conscious of their common ties, they were devoted to one another in love. For these believers to be a believer naturally meant sharing with other believers the life of the coming age.[53]

This loving unity expressed itself uniquely in the sharing of their material resources. Those who possessed land and wealth of their own, upon conversion came to see that their wealth was rather a blessing and a trust to be stewarded for the benefit of others. It seems that the practice of voluntarily selling land in order that the many poorer members of the new fellowship might be provided for soon became commonplace. Although

---

[50] Revelation 5:9-10

[51] G. E. Ladd, *A Theology of the New Testament Revealed* (Grand Rapids, Wm B Eerdmans, 1974) pp. 384-385

[52] Acts 2:42

[53] G. E. Ladd, *A Theology of the New Testament Revealed* (Grand Rapids, Wm B Eerdmans, 1974) p. 388

the fellowship probably comprised of people of many different walks of life and strata of society, this appears not to have inhibited a deep sense of mutual commitment among the believers.

The interrelated unity and diversity of the new *ecclesia* was also apparent in its organization, which took various forms. In the beginning, being barely distinguishable from a Jewish synagogue, the primitive Church would have been presided over by a group of elders. When the leadership gathered for the Jerusalem council, the elders and the apostles shared the role.[54] Paul appointed elders in the Churches he founded in the province of Asia,[55] but when the seven deacons are appointed in Acts 6:2, and then again at the council in Jerusalem,[56] the entire congregation enters into an understanding of the decision reached. This action is critical in quenching the fires of confusion that had been fuelled by enthusiastic Jewish persuaders who were obviously moving amongst the people.[57] In fact, some theologians would suggest that this passage in Acts is the same occasion mentioned in Galatians 2:1-10, although this is difficult to prove.

There is no uniform pattern of government in Acts, so that the Churches are not bound by any formal ecclesiastical structure. It is evident from the apostolic practice of sending Christian greetings and ambassadors among the Churches, sometimes with gifts where there is need,[58] that there is real unity among the different local Churches.[59]

---

[54] Acts 15:2, 22; 16:4

[55] Acts 14:23

[56] Acts 15:12, 22

[57] Acts 15:22-27

[58] Acts 11:27-30

[59] G. E. Ladd, *A Theology of the New Testament Revealed* (Grand Rapids, Wm B Eerdmans, 1974) pp. 388-389

The Breach with Israel

The new *ecclesia*, then, was distinguished first by the quality of its relationships. They are holy in this sense before they are so in any separatist sense.

The disciples show a great reluctance throughout the book of Acts to break away from the Jewish synagogue. The Jews become increasingly antagonistic and the witness of the disciples ever bolder. With Stephen's recognition that temple worship and, implicitly, Torah observance have been rendered obsolete under the terms of the new covenant,[60] persecution breaks out against the Church and the believers are scattered throughout Judea and Samaria. The result is that the Jewish believers are forced to address the question of the status of the Gentiles.

Peter's vision at Joppa, the intervention of the angel of God and the outpouring of the Holy Spirit upon the Gentile believers following the proclamation of the gospel at Caesarea, convince him that Cornelius, his relatives and all his close friends should be baptized[61] – but he nevertheless takes a lot of persuading! "I now know," he says to them, "how true it is that God does not show favoritism but accepts men from every nation who fear Him and do what is right."[62]

Following this event, Peter has to persuade the Jerusalem Church of the legitimacy of his actions.[63] Even having concluded that: "God has granted the Gentiles repentance unto life",[64] the issue of the Church's relationship to Israel and to the law is not resolved until after the planting of several Gentile Churches by Paul and Barnabas. This is the stimulus

---

[60] Acts 7
[61] Acts 10
[62] Acts 10:34-35
[63] Acts 11:1-18
[64] Acts 11:18

and presenting problem for the Jerusalem council.[65] The council concludes that the Gentiles need not bear the burden of observing the law, however they are not yet clear as to the degree of their exemption. The letter drafted to the Churches of Antioch, Syria and Cilicia curiously counsels them to abstain from food sacrificed to idols, from blood and from the meat of strangled animals.[66] Thereafter, Paul continues his practice of going first to the Jews of each city that he visits with the gospel.

It is not until Rome[67] that he pronounces God's judgment upon the nation as a whole[68] with the sober conclusion that, therefore, "God's salvation has been sent to the Gentiles, and they will listen!"[69]

> "It is obvious that the leaders and teachers in the New Testament considered themselves the heirs of a rich heritage. They felt that what they were experiencing and saying was a fulfillment of what was begun in Old Testament times. Jesus himself was master of the Old Testament and wherever there was occasion, He related His work to that of Old Testament leaders. He and His apostles accepted the Jewish scriptures and considered their work as the completion of God's revelation of Himself to the Jewish people."[70]

When the breach with the synagogue finally comes, it is accepted with sad resignation.[71] As Paul quotes from the prophet Isaiah, "this people's heart has become calloused". Even so, as Paul has already explained in his

---

[65] Acts 15

[66] Acts 15:29

[67] Acts 28:11-31

[68] Acts 28:26-27

[69] Acts 28:28

[70] H. I. Hester. *The Heart of the New Testament*, (USA, Broad Man Press, 1950) p. 15

[71] It began with the episode of Stephen's death (Acts 6:13), and continued through constant rejection of the early Christians. By the later chapters of Acts, what began as a seed in Jerusalem became a fertile movement in Rome (Acts 28:28).

epistle to the Romans, it is a hardening only "in part until the full number of the Gentiles has come in."[72] It is Paul's conviction that "all Israel will be saved,"[73] for "as far as election is concerned, they are loved on account of the patriarchs, for God's gifts and his call are irrevocable."[74] These are a people who have been called out and set apart for covenant relationship with God and responsibility for others, and once called out and set apart, the covenant promise is sure and irrevocable. Paul reminds the reader that it is the Gentiles who have been grafted into the olive tree of Israel to share in its nourishing sap, not the other way around.

Concluding Part One 'The Legacy of the Old Testament'

The Old Testament was the sum total of the Bible that existed for the early Church leaders. Undoubtedly, the scriptures figured greatly in their considerations and explanations of what Christ had achieved.

Their newness was not a fad; it was intrinsically linked to the purposes of God as revealed to every generation. The two covenants, old and new, cannot be separated. They represent two crucial reference tools for the believer's spirituality and act as a compass or a satellite navigation system for the spiritual journey. As Andrew Murray states:

> "The two covenants represent two stages of God's education
> of man... the progress and transition from one to another is
> not merely chronological or historical, it is organic and
> spiritual."[75]

---

[72] Romans 11:25
[73] Romans 11:26
[74] Romans 11:28b-29
[75] Rev. A. Murray, *The Two Covenants* (London, Misbet, 1899) p.14

CHAPTER NINE

THE CHURCH: A PEOPLE EMPOWERED

Paul and the Church

Paul's use of the metaphor of the olive tree[1] suggests both unity and distinct identity. The Church is rooted in Israel and lives not only by its nourishing sap, but also by the mercy of God, having been grafted onto the tree by His own loving hand. However, despite the fact that branches were broken off[2] so that the believing Gentiles could be grafted in, it is the root that supports them. Furthermore, if a place could be found for these who do not "belong," how much more readily will God find a place for penitent Jews to be grafted back in again! Indeed, says Paul, this is God's very purpose; it is to the reconciliation of Israel that He is looking forward, when God will gather His people into the New Jerusalem, through faith in Jesus as Israel's crucified and risen Messiah.[3]

The grafting in of wild branches to the natural life of the olive tree anticipates the redemption of those that were broken off. This redemption will result in a more splendid cultivar. In the same way, Paul uses a number of different metaphors for the Church to show that the new

---

[1] Romans 11
[2] Romans 11:17, 19-20
[3] Romans 11:25,26

ecclesia, according to its promises in Christ, fulfils the hopes of the old, while also looking forward. The future will see a more consummate expression of unity, holiness, loving commitment and inclusiveness that is fitting to a people who have been called out and set apart for covenant relationship with God and responsibility for others.

This chapter will examine three metaphors that Paul felt to be especially helpful for understanding the nature of the Church.

Metaphorically Speaking, The Body of Christ

The body of Christ is perhaps the most distinctive of the many metaphors that Paul employed.[4] Astonishingly, Paul claims that the body "of" or "in" Christ is one with the Lord. It is not an exclusive association to the detriment of the broadening of our fellowship with the Trinity. This oneness is in keeping with the prayer in John 17. For Paul, this relatedness of the parts to the head is what grounds the unity of the members of that body.[5] This identity in Christ ought to be shaping relationships with one another. Unfortunately, like the Corinthians, modern day Christians demonstrate a tendency to emphasize their differences instead of the deep ties that bind. Paul argues that God has made each person differently, with different gifts and roles to play, but all are united in one calling.[6] Each one ought to serve the common good and every person's contribution ought to be recognized and valued.

In the Epistle to the Ephesians, Paul develops this line of thought further. Christ is the head of the body and the body is to grow up in every

---

[4] 1 Corinthians 12:12-27
[5] 1 Corinthians 6:15
[6] 1 Corinthians 1:10

way into Him who is the head.[7] The eschatological thrust of this passage is evident, as it looks forward to the final attainment of a unity and maturity, culminating in the whole measure of the fullness of Christ.[8] The reader is reminded that the final goal of Christ's redemptive ministry is to restore order and unity in the whole universe, which has been disrupted by sin.[9] God's plan is "to unite all things in Him, things in heaven and things on earth."[10] This cosmic unity in Christ has already been achieved in principle. He has already been exalted far above every hostile power and has been made head over all things for His Church.[11] However, the very certainty of the eschatological unity demands the effort to realize this unity in Christ in history.[12] Paul encourages the Ephesian believers to work at that unity, "[making] every effort to keep the unity of the Spirit through the bond of peace."[13]

There are a number of interpretations of the metaphorical reference to "the body of Christ." Emphasis is placed on the participation of the believer in the Church. Those who name the name of Christ as Lord in their lives have a societal obligation to play their part for the common good.

> "The participative model of Church requires more than just values and practices that correspond to participative institutions. The Church is not first of all a realm of moral purposes; it is the anticipation, constituted by the presence of the Spirit, and without this presence, even a Church with a

---

[7] Ephesians 4:15

[8] Ephesians 4: 13

[9] Colossians 1:19-20

[10] Ephesians 1:10

[11] Ephesians 1:22

[12] G. E. Ladd, *A Theology of the New Testament Revealed* (Grand Rapids, Wm B Eerdmans, 1974)p. 592.

[13] Ephesians 4:3

decentralised participative structure and culture will become sterile and perhaps more sterile even than an hierarchical Church."[14]

The Temple of the Spirit

In the Old Testament, the temple is regarded as the place of God's dwelling. In 1 Chronicles it is seen how David was denied the privilege of building the temple of God.[15] This trust was given instead to his son Solomon. Mentioned previously, the inheritance of the promise was, in a sense, conditional upon the nation's obedience. First David, then his sons, Absalom and Solomon, stray from the path of righteousness and thus begin Israel's demise. Israel is eventually forced into exile. The destruction of the temple, the banishment of Israel, the inadequacy of the second temple, all spoke of the people's abandonment and of the departure of the presence of God from their midst. As Israel contemplated the horrors of exile, the hope of a messianic deliverance and an eternal Kingdom under Davidic rule is born.[16] This sustains the people throughout the period of the exile and beyond into their partial restoration to the land. Closely tied to that hope was the vision that one day, beyond the inglorious second temple built by the remnant of the people upon their return from exile, there would be a new temple. This would be a temple that would rival that of Solomon.

The prophets spoke of that temple in the context of the coming

---

[14] M. Volf, *After Our Likeness*, (Grand Rapids, Wm B Eerdmans, 1998) p. 257

[15] 1 Chronicles 28:2-3; 6

[16] Ezekiel and Zechariah played an important role in establishing such a prophetic hope. In Psalm 2:6 Zion figures as the centre key of the Kingdom. Refer to Ezekiel 17:22; Jeremiah. 23:5; Zechariah 3:8; Haggai. 2:20-23.

Kingdom of God,[17] but when Jesus comes, announcing the arrival of that Kingdom, it is clear that it is not as they had envisaged. Jesus not only cleanses the temple,[18] He re-forms it in its entirety: "Destroy this temple, and I will raise it again in three days."[19]

Although Paul uses this metaphor to convey that the Spirit of God also indwells the individual believer, insofar as he applies it to the Church, it is clear that he wants to explain that the presence of God has moved from the Jerusalem temple to the Church.[20] The foundation of that temple (Christ) has been well laid by the apostle, but the believers must now be careful how they build. They must avoid the folly of wood and straw (their fascination with wisdom and rhetoric) and build instead with costly and enduring materials (gold, silver and precious stones), imagery taken directly from the building of Solomon's temple.[21] The distinction of the Church of God from the numerous other pagan temples of Corinth is the indwelling presence of God the Holy Spirit.[22]

In keeping with the typological dimension of Paul's metaphors, the temple metaphor also has end-time significance in its identification with heaven. The psalmist describes the Lord in His holy temple, seated upon a heavenly throne,[23] and the writer of the Epistle to the Hebrews describes the sanctuary as "a copy and shadow of what is in heaven."[24] The presence and the glory of God are such that there is no need for a temple in the heavenly Jerusalem, other than the Lord God Almighty and the Lamb,

---

[17] Ezekiel 37:26-27; 40:1; Haggai 2:9
[18] Matthew 21:12
[19] John 2:19
[20] 1 Corinthians 3:9
[21] 1 Chronicles.29:2; 2 Chronicles. 3:6
[22] 2 Corinthians. 6:16–7:1.
[23] Psalm 11:4
[24] Hebrews 8:5

who shield, surround and encompass the people of God.[25]

The Bride of Christ

Paul also compares the Church to a bride. This metaphor, it appears, is derived from Isaiah's prophetic vision of a marriage between Israel and its Lord.[26] This paints a picture of great tenderness as the Lord delights and rejoices over Israel as a bridegroom rejoices over his bride. There is also some precedent in the Gospels for this metaphor. Christ clearly likens Himself to a Bridegroom come among the people, with the implication that they ought to rejoice with Him.[27] On another occasion, in the telling of the parable of the ten virgins, He suggests that the Church must also wait in readiness for His coming again.[28] Paul understands that the bride is promised to one Husband, to Christ, and that it is His task to prepare her for her wedding day.[29] In a more mystical passage in another of his epistles, He likens the love that a husband ought to have for his bride to that which Christ showed for His Church.[30]

The bride is to be virginal, pure and holy, set apart for the love and worship of God, for Christ loved the Church and gave Himself up for her.[31] Both are to love and cherish and prize the love of the other before all things.

This is an incredible picture of the intimacy of God's love and care for His Church. When the Church is revealed in all her beauty, coming down

---

[25] Revelation 21:22

[26] Isaiah 62:1–5

[27] Matthew 9:15

[28] Matthew 25:1–6

[29] 2 Corinthians. 11:2

[30] Ephesians 5:25–33

[31] Ephesians 5: 25–28

from heaven as a bride, beautifully dressed for her Husband,[32] there is the sound of a great multitude, with a voice like the roar of rushing waters and loud peals of thunder:

> "Hallelujah!
> For our Lord God Almighty reigns.
> Let us rejoice and be glad
> And give Him glory!
> For the wedding of the Lamb has come,
> And His bride has made herself ready."[33]

A People Empowered

Having examined the intense commitment on God's part, to fashion a people for Himself "throughout the generations," some basic principles need to be explained. God expects of His people a basic commitment. Relationship with God carries responsibility. God seeks a people who are eager to commit to those responsibilities. Therefore, in order to be covenantal, relationship with God requires the believer to not only commit to God but also to love his neighbour.

Jesus introduces a paradigm shift during His earthly ministry. What forms is the emergence of a dynamic society called Church; a community of believers that has an impact upon the world. They possessed a conscious reality of their responsibility and commitment to affect the world.

It is important now to consider further the historic record of the book of Acts and how it pulsates with the fruitful activity of the Holy Spirit. The

---

[32] Revelation 21:2
[33] Revelation 19:6b–7

empowerment of the believers at Pentecost provided them with an understanding of the divine requirements. Throughout the book, the Holy Spirit is seen to be directing the Church outward, making the gospel effective in reaching the world.

The significant agreement that God made, as referred to in Jeremiah,[34] is realized by the coming of the Holy Spirit on the first Palestinian believers. This new covenant helps the believer to understand the work of the Holy Spirit depicted in Acts. It assists in the understanding of the Holy Spirit, in the dynamic way in which He is at work in the hearts of people to lead them to an understanding of Jesus Christ.

The Church must always align itself in this divine partnership with the Holy Spirit. This will be a safeguard against the temptation to think that it can be effective in the world arena by simply relying on the latest business techniques or eye-catching programs.

The book of Acts in particular, and the New Testament as a whole, reveals the importance of the Holy Spirit in the empowerment process. People such as the Apostle Peter and the Apostle Paul are infused with passion for God's purposes and a compassion for His people. An army of dedicated people come to the fore; they are committed to engage the world with a message of hope, even for those outside of their own cultural mind sets and traditions. Engaging the world is no vision statement placed on the walls of a meeting place. The world for the early Christians was conditioned by The Roman Empire, embedded in the sub soil of Jewish and Greek culture, an inter mingling synchronism of religion; beliefs with cosmopolitism. As Bartlet argues, citing the witness of Seneca, in his treatise on anger, "The world is filled with crimes and vices. Things are too

---

[34] Jeremiah 31:33

far gone to be healed by any treatment."[35]

The Church, then, is a covenantal people who know their God and who become aware of God as they encounter His goodness in everyday life. It is a people who, in spite of adversity, press on with their testimony to Christ, going about doing good to their fellow man.

Clearly, God is at work. He is the builder of the house. The beauty is that He has included people to partner with Him in His plan to reconcile the world to Himself.[36] The first Christians of Jewish descent learned early to co-operate with the Holy Spirit. In God's economy, there shall be no lack of whatever it takes because He has given us everything needed to succeed in our mission. The Church is truly "a people equipped" for the task of worldwide evangelism.

When reading the book of Acts and the accounts in early Church history of what was accomplished, the reader is inspired and reminded that every generation has the inestimable privilege of knowing, loving, and serving God. This is the wonder of it all, that God, in His covenantal way, has intended men and women, in all walks of life, to taste for themselves that the Lord is good. The New Covenant is the realization that God is not far off or detached from the human predicament. He is accessible to all.

Christians are called to awaken to God's agenda. To do so requires taking the time to wait upon the Lord and to have a keen interest in what the Lord is requiring of the believer today. The nature of the true Church needs to be understood properly, especially as His people are to be good stewards of the legacy that has been passed on from previous generations. The way in which the Church relates to and partners with the Holy Spirit

---

[35] JV Bartlet: *Early Church History: A Sketch of the First 4 Centuries* (Frome, Butler and Tanner, 1905) p. 14

[36] Acts 1:8

is significant. It is similar to the confession of Jesus to His followers regarding His own responsibility, when He said, "I must be about the Father's business."[37] This must become the confession of believers today too.

[37] Luke 2:49

CHAPTER TEN

A PEOPLE GATHERED FOR PURPOSE

In the scene prior to "the Ascension" we see a Commander-in-Chief getting together his seemingly beleaguered troops to re-envision them with the purpose of their mission.[1] Preceding the empowerment of the Holy Spirit, it was necessary for a regrouping in order to focus their minds on the task ahead. The interim period was vital to the next phase of their mission. Jesus made certain that He had sufficient time with them over a period of 40 days.[2]

Jesus engaged them in a mission-building exercise. He gave them clear direction as to the basis on which they were to proceed.[3] Essentially, the coming of the Spirit was not to cancel out the engagement of strategic thinking; on the contrary, it would result in an informed faith and a goal-orientated passion for the purpose.[4]

It is a commonly understood principle in any company of people that three things are vital for success: Personality, Purpose and Power. Jesus added this threefold dimension, liberating them to be themselves, as they learned submission to the Holy Spirit.

Jesus was to be the central figure and focus of the Church.[5] The whole

---

[1] Acts 1: 2
[2] Acts 1:3
[3] Acts1:4-5
[4] Acts1:8
[5] Acts 4;10-11

aspect of "Messiah" came into the forefront in the acts of the earliest apostles. Christ was the personality of the Church, with God, the Holy Spirit keeping it "Christ-centered." Unfortunately, the Church has tended to lose touch with its basic identity in this respect. The end result is a community being either focused on the personality and gifting of its leader, or heavily over-promoting its programs.

The banner under which Jesus rallied His apostolic community was "Christ." All believers, in this respect, are "Messianic" – a title that must not be hijacked to satisfy an elitism within Christianity. This is the identity given to the whole Church, be it Jew or Gentile.

The purpose remains central to the success of God's people. Jesus, in all His activity both pre- and post-resurrection, transmitted a sense of purpose and strategy for the energy and focus of the Church. The power element is crucial. It is insufficient for any Church to be focussed around a personality, however full of strategy and purpose. Power provides the ability to produce the end result: In this case, transformed lives, a renewed ideal and a moral certainty that works.[6]

The core reality of the gospel is prayer. That is prayer that changes people and situations,[7] bringing power to heal, deliver and envision. So much so that Paul the Apostle was able to say with full conviction, "I am not ashamed of the *Gospel* of *Christ*, for it is the *Power* of God unto salvation" [emphasis added].[8]

The Church is, of all communities, the embodiment of hope, the harbinger of good news, and the facilitator of power, as it works in union with the Holy Spirit. This hope was embodied in the covenants with God's people; a hope that would transform people's lives and give them a sense

---

[6] Acts 1:8
[7] Acts 4:31
[8] Romans 1:16; 1 Corinthians 1:18

of destiny and the dignity to face the challenges of life and death.

God is faithful to His covenant and He is committed to the long haul.[9] Jesus inspired hope in His followers. Their gathering together fuelled them with hope in the Spirit's power of resurrection and Jesus being lifted up to the highest place, seated in the heavenly places, securing an advantage over His enemies.[10]

The Gift of the Spirit – The Dynamic Impact of the Kingdom

Crucial to the gathering of the disciples was the empowerment of the Holy Spirit and the accompanying high profile in the wider community. This Kingdom dynamic could be measured by the impact that the Holy Spirit was having on the witnessing public.

The corporate baptism of the Holy Spirit was not to the exclusion of the individual.[11] It was obviously broad in scope,[12] whilst at the same time deeply personal and intimate. The Holy Spirit broke the earliest disciples out of self-intimidation and any reluctance to take the lead. He thrust them into the public eye and so avoided the Holy Spirit baptism becoming a private affair. They were indeed a people gathered, experiencing the tangible presence of God at work with them.

"When they heard this sound, a crowd came together in bewilderment, because each one heard them speaking in his own language. Utterly amazed, they asked: 'Are not all these men who are speaking Galileans? Then how is it that each of

---

[9] Acts 2: 39
[10] Phillippians 2:9-11
[11] Acts 2:3
[12] Acts 2:4

us hears them in his own native language? Parthians, Medes and Elamites: residents of Mesopotamia, Judea and Cappadocia, Pontus and Asia, Phrygia and Pamphylia, Egypt and the parts of Libya near Cyrene; visitors from Rome (both Jews and converts to Judaism); Cretans and Arabs – we hear them declaring the wonders of God in our own tongues!'"[13]

The Kingdom of God expanded rapidly as the Holy Spirit continued to provoke the apostles and prophets with a zeal that thrust them into the world and beyond their own strategic limitations. They were prevented from settling down and were constantly pioneering new frontiers for the Gospel of Christ.

The Apostolic Spirit at Work – Strategic Vision

The Apostolic Spirit spearheads the thrust of mission and is constantly equipping the saints for the task that they are called to do. He is the true dynamic of the Kingdom. Christians must avoid solely worshiping the Spirit for His power, whilst at the same time failing to co-operate with His promptings and guidance. This is His principle task for the believer, as Jesus said,

> "All this I have spoken while still with you. But the Counsellor, the Holy Spirit, whom the Father will send in My name, will teach you all things and will remind you of everything I have said to you."[14]

---

[13] *Acts 2:6-11*
[14] John 14:25-26

Much is written on the *ministry* of the Holy Spirit with little reference to the *strategy* of the Spirit. The book of Acts contains the strategy of the Spirit for expanding the Kingdom of God on earth.

The New Testament as a whole and the book of Acts in particular, illustrates that God has His overall plan. As Commander-in-Chief, He still directs the advance and the movement of His forces to fulfill His objectives. The plan of advance is summed up in Acts 1:8:

> "But you will receive power when the Holy Spirit comes on you; and you will be my witnesses in Jerusalem, and in all Judea and Samaria, and to the ends of the earth."[15]

Acts, in its entirety, is about the dynamic of the Kingdom of God. The Holy Spirit Himself is about advancing the Gospel of the Kingdom in the human heart and the wider community. For example, people turning to Christ in large numbers, as recorded in the book of Acts, gather quite a momentum and cannot remain hidden from view. This dynamic was not spasmodic; it was not a shot in the dark. On the contrary, the record is a clear account of a well thought-out plan. It was obviously calculated to have a substantial impact on society as a whole. According to Lantee, "It was God not man who controlled the spread of the Good News and it is God or His Spirit who issues the commands."[16] To this end believers must continue to call upon the Lord and look to God for His direction, remaining open to receiving from His empowering presence in all that they seek to do for Him today.

Paul words it well in Galatians when he refers to the timing of God in the sending of His Son to the earth. His actions show forethought and reveal to us that God is a very thorough strategist.

---

[15] Acts 1:8

[16] Lantee in C S.C. Williams, *The Acts of the Apostles*, (London, A & C Black, 1964) p.17

"But *when the time had fully come* [specific timing], God sent His Son, born of a woman, born under law, *to redeem those under law, that we might receive the full rights of sons* [specific purpose]."[17] [emphasis added]

Jesus specifically gave testimony to the Father's activity in timing events.

"He said to them: 'It is not for you to know *the times or dates the Father has set by His own authority'*."[18] [emphasis added]

What is clear is that God has an agenda and He wants His people engaged in it. He has a clear objective in mind: it is the bigger picture of the advance of the Kingdom. This is the rule of God in the hearts of men and women.

A Divine Imperative for the Church and a Sign for the World

The coming of the Holy Spirit upon the early believers at Pentecost was a significant paradigm shift in God's purposes in the earth. The purpose would soon become evident. God's people, gathered together in unity of heart, were to experience a move of the Spirit so profound that it would challenge the very foundations of secular society.

What was taking place was beyond an individual, subjective experience.[19] It was the initiation of the disciples into a divine activity already in process. The very loud and public declaration[20] of the actual baptism at Pentecost was explained as extraordinary. Even cloven tongues

---

[17] Galatians 4:4-5
[18] Acts 1:7
[19] Acts 2:3
[20] 'Noise' Acts 2:2

of fire came upon the whole community![21] It was a divine interaction that was taking place.[22] God was at work and He would not be hindered in His task. The sound of a "mighty rushing wind" – God was fanning the furnace of divine utterance.

The Holy Spirit transformed this small group of believers, liberating them from intimidation and from the fear that had seized hold of them. No longer would their zeal be stifled and their dreams suppressed.

The work of the Spirit was evidently successful in projecting them into a higher and more visible profile.[23] The people found that they soon aroused curiosity in the public arena. The baptism of the Holy Spirit was never to be a private affair. It was a transformation, the fruit of which was designed to be a public declaration; a total transformation that took place in the life of each person submitted to the work of the Spirit in his or her life.

The Church did not begin, nor was it expected to continue, in isolation from the world. The strategy was always with God, and it was one of thrusting His people into the nations of the world. The believers, by the work of the Spirit, were able to break out of self-imposed limitations, boldly declaring the Lordship of Christ.

The Church was given the responsibility of being a prophetic statement of Christ in the world. This was to truly reflect God's interests and goals, affecting change in the way people thought about God, and introducing them to a life experience of the divine. God's intention is stated clearly throughout the scriptures: "My prayer is not that you take

---

[21] Acts 2:3
[22] Acts 2:4
[23] Acts 2:4-5

them out of the world but that you protect them from the evil one... May they also be in us so that the world may believe that you have sent me."[24]

> "All authority in heaven and on earth has been given to me. Therefore go and make disciples of all nations, baptising them in the name of the Father and of the Son and of the Holy Spirit, and teaching them to obey everything I have commanded you. And surely I am with you always, to the very end of the age."[25]

The mission of the Church became very explicit. God expects his people to line up with the activity of the Holy Spirit. The work of the Spirit would prove to be contagious, attractive and effective in bringing about a change of heart and mind in the lives of people. The Church gatherings were to witness to the reality of God and kindle a fire with fervor for God in their hearts and minds. The Church is called to be a sign – to facilitate clear direction for those unacquainted with the person of Jesus, proclaiming the purpose of His mission and His power to transform lives.

The dynamic interaction between the work of the Spirit and prophetic statements made by the Church leaders[26] had a profound effect on the gathered believers. A deepening faith gripped their hearts, revealing a compelling call to convict the world, which produced a deep searching of the heart, just as Jesus had said the Holy Spirit would be engaged in doing.[27]

It ought to be evident who the followers of Christ represent. In all walks of life, wherever the believer is to be found, there should be an

---

[24] John 17:15,21
[25] Matthew 28:18-20
[26] Acts 2:16, 7, 17:25
[27] John 16:8

acknowledgement that "something is different." The people who believe should possess a tacit sense of their faith in God and an understanding as to the meaning of life.

Redeeming the Lost – The Power to Transform Lives

"But I tell you the truth: It is for your good that I am going away. Unless I go away, the Counsellor will not come to you; but if I go I will send Him to you. When He comes, he will convict the world of guilt in regard to sin and righteousness and judgment." (John 16:7-8)

Jesus stepped into people's situations and brought about change and often the redemption of lives.

Besides rhetorical principles, what provision does the Church have for those who are bound, lonely or lack a sense of purpose? The love of God is not content with words. It must translate into action. Deeds of hope and kindness have an effect on the environment. Jesus was focused and busy in the purpose, yet He always found time for the interruptions and crises in people's lives. So must the Church be willing to be interrupted.

In what ways is the Church demonstrating the love and power of God? Compassion should cause the Church to engage with the world, not seek to escape it.

To Disciple All Nations

In the Church, people of all cultures can be trained in the ways of God. There are no borders to the mission of the Church; there are no off-limit areas to the message of the Kingdom. The mission is not to build the Church; it is to reach out with the message of hope[28]. Christ will see to it that the Church is built. Jesus said, "I will build My Church."[29]

The activity of the Holy Spirit in the world is not one of a confrontational approach. He is steadily working in convicting the world concerning sin[30].

Witnessing to Christ is not necessarily preaching; it bears a deeper meaning. It is about carrying the testimony of the reality of Christ in one's own life. Witness comes from the word *martus*, the English equivalent being *martyr,* denoting "...one who can or does aver what he or she has

---

[28] Matthew 28:19-20
[29] Matthew 16:18
[30] John 16:8

seen or heard or knows."[31] From the very outset, Jesus set the mission of the Church and the prescribed sphere of activity was the world.

> "The spirit of all mature religion is that I am my brother's keeper and my brother is my keeper... Nothing else, but the world should be our parish. Such is the case, because, having discovered the full beauty and the ultimate significance of personal life, one longs to make it a social possession; this is, to desire precisely that kind of life for every man, woman and child who enters the world..."[32]

This then is the Church's mission: to instruct, and influence the world; remembering that in referring to the world, the Church must deal with "the people factor."

A Discipling Community

> "They devoted themselves to the apostles' teaching and to the fellowship, to the breaking of bread and to prayer. Everyone was filled with awe, and many wonders and miraculous signs were done by the apostles. All the believers were together and had everything in common. Selling their possessions and goods, they gave to anyone as he had need. Every day they continued to meet together in the temple courts. They broke bread in their homes and ate together with glad and sincere hearts, praising God and enjoying the favour of all the people. And the Lord added to their number daily those who were

---

[31] W. E. Vine, M. F. Unger, W. White Jnr, *Vine's Complete Expository Dictionary of Old and New Testament Words* (London, Thomas Nelson, 1996) p. 680

[32] J. Ansbro, *Dimensions of Divine Providence* (New York, Orbis Books, 1986) p. 67

being saved."[33]

Meetings and programs are important but they present a limited picture. Time and space is needed in Church agendas if believers are truly to learn together and have a full expression of *koinōnia* ("fellowship"), as was displayed in the life of the Church in Acts. The Church today needs a deeper discovery of one another in order to release the potential of wealth that each person carries, and to draw on their strength and experience.

The early apostles had been schooled in Kingdom thinking throughout their relationship with Jesus. The term "discipleship" was very indicative of the nature of engagement that Jesus used in establishing the foundation of the Kingdom of God in their hearts. He taught them that to make their priorities clear in their lives, they must "seek first the Kingdom of God."[34]

Jesus spent invaluable days with them and used the hustle and bustle of life as their classroom. In such a way, they were nurtured in the culture of discipleship. This was the context in which Jesus revealed the Great Commission of Matthew 28, helping them to understand that the nature of their task was to in turn disciple other men and women in matters relating to the Kingdom of God.

Discipleship today is often shied away from for fear of excesses and abuse. Nevertheless, it is still a key component in the maturing of the saints. The Christian life is so much more than ascribing to a set of beliefs. It calls for the disciplines of the Spirit and the teaching of the flock of Christ. Discipline is the key in Church life, a fact that has been evident in the early community and subsequent ecclesiastical testimonies over the centuries. The sixteenth century reformed Church people considered discipline as a fundamental part of Church life. Discipline ought to form an

---

[33] Acts 2:42-47
[34] Luke 12:31

integral part of today's teaching and education process of believers; they should be tutored in the art of discipline.

The whole Church in the New Testament was essentially a discipling community. Surrounded as it was by a pagan world, the Church seized every opportunity to influence it. The Gospel had a powerful impact and its effects spread rapidly. Tertullian[36], the great Christian apologist, made the following declaration:

> "We Christians are but of yesterday and we have filled your cities, your islands, your fortresses, your towns, your market places, the very camp, palace, senate, forum, and have left you nothing but the temples of your gods."[35]

The Church, therefore, is designed to be a mobile testimony, able to travel to where the people are, and meet them at their point of need. Its message and life-changing experiences will speak to the nations of the world and will be applicable in every age. A lamp is not hidden but is placed in a position where the benefit of its light can be maximized.[36] So, too, the Church is placed in the center of human activity in order that its effect may be felt at every level of human experience. The people who have been called out from the influence of the world are to be so positioned that they provide a signpost, pointing towards a better way of life to those who are still caught up in the world and its thinking. Every Christian is called to contribute.

Essentially, the Church is a model community; an ideal society existing in a hostile environment. The Church must not lose sight of God's original intention. Like the Israel of God, it was always intended that the Church should be of value to the wider community in which it is placed. In God's

---

[35] Backhouse & Taylor, *Early Church History*, (London, West/Newman and Company, 1892) p. 115
[36] Luke 8:16-18

economy there is such a premium put on the value of the community called Church, but the Church was never meant to be a closed, exclusive club. Rather, it is a vital expression of the life of God; an attracting, drawing power to the outsider. This must not be open to abuse.

> "There was no merging of all private possessions in a common stock, but a voluntary and variable contribution on a large scale. That is to say, the ecclesia was a society in which neither the community was lost in the individuals, nor the individuals in the community. The community was set high above all, while the service and help to be rendered to the community remained a matter of individual conscience and free bounty."[37]

Discipleship is something deeper than educating the mind. It is about broadening the mental arena and engaging the heart in a pursuit of God's best for people's lives. In the great awakening that took place at Pentecost, the work of the Spirit was best understood as a continuous urge to disciple one another in the faith. It took the form of sharing together in communal times of prayer, fellowship and breaking of bread in one another's homes, and focusing on what Christ had accomplished in His life, death, resurrection and ascension. It was about establishing a lifestyle that encouraged a community known for its caring and sharing of life together. It saw the formation of friendships that transcended regional or socio-economic boundaries. Today the Church needs to be careful to build the same way, with ownership and participation, not a spectator mentality.

---

[37] F. J. A. Hort, *The Christian Ecclesia*, (London, Macmillan and Co., 1908) p. 48

Further Study

Refer to the following texts on discipleship: Matthew 10:24-25, Luke 14:26, Acts 1:6, Acts 20:1.

- *What can you discover about the nature of discipleship?*
- *What is meant by discipleship in the context of the Church?*
- *Should discipleship be understood in purely Christian context or is there more to understand in terms of discipling on a broader evangelistic plane?*

CHAPTER ELEVEN

THE EMPOWERMENT OF THE HOLY SPIRIT

Clearly, after the Pentecostal outpouring of the Holy Spirit, the Church enters into a new experience that radically increases its effectiveness in the wider community.

> "Then the disciples went out and preached everywhere, and **the Lord worked with them and confirmed His word** by the signs that accompanied it."[1] [emphasis added]

It is a mistake to assume that possessing the principles of the Kingdom is adequate in itself. The Kingdom of God will only be established in the power of God. This is inclusive of His authoritative Word, which is able to impart life to its hearers. In order to assist believers to grasp something of the work of the person of the Holy Spirit in their empowerment, it is helpful to consider the book of Acts. The *style, structure* and *significance* of the book of Acts reveal aspects of the mind of a strategist. These three strands will now be examined in turn.

---

[1] Mark 16:20

The Style of the Book of Acts

The emphasis throughout the book of Acts is one of "divine interventions," which take place in a myriad of ways. They are like hinges on which doorways of opportunity swing open to the gospel message of the Church. Supernatural occurrences are 'part and parcel' of the experience of truly apostolic people, who are cooperative with and open to the work of the Spirit as He directs their mission in life. There are clear hallmarks that are the result of the empowerment of the Holy Spirit; these can be called "divine encounters." Nuttall states:

> "The gift of the Spirit is God's supreme gift to man, for it is the gift of Himself."[2]

Jesus promised that after His departure His followers would experience the Spirit's empowerment. Yet as soon as Jesus was alive from the dead, they witnessed Him pass through closed doors[3] and miraculously provide the fish in their nets.[4] Stephen, as he proclaimed the gospel, was transfixed by a vision of Heaven even though his body was being pelted with stones[5]; and Saul of Tarsus had a sudden and dramatic encounter with the risen Christ, which deeply affected him and prepared him for a new commissioning as an apostle of Christ.[6]

In addition to the examples of empowerment, there are records of special equipping in which people are deeply affected by the Holy Spirit, such as being "filled with awe." "'... We hear them declaring the wonders of God in our own tongues!' Amazed and perplexed, they asked one

---

[2] G. F. Nuttall, *The Holy Spirit and Ourselves*, (Oxford, Basil Blackwell, 1947) p. 1
[3] John 20:26
[4] John 21:6
[5] Acts 7:55-56
[6] Acts 9:3

another, 'What does this mean?'"[7] There was also Peter's experience of an urgency and expedience of the Spirit as he was quickened to convey the truth in a contentious situation: "Then Peter, filled with the Holy Spirit, said to them: 'Rulers and elders of the people! If we are being called to account today for an act of kindness shown to a cripple and are asked how he was healed, then know this...'"[8]

Such provisions of boldness by the Spirit became a matter of regular experience and the disciples were enabled to preach the Word with a new confidence: "After they prayed, the place where they were meeting was shaken. And they were all filled with the Holy Spirit and spoke the Word of God boldly."[9]

In fact, the reference to "boldness" or "with great boldness" occurs often in the book of Acts and frequently refers to a transformation in Jesus' followers' mood and confidence.[10] It shows ways in which the Holy Spirit affects people, equipping them to achieve far greater things than would be possible if left to their own strength. Clearly, their testimony was sharpened and their understanding enriched as they communicated the message with power. Jesus had forewarned them not to be anxious about what they should say, because the Holy Spirit would give them the right words.[11] They certainly lacked for no good thing. Boldness was a part of their enabling for the task.

Such 'equippings' reflect the evidence of the Holy Spirit at work in the believer. The work of the Spirit is not limited by a lack of understanding. His commitment is to assist and enable the believer to achieve individual

---

[7] Acts 2:11-12
[8] Acts 4:8-10
[9] Acts 4:31
[10] Boldly = Acts 9:27,29; 14:3; 18:26; 19:8 Boldness 4:13, 29, 31
[11] John 14:26

and corporate success. Believers must be acutely aware of the value of operating with the Holy Spirit's quickening and empowering.

Powerful enablement was evident each time the people of God sought the Holy Spirit to complete an assigned task. The apostles were given the capacity to move in the realm of healings and miracles.

> "Then Peter said, 'Silver or gold I do not have, but what I have I give you. In the name of Jesus Christ of Nazareth, walk.' Taking him by the right hand, he helped him up, and instantly the man's feet and ankles became strong. He jumped to his feet and began to walk." [12]

> "Then the Church throughout Judea, Galilee and Samaria enjoyed a time of peace. It was strengthened; and encouraged by the Holy Spirit, it grew in numbers, living in the fear of the Lord."[13]

At one stage, Paul was stirred and troubled by a demon-possessed woman who was following him for three days.[14] Then, as the Spirit prompted and enabled him, he was emboldened and powerfully commanded her to be set free. It was evident that the Lord was present with them, confirming with signs and wonders the validity of the message of the Kingdom that they preached.

Particular envisioning was also a key administration of the work of the Spirit. It is necessary at times for God to envision believers since He follows a different pattern of thought. How encouraging to know that God is able to unlock the human "mindset," renewing the mind by the power of the Holy Spirit!

---

[12] Acts 3:6-8
[13] Acts 9:31
[14] Acts 16:17-18

People are often unnecessarily straightjacketed; trapped in webs of small thinking. Such self-limitations and narrow-mindedness are a hindrance to progress. In Acts, the reader finds God bridging the gap and removing the mindsets and entrenchments.

> "[God] communicated directly through words, through dreams, through visions – employing vehicles that those He approached believed in... On occasion He communicated in more unusual ways such as thorough a donkey (Numbers 22), through an angel, or through some miraculous event... But God's preferred way of bridging the gaps is by means of human-beings to human-beings..."[15]

Such was the impact on Peter concerning his attitude to the Gentiles. The "Jewish mindset," with its racial dimensions and cultural divide prevailed. In a vision, the Holy Spirit powerfully revealed to Peter His heart for the Gentiles. Peter was still talking about it when he arrived at the house of Cornelius. He told them that what he was doing was against the Law and all his teachings, but God had told him not to hesitate.[16] Such experiences of God enlighten the believer, enlarge their thinking, and should be part of a daily walk with God.

It is important to remain open to the scrutiny of the Holy Spirit in order that such strongholds of the mind do not hinder His progress and strategy. In this respect, believers, with their traditions and theology, must not be allowed to raise barriers in the way of the Spirit. There are many diverse ways God wants to lead, retaining the believer's 'fertility' and adaptability, without being afraid or overly conservative. Such was the transformation in Peter's life that he could boldly say:

---

[15] C. H. Kraft, *Christianity in Culture* (New York, Orbis Books, 2005) p.135
[16] Acts 10:20-30

"I now realize how true it is that God does not show favoritism but accepts men from every nation who fear him and do what is right."[17]

The culture of the Kingdom by the working of the Spirit was to have an influence on the culture of the day, especially as it was enforced by religion.

To summarize, divine encounters bring people into a powerful experience of Christ and His presence. Equippings help people to receive an impartation of the Spirit, quickening their faith and stirring up their gift through the laying on of hands. Authority in the Spirit allows people to move with confidence in the realm of the Spirit with the authority of God. Envisioning is an essential approach of apostolic ministry – a people enlightened to their destiny and purpose in life.

Further Study

Research the words "endowment" and "equipping" and find your own illustration for what they mean. Give particular reference to Genesis 30:20; 2 Chronicles 2:12-13; Luke 24:49.

The Structure of the Book of Acts

The book of Acts is about days of empowerment. The book itself is divided into 28 chapters and appears unfinished, serving as a reminder that the work of God has not ended. As it is read, great encouragement can be taken from the fact that whatever the obstacles or the difficulties, whatever

---

[17] Acts 10:34-35

the persecution, it is always possible to overcome because God is with his people. In Acts, a new day was dawning, and God was arousing the people from their apathy. They were beginning to enquire for themselves what God was doing.

Within the space of 28 chapters, 75 questions are asked and 21 Old Testament prophecies are referred to. The number of questions reflects the profound effect that the Spirit and the Word were having on people's minds. They were shaken and disturbed by what was taking place. It was no small debate that was held. Often rigorous scrutiny was the preoccupation of the Pharisees. Mental rigorous research in and of itself is not harmful, as all of humanity ought to be subject to scrutiny. It is debate for debate's sake that becomes harmful, especially when it reaches speculation and becomes far removed from the parameters of the biblical text. Brueggemann puts it in a poignant way when he reflects on how Jesus dealt with the paralysis of analysis. He states:

> "Jesus came to those paralyzed by the over punctilious requirements of some forms of Judaism that had been diverted from the claims of God and neighbor, and by the comprehensive ideology of the Roman government, which wanted to eliminate the God of the Jews from its horizon...."[18]

Today is no different. This is a time when ideologies abound and when Christianity is often marginalized. Without the aid of the Holy Spirit, believers are prone to settle for less than what God intends. Religion without the work of the Spirit blankets the mind and stupefies creative faculties.

One of the first signs of an awakening of the Spirit of God is to stimulate a healthy enquiry regarding the supernatural, a type of quest,

---

[18] W. Brueggemann, *The Word Militant*, (Minneapolis, Fortress Press, 2007) p. 162

and to begin to examine and consider what is taking place. Often, when God is doing something new, people become perplexed as they attempt to process it.

The New Testament Church was experiencing a major paradigm shift. "The fullness of time"[19] was a phrase used to express the strategic timing on God's part in the preparation of the world for the coming of Jesus and the Gospel of the Kingdom. The infrastructure and the political landscape[20] at that time helped the message spread beyond Judea along the trade routes. Expertise in communication, achieved by the technological breakthroughs that have taken place today, also leads to yet greater possibilities for the spread of the Gospel of the Kingdom today.

Even more significant was the prophetic framework in which the apostles were moving. The large number of Old Testament references shows the great pains they took to research the Word of God and apply it to the dynamic happenings that were taking place in the power of the Spirit.

The Jewish mind was very attuned to the importance of the Old Testament prophecies. This was demonstrated in the teaching that Peter received from Jesus. Paul was also so well trained by his Pharisee teachers regarding the prophecies from the Old Testament that, later on, he frequently referred to them in his writings. He was viewed as having a scholarly mind – a "Hebrew of the Hebrews."[21]

The events recorded in the book of Acts are eternally profound. There is a divine inflow of the Spirit cascading across the landscape of time,

---

[19] Galatians 4:4-7

[20] Pax Romana – Roman peace – for the first time in centuries it meant that was easier to travel across borders without encountering suspicion or threats from rival kingdoms and bandits and thieves were often curbed by the Roman military presence throughout the empire.

[21] Philippians 3:4-6

flooding into regions beyond with an irresistible force and an inspiring message of hope that could not be contained in one culture, one nation or in any single part of the world. What is seen in the book of Acts is not just the inflow of the Spirit, but also its apostolic outflow.

The Significance of the Book of Acts

The significance of the book is that it is a firsthand account written by Luke, who was present in the development of the work and its expansion. This provides one of the earliest records of the spread of Christianity.

It is historic, covering the beginnings of the work of God in a small group of disciples, to an eventual worldwide movement affecting key world centers, such as Caesarea, Antioch, Ephesus, Philippi and Corinth.

The curtains are drawn back on the stage of the gathered believers, revealing a dramatic turning point that sets the pace for generations. The scene set is so vivid, revealing the power of God at work, highlighting the ascension of Christ (Exaltation) and the outpouring of the Holy Spirit (Empowering). The Holy Spirit is at work in the marketplace, the home, in prison and in upper room gatherings. God is working with His people to establish His Kingdom.

CHAPTER TWELVE

A STRATEGY THAT WORKS

The advance of the work of God is unstoppable and this is apparent, particularly in Luke's writings in Acts, and in the New Testament as a whole. The fledgling Church was plagued by challenges within and without. Firstly, persecution was harsh, claiming the lives of notable figures in the Church. Secondly, heresy was a constant threat to the wellbeing of the community. There were also considerable pastoral challenges that the Church faced as converts from paganism came into contact with believers who were conservative in their Judaistic traditions. Nevertheless, not even human limitations could be allowed to hinder God from fulfilling His purpose. God has a strategy – and it succeeds, even when the Church struggles to understand what He is doing. Luke highlights on more than one occasion the need and the strain placed upon leadership to catch up with the direction and work of the Holy Spirit.[1]

In examining the structure of the book of Acts, a discernable strategy emerges. An essential part of the equipping of the Church is that it must be equipped with a workable plan if it is to remain effective in reaching the nations.

Consider Figure 12.1, which illustrates the directional flow of the Spirit. The account of Luke emphasizes that there is nothing haphazard

---

[1] The conflict between Peter and Paul; Thomas' doubting Christ's resurrection. leadership challenged by Cornelius.

about what is taking place. The book of Acts is about a powerful release of the Life of God – "Life" with a capital "L."

Figure 12.1: An Outline of the Book of Acts
*numbers relate to chapters in Acts

Holy Spirit Inflow	Holy Spirit Outflow		
1: Direction	8: Ethiopian	15: Council	22: Castle
2: Descent	9: Saul	16: Philippi	23: Council
3: Demonstration	10: Cornelius	17: Athens	24: Felix
4: Deliverance	11: Council	18: Corinth	25: Festus
5: Discernment	12: Persecution	19: Ephesus	26: Agrippa
6: Deeds	13: Antioch	20: Macedonia	27: Storms
7: Death	14: Lystra	21: Temple	28: Rome

Outflow Unhindered

A Clear Set of Directions Given: Acts 1

Jesus directs the mission and keeps things in clear focus. The disciples are able to identify His orders, given by the Spirit, and to comprehend them by the enablement of the Spirit. This is illustrated in the opening remarks of Luke in Acts 1. Jesus communicates with a passion the key issues, the things concerning the Kingdom.

The Kingdom of God occupies His parting instructions and the focus is consistent with the whole of scripture. The real nature of God's redemptive acts toward people has always been a revelation of His Kingship. The followers of Christ are called to recognize their proper place as citizens in the Kingdom, which is an integral part of God's deliverance, as the song of Moses illustrated when it spoke of God's kingly rule in the earth:

"The LORD will reign forever and ever."[2]

This reality was impregnated in the mind of the psalmist when he applauded the reign of God over the entire world. His passion and vision was for nothing less.

"The LORD has established His throne in heaven, and His Kingdom rules over all."[3]

Such a prophetic revelation of world government was entrusted to the prophet Daniel. He stated clearly that God had chosen His King to reign over the affairs of men; it would be no ordinary person who would connect with the Divine.

"In the time of those kings, the God of heaven will set up a Kingdom that will never be destroyed, nor will it be left to another people. It will crush all those kingdoms and bring them to an end, but it will itself endure forever." [4]

"In my vision at night I looked, and there before me was one like a Son of Man, coming with the clouds of heaven. He

---

[2] Exodus 15:18

[3] Psalm 103:19

[4] Daniel 2:44

approached the Ancient of Days and was led into His presence."[5]

Jesus is truly the anointed King talked about in the prophetic writings. Hence the apostles did not hesitate to declare His Lordship: "... that at the name of Jesus every knee should bow, in heaven and on earth and under the earth".[6]

This message of the Kingdom, so profound yet so accessible to "whosoever", was to be taken throughout the world with a truly transforming effect upon people, who were then able to participate with God in His work on the Earth.

The Descent of the Spirit: Acts 2

The coming of the Holy Spirit proved to have a profound effect in dealing with people's inadequacies. Jesus had prepared the thinking of His disciples in explaining the advocacy of the Spirit as Him coming alongside them as a personal guide. He explained that the Spirit would give them the equipping necessary to achieve the task and that he would enable them to be a truly prophetic people.

Throughout chapter two, there are several references made to a newfound eloquence; it was something that was not taught but caught.

The baptism at Pentecost was prophetic in the sense that it gave witness to the ascension of Christ. Jesus bestows His royal blessing of power and authority. His people could now have confidence in a divine wisdom, and 'laser-like' power and accuracy in their communication of the

---

[5] Daniel 7:13
[6] Philippians 2:10

Lordship of Christ. Peter cites this in his first oration, explaining what was taking place: a baptism of power by the Holy Spirit.

> "Exalted to the right hand of God, He has received from the Father the promised Holy Spirit and has poured out what you now see and hear... Therefore let all Israel be assured of this: God has made this Jesus, whom you crucified, both Lord and Christ."[7]

The baptism was prophetic in the sense that it was a whole new epoch of divine activity within the human heart. Men and women, young and old, were finding their place, partnering with God in His purposes for their generation. "The-Called-Alongside-One" (the Paraclete), the Holy Spirit became the indwelling Spirit. The people who believed were empowered and equipped in order to connect with others, carrying with them an understanding of the gospel. "Even on my servants, both men and women, I will pour out my Spirit in those days, and they will prophesy."[8]

This was God's strategy for success and it needed to influence their thinking and imagination. The baptism was prophetic, not only in the release of the tongue, but in the opening of the mind and perceptive skills of people touched by the power of the Holy Spirit. It still remains the same for the Church today. The same power of the Holy Spirit will help men and women participate with the Divine purpose, which is to spread the gospel of the Kingdom of God.

> "... your young men will see visions, your old men will dream dreams."[9]

---

[7] Acts 2:33, 36; This was the fulfilment of Christ's predictions found in John 13:5 and 16:7
[8] Acts 2:18
[9] Acts 2:17

The baptism is prophetic today in that it carries a sense of continuity with the past. It can be verified in the scriptures as relevant and wholesome. It was an opportune moment for Peter to expound to the people that this baptism of the Holy Spirit was a sanctifying work in line with what God's Word had predicted. "'These men are not drunk, as you suppose. It's only nine in the morning! No, this is what was spoken by the prophet Joel.'"[10] Peter goes on to explain that such an anointing would take place for generations to follow.

The baptism of the Spirit also immerses people into a whole new redemptive experience. A new wineskin needed to emerge, thus enabling people to taste the powers of an age to come.

The baptism is prophetic in the sense that transcendent joy accompanies it in both an individual and a corporate setting. They became a people who were not only envisioned by God, but who also enjoyed the experience of living with Him and serving Him. "'You have made known to me the paths of life; you will fill me with joy in your presence.'"[11] In the words of the chorus: "There is joy in serving Jesus as I journey on my way; joy that fills my heart with praises every hour and every day..."[12]

The baptism was prophetic in that it had a deeply transformative effect on attitudes and behavioral patterns. A truly prophetic people are literally committed to doing God's will, and with great joy they devote their lives to help make a difference. Consider this sense of pulling together; it revealed the effect that the move of God's Spirit was having on the Christian community. Luke refers to it here:

---

[10] Acts 2:15-16
[11] Acts 2:28
[12] O. J. Smith and B. D. Ackley, *"There is Joy in Serving Jesus"* (Public Domain, 1931)

"They devoted themselves to the apostles' teaching and to fellowship, to the breaking of bread and to prayer. Everyone was filled with awe, and many wonders and miraculous signs were done by the apostles. All the believers were together and had everything in common. Selling their possessions and goods, they gave to anyone as he had need. Every day they continued to meet together in the temple courts. They broke bread in their homes and ate together with glad and sincere hearts, praising God and enjoying the favour of all the people. And the Lord added to their number daily those who were being saved."[13]

Here is a valuable trilogy successfully at work, consisting firstly of clear objectives, secondly of empowerment for the task, and thirdly, of a practical outworking which becomes clearly visible by the demonstration of the Holy Spirit in people's lives.

The Demonstration of the Holy Spirit: Acts 3

This is a clear record of the demonstration of the power of God. There was profoundness in the preaching, and a Spirit-led enabling of them to generate faith for the physical healing of the lame man. The practical outcome was a healing that was focused not on man's ability, but on God's.

This is a far cry from what is often the case for the Church at large today. Admittedly, power can, all too easily, cause the believer to be caught up with the charisma and the personality, who can, all too easily, become the center of attention. This should be contrasted with the first

---

[13] Acts 2:42-47

apostles who insisted on giving the credit to the ascended Christ. Believers can all learn a lesson in humility from them, and this will serve far more effectively in revealing Christ to a lost world.

> "By faith in the name of Jesus, this man whom you see and know was made strong. It is Jesus' name and the faith that comes through Him that has given this complete healing to him, as you can all see."[14]

God's power is restorative in nature. It is a sign of God's Kingdom and His ultimate intention to restore. "He must remain in heaven until the time comes for God to restore everything, as He promised long ago through His holy prophets."[15]

Powerful deeds of healing miracles are 'part and parcel' of God's Kingdom at work to this day. This particular miracle that Luke refers to expounds for the reader the power of the Kingdom, and the ability of God to bring transforming and radical change to the condition of people. "Indeed, all the prophets from Samuel on, as many as have spoken, have foretold these days."[16]

The chief demonstration of healing is not only to set people free, it is also to make a statement, sometimes referred to as a sign. The mandate is clear that the Kingdom of God will carry with it a message of blessing and hope to a hurting and a needy world. God's people who work in faith with Him are to become a blessing to the world around them.

> "And you are heirs of the prophets and of the covenant God made with your fathers. He said to Abraham, 'Through your offspring all peoples on earth will be blessed.' When God

---

[14] Acts 3:16
[15] Acts 3:21
[16] Acts 3:24

raised up His servant, He sent him first to you to bless you by turning each of you from your wicked ways."[17]

Luke was emphasizing that this long awaited arrival of the Kingdom was taking place before their very eyes, as it was foretold by the prophets of old. The Kingdom of God is not a religion that is weak and anemic, or devoid of transforming qualities. On the contrary, the Kingdom of God is meant to be characterized by the dynamic working of the Holy Spirit. The Kingdom comes near to the human predicament with a radical message. It precipitates a response of the heart.

"Anyone who does not listen to Him will be completely cut off from among his people. "[18]

God's strategy was always "incarnation". He always intended "to abide" with us in our earthly pilgrimage, precipitating a lifestyle which is in touch with reality: a reality which speaks volumes about Him and His people. "The Kingdom of God is ... righteousness, peace, and joy in the Holy Spirit."[19] These dynamic ingredients are infinitely attractive to people:

Righteousness – the antidote to corruption

Peace – the calm, in spite of the outward stress of life

Joy – The liberation of being

These three distinct qualities of righteousness, peace, and joy are crucial to the wellbeing of the Christian community for the following reasons:

Righteousness: God's Kingdom insists on a new basis of operation. It calls for a radical adjustment in the believer's frame of mind, a new reliance on

---

[17] Acts 3:25-26
[18] Acts 3:23
[19] Romans 14:17

Christ and for His righteousness that is imparted to those who believe in Him.[20] God's Kingdom affects the inside; believers must learn to utilize effectively what God has given by His Spirit. The Kingdom is not an outward ceremony; it is an inward dynamic that alters the way believers live in the world.

Pervasive Peace: The circumstantial pressures did not cause it to fail, nor could the pagan quench it. The peace of God is foundational. It was obviously so in Stephen during his martyrdom.[21] It became the evident blessing on the Churches throughout Judea, Galilee and Samaria. God's people were protected from evil intrusion and political harassment. The peace of God contributed to the establishment of the Church.[22]

Contagious Joy: This is a chief characteristic of the work of the Spirit. It was so evident at the baptism of the Spirit at Pentecost, as well as in subsequent visitations and outpourings. God's work generated a sense of celebration. This in itself became an attractive magnet. The apostles who had been jailed carried this note of joy, which overflowed into every prison cell and resulted in the eventual conversion of the hardened jailer.

The Deliverance from Prison: Acts 4

The troubling of the believers has been predicted since the time of Christ's work on earth.

> "If the world hates you, keep in mind that it hated me first. If
> you belonged to the world, it would love you as its own. As it

---

[20] Luke 17:21

[21] Acts 7:55, 56

[22] Acts 9:31

is, you do not belong to the world, but I have chosen you out of the world. That is why the world hates you."[23]

Popularity will never be the measuring rod of success, nor persecution the proof that the devil is stronger than Christ.

"I have told you these things, so that in me you may have peace. In this world you will have trouble. But take heart! I have overcome the world."[24]

The key is that Jesus has called believers into His Kingdom for such a time as this. "Jerusalem... will be rebuilt... in times of trouble"[25] The key lies in the reality that Christ and His people are overcomers in times of suffering, persecution and hardship. They will possess the power to endure. Their prayer shall be "deliver us from evil..."

The great testimony is that believers are more than overcomers. It became powerfully evident in the New Testament Church that such a powerful outworking could only be attributed to the tenacity of the Holy Spirit in the life of the followers of the Risen Christ. The Spirit's immanence is the reassurance that He will strengthen the people of God; remarkably so that, at times, if it becomes absolutely necessary, He will intervene and rescue His people. Observe the boldness and sharp thinking of Peter when the Holy Spirit empowers him: "Then Peter, filled with the Holy Spirit, said to them: 'Rulers and elders of the people!'"[26]

Peter was supplied with wisdom from above; he was able to give answer to the senior official with clarity of proclamation. He arrested the attention of the hearers by appealing to the covenant agreements, as seen

---

[23] John 15:18-19
[24] John 16:33
[25] Daniel 9:25
[26] Acts 4:8

recorded in the scriptures. He displayed courage as he stood before the people and dealt with their objections. "When they saw the courage of Peter and John and realized that they were unschooled, ordinary men, they were astonished and they took note that these men had been with Jesus."[27]

Prayer also proves to be an integral part of the strategy of God for His people and a vital key to deliverance, strengthening and the intervention of God. "This poor man called, and the Lord heard him; he saved him out of all his troubles."[28]

The effect of persecution becomes obvious in Acts 4:32-36. Adversity not only causes the believer to draw on faith towards God, it also brings about character formation that shapes the very soul of the community. People who suffer together become bonded in a deeper commitment to each other. Resolve, once it is strengthened, causes people to become even more focused on the task, and their prayer life is transformed. "When they heard this, they raised their voices together in prayer to God. 'Sovereign Lord,' they said, 'you made the heaven and the earth and the sea, and everything in them'".[29]

Such belief is not theoretical; they fully understood that the Lord is sovereign and that He remained the key to their deliverance. Oppression by the authorities served only to advance the message, revive the Church and strengthen their resolve to witness to Christ. "Now, Lord, consider their threats and enable your servants to speak your word with great boldness.'"[30]

---

[27] Acts 4:13
[28] Psalm 34:6
[29] Acts 4:24
[30] Acts 4:29

Discernment at Work: Acts 5

This chapter, in a shocking way, shows the need for discernment to be exercised in Church life. There was a genuine spirit of generosity in the people and abuse was not tolerated. The Kingdom of God can only progress where there is the integrity of Christ's Spirit. It is an offence to God's Spirit to deceive others.

> "Then Peter said, 'Ananias, how is it that Satan has so filled your heart that you have lied to the Holy Spirit and have kept for yourself some of the money you received for the land?'"[31]

> "Peter said to her, 'How could you agree to test the Spirit of the Lord? Look! The feet of the men who buried your husband are at the door, and they will carry you out also.'"[32]

> "You stiff-necked people, with uncircumcised hearts and ears! You are just like your fathers: You always resist the Holy Spirit!"[33]

Discernment is a vital gift, evidently needed to keep the Church pure in motive, to protect the credibility of the community of God, and to safeguard the things of the Spirit from falling into abuse. Seldom do people in Christian circles see the enemy within hinder the advance of God's Kingdom less than the enemy without. Deception has many guises, but none more threatening than when it is dressed up in its best Sunday clothes.

---

[31] Acts 5:3
[32] Acts 5:9
[33] Acts 7:51

Ananias and Sapphira are found out in an act of deception, attempting to hold onto that which should have been released. They manipulated the facts to make good their appearance.

Death is a feature in God's dealing with religion, especially a form of godliness that denies His power.[34] King David found this to be the case in the moving of the Ark of the Covenant.[35] Jesus Himself equated some of the behavior of the Pharisees and scribes as reflecting that of whitewashed gravestones full of dead men's bones.[36]

Further Study

1   *What lessons can be learned about dealing with unrighteousness?*

2   *Consider and discuss the following:*
   * *Never use a wrong reaction to seek to expose evil.*
   * *Remember God in His sovereignty will deal with deception.*
   * *Never promise what you are not wholeheartedly willing to deliver.*

Deeds of Service: Acts 6

Administration is extremely important as the work of God expands. Everything needs proper administration or things will clog up and cause frustration. In chapter 6 there is a beautiful picture of a body of people expressing need. The call to leadership is to provide a solution that is wise. Practical suggestions and strategies emerge from the community as

---

[34] 2 Timothy 3:5
[35] 2 Samuel 6:6-7
[36] Matthew 23:27

creative thinking and dialogue is encouraged. This is so beneficial for development.

A healthy community will foster a creative administration, with such elements as a freedom to speak plainly about strengths and weaknesses; a leadership that is approachable and sensitive to genuine needs; an ethnic diversity and awareness with a greater understanding, avoiding elitism of one group over another; a ministry that is clear as to its primary call, protecting that which is truly important; a continual recognition and development of emerging ministries; a servanthood approach to leadership.

Success always has its own set of challenges. This is seen especially with the linguistic and cultural challenges that emerged through the spread and embrace of the gospel from the Hebraic community to the Hellenistic. The terms 'Hellenists' and 'Hebrews' are introduced suddenly by Luke and without explanation. [37]

F.F. Bruce comments further: "The Hebrews were evidently Jews who habitually spoke Aramaic, whose home land was Palestine. The Hellenists, on the other hand, were Jews who spoke Greek and whose way of life, in the eyes of stricter Palestinians, smacked too much of Greek customs."[38]

Serving is the key to the success of any community, especially the community of Christ. Amongst Christians, there ought to be no greater ambition than to serve. What is found illustrated in this chapter ought not to be limited to the early Church. If the Church is seeking to be useful to God, then it must be prepared to start by being available to others. Activity, zeal and desire for God must not blind the Church to the opportunities that are at its feet.

---

[37] Acts 6:1

[38] F.F. Bruce, *New Testament History* (UK, Double Day Books, 1969) p. 217

Death of a Prominent Leader: Acts 7

God's strategy often calls for crisis to unlock the Church. The death of Stephen in chapter 7 was a terrible incident. It would seem that everything was against the expansion of the gospel. But God was at work. What seemed a serious setback actually resulted in progress; a movement and a dynamic is at work, it results in a shift of the focus of missional activity from Jerusalem to Antioch.

Stephen's martyrdom was to prove a turning point and was the release of a whole new phase of expansion. The seed that had fallen into the ground and died did not remain alone; it sprang up, bearing much fruit.[39] His apologetic did expose an underlying conviction within the early Church, that the old structures and approach of temple worship was incompatible with the teaching of Jesus.

This, coupled with a renewed persecution of the Church, forced Jewish Christians to scatter. Wherever they went their influence spread and many people were born again. This mass movement of testimony to the regions beyond fulfilled the command of Christ that was over them, which was for them to go into the entire world making disciples.[40]

In this respect, it is worth looking at how, in certain chapters, Luke draws the reader's attention to specific nations or key people who were affected by the proclamation of the gospel.

---

[39] John 12:24
[40] Matthew 28:19

The Conversion of Key People: Acts 8-10

The Kingdom's greatest resource is people, especially those who are well equipped and schooled in the realities of life. In the space of three chapters there is a cross-cultural perspective given of the intention of the Spirit to reach across the world with the message of the gospel of the Kingdom:

Chapter 8	– the Ethiopian, who proves to be a key player, representing the African continent;
Chapter 9	– Saul of Tarsus who is representative of the Asiatic;
Chapter 10	– Cornelius, a centurion of the Italian cohort, is representing the European continent.

Consider **the Ethiopian**. He was a very important person in his nation. His conversion would be strategic because of his influence in high places.

> "Now an angel of the Lord said to Philip, 'Go south to the road – the desert road – that goes down from Jerusalem to Gaza.' So he started out, and on his way he met an Ethiopian eunuch, an important official in charge of all the treasury of Candace, queen of the Ethiopians. This man had gone to Jerusalem to worship, and on his way home was sitting in his chariot reading the book of Isaiah the prophet."[41]

Philip is caught up in the Spirit and directed by the Spirit's command as he educates the Ethiopian concerning Christ. Philip was unaware of the amount of preparatory work the Holy Spirit had already undertaken in regions beyond. The Holy Spirit interrupts events and helps Philip make a more strategic move. It is imperative that believers stay sensitive to the

---

[41] Acts 8:26-28

Spirit's leading and do not become trapped by success and individual agendas within the work of God.

The Bible is a unique source of information when it comes to how to operate strategically. Perhaps the Church has become too professional in what it feels it can do for God, or how it should present God to the world?

The work of the Holy Spirit remains committed to the process of the enlightening of the individual. There must be room for revelation and information to stimulate the believer's thinking. There must be a right balance between the use of natural skills in serving God and possessing a heightened sensitivity to the person of the Holy Spirit.

Saul was also a vital person in the expansion of the Kingdom into Gentile regions. He was, prior to his conversion, the "crème de la crème" of the religious establishment, an activist against the newly established Christian community. Yet God's choice is the best one, despite the fears, anger and suspicion of the Christian community. Paul will prove to be a greater blessing than he ever was a threat to them. Such is the grace of God in forming a Kingdom through the persecution of the early Church. God took hold of one man – Saul of Tarsus – making him the champion of the gospel to the Gentiles. How amazing is the grace of God in people's lives. For over a quarter of a century Paul travelled extensively and worked tirelessly for the cause of Christ and for the care of all the Churches. He helped in the early formation of Christian thought and tradition during the early years before meeting with his death at the hand of Rome.

Cornelius the Centurion was another turning point for the advance of the gospel to regions beyond. Peter's encounter with him broke every religious and legal barrier. God, the Holy Spirit, took the initiative in leading Peter into a whole new society. People were enquiring after God from beyond the Jewish sector. The Holy Spirit had to help the leadership to break out of their current mind set.

> "At Caesarea there was a man named Cornelius, a centurion in what was known as the Italian Regiment. He and all his family were devout and God-fearing; he gave generously to those in need and prayed to God regularly. One day at about three in the afternoon he had a vision. He distinctly saw an angel of God, who came to him and said, 'Cornelius!' Cornelius stared at him in fear. 'What is it, Lord?' he asked. The angel answered, 'Your prayers and gifts to the poor have come up as a memorial offering before God.'" [42]

Cornelius is deeply affected by "the reality of God". He is earnest in his quest to make a proper connection with God. This was no flash of brilliance; it was a deep yearning of his heart and life. He was not content with the status quo. He shared a deep commitment to change and a human dedication to God and fellow men, which reflects a certain attitude of life that attracted divine attention. Cornelius touched God's throne, and both he and Peter found a divine strategy for the way forward in their praying.

God's purposes are not detached from the deep longings of His people. His people often carry burdens, desires and longings for God that He has placed in their hearts. This is the prerequisite for change. The language often used to describe this is "hunger and thirst."

Prayer was not a theoretical exercise; it was linked to a self-less lifestyle. Their prayers were in line with the interests of God. To Peter it was a strategic way of keeping in touch with Christ.

---

[42] Acts 10:1-4

Prayer preceded one of the greatest advances of God's Kingdom into the Gentile world. It was the key that unlocked a greater move of God.

Prayer was the prerequisite for the outpouring of the Spirit in great measure on this whole household. Prayer such as this serves to remind believers that prayer engages the activity of the heavens.

The Angelic presence and the vision from Heaven were all born out of an appeal to God in **prayer**.

Luke explains the importance of the vision given to Peter; God was preparing his mind for a cultural leap from Judaism to Gentile ministry. There is no exclusivity with God. The four corners of the sheet in the vision refer to the universality of the gospel message. International borders or cultural boundaries will not limit it. The sheet came down from heaven, the place that initiates all blessing in our world. It shows a unity in diversity being the quality of expression to be enjoyed in God's Kingdom.

A new season was springing upon the Church. It needed to become unshackled from its own intensity and be released to touch the unsanctified. It was essential for the Church to broaden its influence and reach beyond the borders of its own Jewishness. God wanted them to touch hurting humanity, and that meant those who were considered outsiders: Gentiles. God calls for a gracious acceptance of those who are different.

CHAPTER THIRTEEN

THE GIFTS OF ENABLEMENT

A constant expansion of the horizon took place as the Holy Spirit equipped, envisioned and thrust the ministry of the Church outward.

The Key Involvement of the Spirit in the Church – Focus

The Holy Spirit, whilst His focus was on Christ and His agenda for the Church, was never viewed as a silent, impersonal force at work in the Church. In fact, the Holy Spirit's dynamic was tangible.

> "After they prayed, the place where they were meeting was shaken. And they were all filled with the Holy Spirit and spoke the Word of God boldly."[1]

His presence had a powerful and effective charge in the gatherings.

> "As I began to speak, the Holy Spirit came on them as he had come on us at the beginning."[2]

> "When Paul placed his hands on them, the Holy Spirit came on them, and they spoke in tongues and prophesied."[3]

---

[1] Acts 4:31
[2] Acts 11:15
[3] Acts 19:6

Strategic Direction

The strategic direction that they received as a community came from the person of the Spirit. The Holy Spirit, not a flash of brilliance or ingenuity, determined the agenda.

> "While they were worshiping the Lord and fasting, *the Holy Spirit said*, 'Set apart for me Barnabas and Saul for the work to which I have called them."[4] [emphasis added]

Great premium was put on inquiring after God in periods set apart for this purpose. Fasting was not a heavy session of waiting. It was peppered with a beautiful spirit of worship and celebration.

The space given to the Lord during these times was considered vital and preceded plans for expansion. New commissioning and exploits were birthed in the presence of God. New partnerships were forged in times set apart to hear from the throne of God.

Calling was not a manmade choice for a convenient decision. It originated from God and was confirmed by His Spirit.

> "*It seemed good to the Holy Spirit and to us* not to burden you with anything beyond the following requirements..."[5] [emphasis added]

---

[4] Acts 13:2
[5] Acts 15:28

Strengthening of Resolve

The Holy Spirit brought a sense of wellbeing to the Church through His executive leadership. One of the key marks of the Spirit of God at work is this pervading sense of alignment, and the atmosphere of a wholesome respect for God.

> "Then the Church throughout Judea, Galilee and Samaria enjoyed a time of peace. *It was strengthened; and encouraged by the Holy Spirit*, it grew in numbers, living in the fear of the Lord."[6] [emphasis added]

This constant interaction with the Holy Spirit, as the One called alongside, was a profound source of strength and encouragement to the believers. The words of Jesus must have constantly revisited the Church: "when He, the Spirit of truth, comes, He will guide you into all truth."[7] They were truly a people of purpose and presence.

The Practical Advantages of People Filled with the Spirit: A Spirit of Servanthood Becomes Evident

The advantages of the Spirit-filled life are very practical. Acts 6 is a significant passage in showing us the priority God places on ministry in His community – Believers cannot fulfill their obligations without the anointing of the Spirit.

The apostles were faced with the need to embrace change as the work continued to expand. These Spirit-filled men did not just seek out gifted

---

[6] Acts 9:31
[7] John 16:13

people; they were interested in responsible people who were willing to serve, filled with the Holy Spirit and with wisdom.

People filled with the Spirit of Christ will take a keen interest in the lives of others. They will first seek out the solutions by listening to the problems that people are facing, and then accept the responsibility to make the necessary changes.

"In those days when the number of disciples was increasing, the Grecian Jews among them complained against the Hebraic Jews because their widows were being overlooked in the daily distribution of food. So the Twelve gathered all the disciples together and said, 'It would not be right for us to neglect the ministry of the Word of God in order to wait on tables. Brothers, choose seven men from among you who are known to be full of the Spirit and wisdom. We will turn this responsibility over to them and will give our attention to prayer and the ministry of the Word.'

"This proposal pleased the whole group. They chose Stephen, a man full of faith and of the Holy Spirit; also Philip, Procorus, Nicanor, Timon, Parmenas, and Nicolas from Antioch, a convert to Judaism. They presented these men to the apostles, who prayed and laid their hands on them.

"So the Word of God spread. The number of disciples in Jerusalem increased rapidly, and a large number of priests became obedient to the faith."[8]

Consider several traits noticeable in the local situation (Acts 6):

---

[8] Acts 6:1-7

- The leaders, with *sensitivity to the Spirit*, show respect to the work of Christ's Spirit in the Church. They give Him His rightful place of authority. "Choose seven men from among you who are known to be full of the Spirit..."

- Philip, who was subsequently chosen, *reached out to others* in evangelism. He attracted people of stature into the gathering such as large numbers of priests who were converted through his commitment.

- *Morale is uplifted* when Spirit-filled people are appointed to the task of overseeing, and the people know that their needs are being considered and changes are being made that will improve their situations.

- There is a *sense of security* when a Church's leadership exercises authority whilst remaining open to entreaty. People should not be afraid to ask questions and appeal to leadership, or to express their concerns. Leadership will advance on every front when it is not afraid to serve or give attention to menial tasks.

The Holy Spirit enables people to prioritize, as it is recorded in this chapter of Acts. The apostles were released from the detail of administration. The time given to the Word and prayer was not neglected. Everyone was willing to serve in some capacity, which released everyone to concentrate on the individual tasks that the Lord had appointed for each one.

The results of the leading of the Spirit were tangible. The emphasis was kept on breaking new ground, yet sufficient time was given to explain God's Word to the people. When the Spirit is lacking in any work, principles of the Word become threadbare and lack-luster. However, when the Church is moving in the Spirit, the gospel principles become sharper and more exciting.

The Disadvantages of Neglecting the Work of the Spirit

When the Spirit is hindered, advancement is obstructed and the inspirational elements of the work of the Spirit become sidelined by the business of administrative tasks.

When sensitivity to the Spirit is restricted, fruitfulness is affected which is made obvious by the evident lack of new birth in the Church community. The Church community loses its sticking power, people drift and any new additions soon fall away. The sense of God's direction is lost. The prophetic element ceases to be effective in the meetings. People become weary of event-orientated meetings.

Resisting the Holy Spirit was referred to strongly by Stephen who was offensive to the religious establishment when he said, "You stiff-necked people, with uncircumcised hearts and ears! You are just like your fathers: You always resist the Holy Spirit!"[9].

Ignoring the Spirit Must be Avoided

Ignoring the Spirit of God is a serious charge to make; it is the last thing that the believer would want to admit to. Certainly, believers would never knowingly or willfully resist the Holy Spirit, but individuals are not always aware when they are doing so. The idea of willfully resisting the

[9] Acts 7:51

Holy Spirit, which is so foreign to believers today, was no doubt what created such a reaction against Stephen and resulted in his martyrdom.

May God deliver Christians today from discriminating against what He is doing in people's lives. Stephen became a martyr of people's prejudice. Christians must avoid the habit of marginalizing others, even in their thinking. And they must also guard against reacting to an uncomfortable confrontation of God's Word in their lives. As Paul referenced in his address to Agrippa in Acts 26:14: "Saul, Saul, why do you persecute me? It is hard for you to kick against the goads."

Stephen was part of an emergence of the wider gifting to the Church.

A Good Administration Cooperates with the Spirit

Every Church community must be careful not to over-administrate the work of the Spirit. Management is good, but it must make room for the Holy Spirit to redirect and refocus the Church.

A clear recognition and respect of gifted ministries is needed. This calls for a constant cooperation with the work of the Spirit. All believers must seek the mind of the Spirit in each given Church situation.

Apostles who learn to ride in tandem with the Spirit will keep in pioneer-mode and will be able to advance God's purpose. The dual operation of the Spirit will keep the Church on track. He will direct the affairs of its ministry, sometimes by holding back activity and sometimes by compelling the believers to action.

Consider the dual role of the Spirit as seen in Acts 16.

Restraint – The Confinement by the Spirit

"Paul and his companions travelled throughout the region of Phrygia and Galatia, having been kept by the Holy Spirit from preaching the Word in the province of Asia. When they came to the border of Mysia, they tried to enter Bithynia, but the Spirit of Jesus would not allow them to."[10]

It is easy to press ahead with what appears a good idea, only to find that it does not have the ownership of God on it. It is important to learn the voice of the Holy Spirit in restraint, enabling the Church to know what to give its energy to and what to withhold it from. This is its mission.

This sensitivity to strategy and to the Holy Spirit is precisely what is needed today. The Church must be prepared for redirection if it is to avoid entrenchment. The Holy Spirit will sometimes keep the Church from a particular action. At other times He will direct the Church with specific details. Flexibility and availability are required if God's people desire to be useful to the Lord.

"The two of them, *sent on their way by the Holy Spirit*, went down to Seleucia and sailed from there to Cyprus."[11] [emphasis added]

Constraint – The Compelling Urge of the Spirit

This requires learning to yield to the gentle pressure of the Spirit.

"After Paul had seen the vision, we got ready at once to leave

---

[10] Acts 16:6-7
[11] Acts 13:4

for Macedonia, concluding that God had called us to preach the gospel to them."[12]

Believers must never be too quick to engage themselves when there is often a legitimate reason why the pathway is being obstructed. The apostle referred to times when he wanted to pursue a course only to be hindered by Satan, witnessing persecution and violence. However, he also confessed to the direction of the Holy Spirit, recognizing the leading of the Spirit. God always calls His Church to focus its attention and channel its energies more appropriately.

Sometimes with forcefulness and vivid illustration, the Spirit came across in prophetic utterance, such as with Agabus:

"After we had been there a number of days, a prophet named Agabus came down from Judea. Coming over to us, he took Paul's belt, tied his own hands and feet with it and said, 'The Holy Spirit says, "In this way the Jews of Jerusalem will bind the owner of this belt and will hand him over to the Gentiles."'"[13]

Indicative of the prophetic nature of the strategy of the Spirit, is the directional word. Such is the incident recorded about Agabus. Clear specifics and meaning are given in what the Holy Spirit is saying to God's servants.

---

[12] Acts 16:10
[13] Acts 21:10-11

The Targeting of Key Cities

Antioch was an important place for the move of the Spirit. It was the doorway into the Gentile world and the capital of Syria. It was to be a springboard for the outreach of the gospel. It was not long before a Church was established there, becoming a base of operation for the Apostle Paul. In fact, the first record of activity in Antioch and Syria highlights the evidence of the hand of God at work with a great response from the people towards salvation. With such a resource available to him, Paul was able to use Antioch as a base for his three missionary journeys.

> "In the Church at Antioch there were prophets and teachers: Barnabas, Simeon called Niger, Lucius of Cyrene, Manaen (who had been brought up with Herod the tetrarch) and Saul. While they were worshiping the Lord and fasting, the Holy Spirit said, 'Set apart for me Barnabas and Saul for the work to which I have called them.' So after they had fasted and prayed, they placed their hands on them and sent them off."[14]

Corinth was a famous Grecian city and another important place. The commercial center for Greek enterprise, it was also the capital of Achaia, one of the two great provinces into which Greece was divided by the Romans, the other being Macedonia.

> "It was the centre of business and political power. What Jerusalem was to the religious Jew, Corinth was to them commercially."[15]

---

[14] Acts 13:1-3
[15] D. Thomas, *The Acts of the Apostles* (London, Dickinson, 1889) p.304

It was also clear that the best means of penetrating the Greek culture was to start at Corinth, as it was the meeting place of the philosophers of the day.

Ephesus opened up an avenue for the gospel into Asia. The Holy Spirit was clear in His objective in establishing the Church at Ephesus. It was the seat of government for the whole of the province of Asia and therefore very strategic.

> "What Jerusalem was to Peter, Ephesus became to Paul, the place where Christ did by him His mightiest acts – the manifest outpouring of the Holy Ghost – manifold and wonderful healings – and the destruction of heathenism and its magical arts.[16] Ephesus gained in importance for Christendom as Jerusalem lost its central place..." [17]

A helpful illustration of the chapters in Acts is demonstrated in the following outline. This provides a context and a gauge that shows the strategic expanse of the work of the Spirit through the apostles.

Chapters	Time Span	Regions
Acts 1-8	AD 33-35	Jerusalem
Acts 8-13	AD 35-48	Judea and Samaria
Acts 13-28	AD 48-72	Uttermost parts

[16] Acts 19:18-19

[17] H. W. J. Thiersch, *A History of the Christian Church in the Apostolic Times*, (London, Thomas Bosworth, 1883) p. 138

Acts 11 to 19

A trace of the activity of the Spirit on the geographical landscape is quite rewarding. The message of the gospel being preached and the signs that followed had a major impact and it is not long before a pattern emerges, and the strategic way of the Spirit can be seen.

Jerusalem was the city of Judaism. Christianity was to affect both the religious and political communities. Such was the power dimension at work that the early disciples were accused of filling Jerusalem with their gospel. The effect on society was overwhelming. It was not long before the Church was drawing attention on a worldwide scale.

The Jerusalem Church was stretched as it struggled to come to terms with the spread of the good news. It was on a challenging learning curve, constantly needing to reconsider its terms of reference. The conversion of the gentiles was a case in point, and it was disturbing the status quo, resulting in the need for consultations, such as in Acts 15. As time progressed, the Christians in Jerusalem were outpaced by the move of the Spirit. They criticized Peter for 'breaking out of the box' of their Jewish law, and summoned him before the council. He then explained to them the hand of God in the things that were taking place before they acquiesced.

> "The apostles and the brothers throughout Judea heard that the Gentiles also had received the Word of God. So when Peter went up to Jerusalem, the circumcised believers criticized him and said, 'You went into the house of uncircumcised men and ate with them.'"[18]

The problem the Jews encountered is one that is familiar to believers

---

[18] Acts 11:1-3

today: used to seeing things their own way, they can become static and inflexible in their thinking. God needs to intervene and lift the believer's vision. It is interesting that the Holy Spirit had to use persecution to instruct the Church at Jerusalem regarding their need for change. James is killed and Peter is imprisoned and, as a result, the Church turns to prayer. It takes an angelic visitation to break him out. It is an illustration in the natural of what God then does in the spiritual. They needed to break out of their self-imposed limitations, so God did what they did not expect or grasp in order to take them to a new level in their understanding.

However, it cannot be said that the Jerusalem Church became ineffective in comparison to the missionary dynamic that was taking place in Antioch (the Antiochan Church later became an active apostolic base). On the contrary, throughout the Book of Acts, Jerusalem remains a crucial center. Its influence spreads beyond the efforts of Paul and Barnabas. But the center of evangelistic gravity shifted to Ephesus, the gateway to the East, until the Church at Rome rose to ascendancy in the third century.

Further Study

- *Consider the area where you reside. What are the advantages of such a place for gospel outreach?*
- *Discover the key places where people frequent. What is the character of the region?*

A Redefinition for Mission

The Holy Spirit is in advance-mode and will not allow stagnation. Often leadership involves catching up with what God is already doing in the hearts and minds of people. It serves to keep the Church humble and casts

God's people upon Him for direction. The choosing of Paul and the conversion of Cornelius emphasizes this point, showing how much the early apostles needed to understand the enormity of the task. They needed to be stretched in order to embrace the broader pursuit of the Spirit into the regions beyond.

The wisdom of the Spirit calls for objective planning. Time must be set aside to observe what God is doing and the reasons for His actions. At the same time, the Church must keep alert to what is taking place in the political and social arenas.

Believers today must learn from the difficulties of expansion in the Jerusalem Church. The Holy Spirit had to maintain the spread of the gospel in line with the mandate that Jesus had given to the early apostles. He had to 'break them out of their boxes' and deal with their narrow thinking. Consider what it took to get Jerusalem and the leadership to catch up and come to terms with the fact that the Spirit was leading the Church:

- The death of Stephen.

- The Holy Spirit moving on Philip to release him from a revival and crusade mindset to more strategic link-ups.

- God shows Peter the vision three times before he realizes what God is saying. It was the same provincial mindset seen when Saul is converted. People's fears come to the surface, hindering objectivity and adventure.

The true nature of the stimulus of the Spirit in revelation is to feed the soul and to move the believer's feet to action. The revelation of the Word of God is only one aspect; the other is to awaken the present reality of what God wants His people to do, and how they are to go about accomplishing it. This cannot be generalized; it is often very specific, as in the cases previously examined. Are God's people afraid of waiting on Him? Are they afraid to receive from Him specific direction? The Church should seek what God has planned and *then* ask for His blessing, rather than trying to organize God and ask for His blessing at a later stage. Strategy meetings should make room for the Holy Spirit to direct the Church concerning specific people and emerging missions.

The prophetic nature of the Holy Spirit's strategy with the Church continues throughout the book of Acts. Certainly, Paul and his team experienced the dealings of the Spirit as they sought to spread the good news abroad.

Acts 20 to 28

Throughout chapters 20-28, the reader sees a colorful picture of the exciting experiences of the Apostle Paul. He was tireless in his efforts to work with the Spirit in the spreading of the gospel to the regions beyond. He used every means, popular or otherwise, to serve the purposes of God. Consider further the three strategic phases of his work as we find them outlined in the remaining chapters of Acts.

Figure 13:1   The Strategic Phases of Apostolic Ministry

Phase One	Phase Two	Phase Three
AD 48-49	AD 50-52	AD 53-57
Chapters 13-14	Chapters 16-18:52	Chapters 19-28
Regions of Galatia, Pisidion, Antioch, Iconium, Lystra, Derbe	Regions of Galatia (2nd Visit), Macedonia, Greece, Philippi, Thessalonica and Corinth	Regions of Macedonia, Greece, Rome (imprisonment)

Acts chapter 15 carries significance in its own right. It provides insight into the time and energy expended by the Jerusalem Church as it sought to expand the work and meet its challenges (such as the clash of cultures). The urgent need is evident for a common approach in the core beliefs, and for a greater degree of cooperation, which is vital in order to avoid unnecessary hardship and conflict. Success always has its own complexities that need to be faced. It is by no means dissimilar to today's challenges. In reflecting on the situation that the Church was faced with, issues that must be faced in the Church today can be seen.

Accountability is not a private matter. It is a broader issue than seeking to maintain sameness or to protect our own turf. True wisdom requires a willingness to be open to change, to adjust one's position when called for, and to respect others who approach matters from a different standpoint.

What is done for the Lord by individuals has repercussions on others. The Word of God must become the ultimate arbiter on issues of disagreement. It will require that one goes beyond the emotion of the moment and submits oneself to the scriptures. The leaders in the book of Acts possessed the presence of mind to make time in their busy schedules to facilitate a meeting for essential consultation. The integrity of their testimony was at stake; therefore, they did everything possible to protect it. There are no shortcuts in this respect.

The latter aspects of Acts in chapters 21-28 remind the reader of the suffering and hostility that often accompanies times of great advance of the gospel. Faith must lead to reality. Faith is essential to keep God's servants on track, especially when being misunderstood, wrongly treated, abused and persecuted. Towards the end of his life, Paul was, in fact, severely restricted by his house arrest but this never compromised his faith.

The Significance of the Book of Acts

The Book of Acts is the bridge between the Gospels and the Epistles. The record is a transition from the earthly life and work of Christ, to the works of the ascended Lord, resulting in the establishment of the Church.

There is much that is not mentioned in Acts about the activities of other ministries during the same period of time. Luke's reference is to that which he personally witnessed. He emphasizes the expansion of the gospel from the Jerusalem base into gentile territory, as far as Rome itself.

"The reliability of Acts has often been challenged, but it has never been successfully impugned... The main narrative of Acts is concerned with the mission which took the gospel northward through Antioch, Asia Minor and then to Macedonia, Achaia and Rome."[19]

The Acts of the Apostles makes the Epistles intelligible to us. There is great benefit to be had from tracing the Churches mentioned in the book of Acts through to the Epistles that were written to them.

God works with personalities in order to establish His Kingdom. Divine strategy is about people and places. The work of the Holy Spirit is beautiful to behold. Great grace is at work in and through the human soul.

"The earliest beginnings of the Church in which the expansion of the Gospel of the Kingdom took place developed from the rural and village culture of Palestine. Differences existed between the culture of the city and the culture of the village."[20]

It appears that the key to adapting to the changing cultures of the day was found in the family unit. It was small enough to be flexible and agile. The home became a safe and friendly environment for travelling ministries.

---

[19] M. C. Tenney, *New Testament Survey* (Grand Rapids, Wm B Eerdmans, 1961) p. 232

[20] W. Meeks, *The Moral World of the First Century* (London, SPCK ,1986) p. 38

CHAPTER FOURTEEN

A COMMUNITY WITH A MESSAGE

Maintaining the Integrity of the Gospel

The circumcision issue[1] illustrates the need for cooperation across the vast network of apostolic Churches. The Church cannot operate in isolated communities. Christians have a responsibility together to maintain the integrity of the gospel in its message and its practices.

Apostles, prophets and elders are important in maintaining the unity, diversity and accountability of the people of God in any given region. The collective involvement of the five-fold ministries helps maintain the integrity of the gospel, safeguarding it from extremes, abuses and practices that violate the scriptures. However, it is God's Word that becomes the authority. When God's Word is the measuring rod on Church issues, it is precisely that that keeps a sense of common values and beliefs.

> "Then the apostles and elders, with the whole Church, decided to choose some of their own men and send them to Antioch with Paul and Barnabas. They chose Judas (called Barsabbas) and Silas, two men who were leaders among the brothers. With them they sent the following letter:
>
> "The apostles and elders, your brothers,

---

[1] Refer to Acts 15

To the Gentile believers in Antioch, Syria and Cilicia:

Greetings.

We have heard that some went out from us without our authorization and disturbed you, troubling your minds by what they said."[2]

Wayne Meeks refers to the knock-on effect of the expansion of the gospel and the challenges that the clash of cultures unintentionally brings to the integrity of the message and practice of the Church as a whole.

"The first Christian groups did not exist on islands or in deserts. They lived in villages or cities. In the villages, daily behavior was controlled by the routines of necessity. The cycles of seasonal labor in the fields, customs as old as the oldest memory."[3]

(Christian communities in today's new millennium have to learn to deal with the pace of communication between its peoples. The Internet reaches the homes of virtually all people. Today it is not so much about the letters received, but the scale of e-mails and the daily communications via all things web-related.)

Apostolic ministry and prophetic activity sought, therefore, to maintain correct practice in the Church, which in turn avoided fragmentation of the body of Christ between the differing cultures. In this respect, they also helped to provide definition as to the nature and practice of Church life.

---

[2] Acts 15:22-24

[3] W. Meeks, *The Moral World of the First Century* (London, SPCK ,1986) p. 12

"Through him and for his name's sake, we received grace and apostleship to call people from among all the Gentiles to the obedience that comes from faith."[4]

Obedience is a vital ingredient for healthy Church life. Principles of faith call for a practice that does not contradict the unity of the body of Christ.

A Community with a Message of Hope

The proclamation of God's Word in society remained a priority. The writer of the book of Acts was quite selective about the speeches recorded; capturing a strong emphasis on what motivated the early apostles. Their cover was not just about belief but their commitment to discipling people into a revealed purpose.

Consider the summary of speeches made as recorded throughout Acts. Here, speeches carry a sense of the importance of God's Word being expanded, and the subsequent outcomes were of an impartation of a genuine hope, encouragement and faith to the recipients.

Peter in Jerusalem – chapters 2-3: He associates with them as "Fellow Jews". He does not seek to alienate the message of the New Covenant from the message of the Old Covenant.

Stephen – chapter 7: He addresses their potential inquiry. He is also very direct in explaining the need for change in the light of God's long-term commitment to a people obedient to His Word.

Peter in Caesarea – chapter 10: He substantiates practice in line with the

---

[4] Romans 1:5

prophetic Word and purpose of God. The content is rich in the values that were to shape God's beautiful society.

Paul in Pisidian Antioch – chapter 13: He used Old Testament scriptures to emphasize the Messiah-ship of Jesus. He tackles a contentious issue, making plain the relevance of Christ in the establishment of God's Kingdom.

Paul speaking to the superstitious pagans – chapter 14: He explains the centrality of the cross as the door of hope to the world.

Paul to the educated Greeks in Athens – chapter 17: He points to the sovereignty of God in arranging events that have taken place. He does not appeal to a sentimentality. He calls for a sober assessment of how God is advancing into the future.

Paul to the Church leaders – chapter 20: He emphasizes the Lordship and Kingship of Christ. Jesus is not just the problem solver of people's lives. He is the One who is in charge.

Paul to the Jewish mob – chapter 22: He explains the power and presence of God's Spirit on all people. He emphasizes that God, in His grace, is at work across the nations.

Paul to Roman and Jewish judges – chapters 24-26: He appeals for a worthy response to God's prophetic Word.

The ability of Paul as a communicator was "par excellence". Roland Allen emphasizes ten elements of Paul's preaching that took place in the synagogue, as recorded in Acts 17:2-3.[5] These elements are:

1. An appeal to the past;

---

[5] R. Allen, *Missionary Methods: St Paul's or Ours?* (Grand Rapids, Wm B. Eerdmans, 1962) pp 62-64

2. A statement of facts;

3. Inevitable objections and their answers;

4. An appeal to the spiritual need of man;

5. A grave warning to those who reject God's message;

6. The centrality of the cross (you will find that it is true in all of Paul's writings);

7. The power of God, and of the name of Jesus (Acts 4);

8. The Lordship of Christ in the context of the Kingdom of God;

9. All activity of the Spirit is based on the Word. The Holy Spirit is provoking people, causing them to appeal to the scriptures in order to gain an understanding of His righteousness;

10. An end time community.

> "As for Jesus and the twelve, so also for St Paul, the eschatological message stands in the forefront. The day of judgment is at hand, when each single individual, whether living or dead, shall have to appear before God's throne and give account of all that he has done".[6]

The need remains for the Church and its leaders to appeal to the Word and to examine it with understanding, in order for them to make things clear to the people what God requires of them. Best practice and proven techniques must never substitute the dual issues of dependence on the Holy Spirit and possessing an adequate accountability to the Word of God.

---

[6] P. Vernle, *Beginnings of Christianity* (New York, Williams and Norgate, 1914) p. 178

The Spirit arouses inquiry from individuals, such as took place with the Bereans. They searched the scriptures to see if these things should be;[7] whereas the disciples had considerable knowledge from Jesus concerning the outpouring of the Spirit, which served them well regarding that which was to take place in the Church (John 15 and 16 give a little insight into the instruction that they received).

Christians today must not underestimate the importance of researching God's Word and engaging dialogue. It is as crucial for the Church today as it was then to set aside time for the public and private reading of the Scriptures.

Further Study

Research one of the nine sermons referred to in this section. Outline its content and explain the core emphasis of the sermon.

In the first chapter of the book of Acts, Luke writes that the apostles were concerned to fulfill the Word of God. This can be seen from an observation of the way in which the first apostles elected a replacement for Judas Iscariot. It was their desire and deliberate intent to fulfill the prophetic expectation as recorded in the scriptures.

It does seem that the appointment of the twelve was not without significance: it was to symbolize a new phase of God's establishment of a holy nation. Peter explains what was happening at Pentecost, expounding the Word of God as he did so. This was a characteristic of the Church of the New Testament, as it sought to safeguard its practice in line with the scriptures. Other examples of appealing to the scriptures for a greater understanding of events can be found in the following passages:

---

[7] Acts 17:11

Acts 1:15-16 "In those days Peter stood up among the believers (a group numbering about a hundred and twenty) and said, *'Brothers, the Scripture had to be fulfilled* which the Holy Spirit spoke long ago through the mouth of David concerning Judas, who served as guide for those who arrested Jesus...'"[8] [emphasis added]

Acts 2:16-17 "No, *this is what was spoken by the prophet Joel:*

'In the last days, God says,

I will pour out my Spirit on all people.

Your sons and daughters will prophesy,

Your young men will see visions,

Your old men will dream dreams.'"[9] [emphasis added]

Acts 17:11-12 "Now the Bereans were of more noble character than the Thessalonians, for they received the message with great eagerness and *examined the Scriptures every day to see if what Paul said was true.* Many of the Jews believed, as did also a number of prominent Greek women and many Greek men."[10] [emphasis added]

The emphasis of this last verse, being inclusive of women, is a significant point noted by the writer. The liberation that took place empowered men and women to play a significant part in the witness to Christ and His activity in our lives.

Crucial to success, expansion and the furtherance of the gospel is having a right attitude to all that God is doing. Egocentricity and exhibitionism must not be allowed to dominate the testimony of the

---

[8] Acts 1:15-16
[9] Acts 2:16-17
[10] Acts 17:11-12

Church, or else it will result in impeding the health and vitality of its members.

The Apostolic Sphere

Expansion requires apostolic cooperation

There was something powerful about the genuine apostolic sphere that emerged in the birth, expansion and establishing of the early Christian communities. The release of power was so evident. The Church continually benefited from a leadership that respected each other. They took care to consider what God was saying and doing in each other's lives. They consulted on matters that were vital to the growth of the Church (Acts 15).

Prophetic direction and strategy

The prophetic nature of the Holy Spirit's strategy with the Church continues throughout the book of Acts. Certainly, Paul and his team experienced the dealings of the Spirit as they spread the good news abroad. Consider the number of dreams, visions and Holy Spirit initiatives in the first instance with Peter and in a quite remarkable way with Paul – not just in Paul's conversion, but in the guidance that lead him throughout his missionary journeys.

The contemporary society

The context in which the gospel spread was a cocktail of politics and religion. Firstly, the greater part of the known world was subdued by Rome and dominated by Paganism.

"The chief cities were adorned with magnificent temples,

erected in honor of 'those which are no gods', embellished with 'graven images' of marvelous beauty. Judaism also had its great ecclesiastical buildings. Besides the temple of Jerusalem, stately synagogues, having massive pillars and cornices richly sculptured, had risen up in many towns".[11]

Secondly, in Jerusalem alone it was said that there were over 480 synagogues. One would be opened if at least ten people requested it. Sometimes they existed as a "house group" type concept. Such congregations of Judaism could be found all over Alexandria, Rome and Babylon, throughout Asia Minor, Greece Minor and Italy.

> "To the contemporary Jew, the disciples of Christ would be regarded as the Jewish sect or synagogue, the synagogue of the Libertines.[12] The synagogues were very numerous at Jerusalem. There were already the Cilician Synagogue, Alexandrian Synagogue and to those were added the Nazerean Synagogue or the Synagogue of the Galileans."[13]

Thirdly, with all that was taking place amongst the Gentiles, their close proximity to the Jewish Christians and the dispersion of Jerusalem Christians into the regions beyond would prove to be great resources needed for the establishing of the Gospel among the Gentiles. The Jewish Christians had become accustomed to travelling and adapting, not only in terms of trade and commerce, but also with their faith in Christ.

Their testimony was proving instrumental in the spread of the Gospel all over the world. It gave a solid base from which the Gospel could expand. In particular, the Church flourished in the home.

---

[11] Backhouse and Taylor, *Early Church History* (London, 1982) p.4

[12] See Acts 6:9

[13] W. J. Conybeare, *The Life and Epistles of St Paul, Vol. 1* (London, Longmans Green and Co., 1877) p. 81

CLOSED

Please scan

for location no.

CHAPTER FIFTEEN

APOSTOLIC NETWORKING

The Church in the Home – A People at Grass Roots Level

The popularity of the gospel, and the speed at which it spread throughout the Roman Empire, was significant and attractive to the communities at large. "The house-to-house expansion of the early Church quickly spread Christianity from the shores of Galilee to remote corners of the Empire"[1]

The home context was to prove a very useful means of influencing the Gentiles with the gospel of Christ. See 3 John for an insight into this phenomenon and the way in which the Church grew in the grass roots dimension of the home. The significance of the house Church was its informality, neighborhood context and flexibility of the household unit. These factors and many more added to the societal impact of the early Church. In other words, the family became the contact point, one which was much more hospitable than an austere building for meetings.

Hospitality was a vital key in holding a meeting or having a meal.[2]

"The early believers met in houses not by default alone... deliberately, because the house setting provided the facilities

---

[1] Gill and Gempf (eds), *Acts in a First Century Setting, Vol II* (Grand Rapids, Wm B Eerdmans, 1994. p.120

[2] Romans 16:13, 23; 1 Timothy 5:10; 1 Peter 4:9

which were of paramount importance for the gathering. Furthermore, the house gave the early believers an inconspicuous place for assembly".[3]

Church historians would say that the upper room frequented by the early apostles accommodated at least 120 men. In fact, some domestic dwellings were remodeled to cater for the growth of the Church. Rome itself, by 250 AD, accommodated over 30,000 Christians.[4]

In spite of the expansion of the work, there were crucial unifying elements of the life and practice of the early believers. There were such things as prayer,[5] singing,[6] scripture reading,[7] breaking of bread/Eucharist,[8] baptism,[9] and the practice of spiritual gifts.[10]

A Community, not just a Congregation

Congregations to this day remain a vital part of the Christian community, but if that is the whole view held of the Church, then the picture is distorted. Peoples' thinking of Church is often confined to when it meets and, therefore, tends to be congregational in nature. This may seem a small, semantics issue, but if it remains unchallenged it will result in a lack of understanding and progress for the people of God.

---

[3] Gill and Gempf (eds), *Acts in a First Century Setting, Vol II* (Grand Rapids, Wm B Eerdmans, 1994. p.121

[4] A. Harnack, *The Mission and Expansion of Christianity in the First Three Centuries, Vol II* (London, Williams and Norgate, 1908) p. 329

[5] Matt 6:6, Acts 1:14, Acts 2:42, Acts 6:4, Acts 12:5

[6] 1 Corinthians 14:15, 26, Ephesians 5:19, Colossians 3:16

[7] Acts 15:31, Colossians 4:16, 1 Timothy 4:13, 2 Timothy 3:16,

[8] Matt 26:26-30, Acts 10:41, 1 Corinthians 11:25

[9] Acts 2:38, 1 Corinthians 1: 13-17, Colossians 2:11-12

[10] 1 Corinthians 12:8-10, Acts 11:27, Romans 12:6

The Church is first and foremost a prophetic community of redeemed people. If it becomes only congregational in its lifestyle, it will cease to be prophetic. It then becomes a social organization, devoid of power or efficacy, which will eventually work against the Church's own true apostolic and prophetic nature.

A sense of family and caring should be the hallmark of such a community, meeting the needs of the *whole* life and not just the soul life. "The task of Christians is to be the sort of people and community that can become a real option and provide a real confrontation for others. Unless such a community exists, then no real option exists."[11]

It was Christ who designed the Church and its function. He made it perfectly clear to the first bearers of the gospel: they were to exhibit a special kind of quality that spoke to the world of a better way.

"By this all men will know that you are my disciples, if you love one another."[12]

The focus of the Church, whether it was gathered or scattered, was to do with living. The people exhibited a clear set of values as embodied in the life of Christ.

Further Study

What is meant by the phrase, 'a prophetic community of redeemed people'? Write a short paragraph explaining each element of this phrase and then explain how the elements relate to one another in their outworking.

---

[11] S. Hauerwas, *A Community of Character* (London, Notre Dame Press, 1981) p. 105
[12] John 13:35

Congregationalism – What is it?

In the "congregational" model, all planning, programs and thought are locked into the context of the corporate meeting. People lose their cutting edge as the platform personality is elevated and participation is discouraged, except by the elite. In large gatherings platforms are necessary, yet the real vitality of a Church must be measured by the quality of the participation of the "whosoever wills".

In this model, visibility of the leaders supersedes the discovery of emerging gifts in the body. Leadership should not be the main focus in Church gatherings. The leaders' finest role should be in their ability to connect with people and to safeguard the integrity of the gospel. Beyond the leadership, the total ministry of the body of Christ must be unlocked. Initiatives must be birthed and they do not need to begin with the leadership's instigation.

In this model, leaders become governors of the meetings instead of overseers of Church life. The majority of most leaders' time is spent in planning and the management of meetings. This is wholly disproportionate to God's priorities, which are praying for, caring for, feeding and instructing the flock. The societal development of individuals and families are seldom considered. Of paramount importance is putting on a good show, with little thought to character development and sanctification.

In this model, the Church's sense of responsibility to the world is diminished, as people focus more on the gathered Church rather than the scattered Church. It is too easy to satisfy the conscience and measure spirituality by attendance and responsiveness in meetings. The life of the Church is manifest in its ability to cope with everyday life in the wider community.

In this model, spirituality is measured by attending meetings rather than a deepening and devoted life in God. Our devotion to Christ is all about growing up in Him. Ministry, therefore, is to empower people to live mature lives.

In this model, social skills and civic service find no encouragement or enhancement as people focus on gifts of the Spirit rather than talents in the world. On the contrary, a healthy Church will become increasingly aware of the wider community, using its resources and skills to affect change and bring hope into people's lives. Credit should go to Christians who have got involved in their community centers, school governorships, and medical ethics committees.

> "The mark of a truthful community is partly seen in how it enables the diversity of gifts and virtues to flourish."[13]

In this model, people are not discipled in life. They are shaped into the required mould based on the type of meetings and the expectations of the leaders. The essential target of the ministry input into the Church should instead be to release the people into doing good and so show the love of Christ in action.

> "Any community and policy is known and should be judged by the kind of people it develops."[14]

The Corinthian Church was very vocal, charismatic and engaged in the dynamic of the Spirit. Yet its greatest need was to deal with its lack of maturity, its self-centeredness, and its relational breakdowns.

In a Church that has been accustomed to focusing on meetings, people are encouraged to be fed rather than to come with a responsible

---

[13] S. Hauerwas, *A Community of Character* (London, Notre Dame Press, 1981) p. 3
[14] *Ibid* p 2

contribution. The whole element of "body participation" needs to be rediscovered, both in and outside of the context of meetings.

Personal faith and social skills will only be developed in a community, not a congregation. To exhibit a truly "Christ like" expression, the people must be encouraged to exercise their faith in their everyday situations.

Structure controls rather than serves. In a body, the head controls, not the skeletal system. Control is a bigger issue in Church life than believers are often willing to admit. Religiosity and zeal to get things right can become the biggest "hang-ups". Especially so if a culture of dependency is created, where people are not allowed to make decisions for themselves. Sometimes believers try too hard to iron out the creases in their pursuit of a "great Church." Sadly, the element of human imperfection that helps outsiders relate to members of the Church as normal people is then lost.

Congregationalism creates a two-tier system of performers and audience. This may, at first, appeal to the average Christian, but it will ultimately work against the healthy growth of the community.

Church as Community

The early Church thrived and exported its gospel on the reputation of a very healthy and growing sense of community, as seen in the book of Acts and Epistles of John.

Contemporary Christians must settle once and for all the issue concerning their involvement in government, politics, the arts and sciences. Leaders must not discourage those who are inclined to take high office, or pursue their careers in the political arena. The Church needs apostles and prophets in *every* walk of life. The Church cannot divorce itself from comment on the political policy and leadership of a country. Jesus did not hesitate to confront Pilate or speak strongly about the nature of Herod.

The Church cannot afford to ignore the plight of the hungry, burdened and homeless. God himself is committed to the plight of the oppressed and underprivileged peoples.[15]

Jesus expressed the importance of the Kingdom of God in its interaction with the disenfranchised: "For as much as you do it unto the least of these..."[16] It became foundational to apostolic concerns that the community of God's people did undertake their social obligation to the needy around them. James exhorted Paul not to ignore this aspect of humanitarian aid.[17]

Further Study

Discuss the meaning and the implications of the following quote on your outlook on and the practical outworking of Church life:

"The Church is the only society that exists for the benefit of non-members"

A Time for Apostolic Networking

Apostolic ministry was not a superficial designation. It remained a vital element in the maturing of the faith in the hearts of God's people, and it kept the Church in expressive thinking. It fostered a sense of cooperation in the ever-multiplying populations of Churches across international

---

[15] Psalm 9:9, Isaiah 58:10, Psalms 68:10, Psalms 82:3, Luke 4:18

[16] Matthew 25:40

[17] Galatians 2:10

borders. As the Kingdom message spread, the apostolic community had to adjust and learn that, in the overlap of operation, cooperation and mutual respect would be requisite. One's commissioning should not be exclusive of others'. A greater degree of wisdom needs to be found in cooperation.

The wisdom of God is clearly seen in the way in which the ground is prepared for Paul to be effective in the fertile soil of the Gentile community.

Peter the Forerunner

Peter was viewed as an essential pillar in the early Church community. The Jewish converts to Christianity were still associated with the synagogue and Jerusalem. There was a general acceptance by now, even in traditional circles, of this cult known as "The Followers of the Way." This terminology would soon be changed to "Christians."

However, God interrupted the convictions of Peter and his strict understanding of the gospel in terms of its appeal to the Jews. It was necessary to broaden Peter's horizons and to enlighten his mind for the expanse of the gospel into regions beyond.

It took the keen activity of the Holy Spirit in the form of visions and words of knowledge to break down the mindset of Peter. He needed to be given the confidence to break out of the limitations of the Jewish community and reach to the Gentiles. Peter would not deny the intrusion that took place in terms of his doctrine.

The Holy Spirit was the pacesetter and Peter was provoked to quicken his step in order to keep up with the pace and direction that God had determined.

- *From observing Peter's challenges, what can we learn about dealing with transitions?*

- *What do you consider to be the fundamental pressure on Peter when undergoing the rebuke from Paul (Galatians 2)?*

- *Cite two occasions in which Peter practices accountability with others.*

- *What character traits did Peter show in the way in which he responded to correction?*

Barnabas the Link Man

Barnabas was to prove instrumental in leading the way for Paul to come into position, ready for the next major phase of the Holy Spirit's penetration beyond Jerusalem. Eventually, Antioch in Asia was established as a strong base to reach the regions beyond.

The wisdom of God provided Paul with a well-seasoned friendship with Barnabas, who was a very resourceful man. Barnabas had knowledge of the development of the early Church prior to Paul's conversion. He proved useful to Paul and introduced him to the inner strategists of the Church in their day. Barnabas was also a very generous-hearted man, besides being filled with the Spirit. He contributed much to the advance of the work of God in his generation.

As the people of God, believers must learn to identify such people today, and use them in their gifting without being threatened by them. Observe that not every apostle is the same. It is a blessing that there is such diversity of personality and gift. Barnabas, whilst of a gracious disposition, was clearly rated highly in the work of God. He showed courage in introducing Paul to the Church at a time when most Christians were suspicious of him. He was fearless in his ability to stand in disagreement with Paul over Mark, revealing an inner strength.

Paul the Irrepressible

Trained since his youth in a Jewish mind-set and religious law, Paul was repositioned by God to champion the Gentile cause. He needed to be irrepressible because so much would come against him in the paradigm shift necessary for the gospel to be established amongst the Gentiles. He knew every legalistic, purist argument and used it all as tools to open the doors for the spread of the gospel beyond the Jews, unto the nations.

Corporate Input of Leadership

A healthy interaction between different ministries should foster a sense of diversity in leadership gifting and functions. No one ministry is sufficient on its own to sustain the wellbeing of the community. The local leadership ought to have interaction with trans-local gifting. Yet there should be certain safeguards put in place to protect the Church, as seemed to be evident with the Apostle Paul. The ministry gift should display a genuine heart to provide for the blessing of the Church. Such input should maintain continuity and ought not to be disruptive or foster a "free for all" mentality.

> "I thank God, who put into the heart of Titus the same concern I have for you... And we are sending along with him

the brother who is praised by all the Churches for his service to the gospel."[18]

Paul was genuinely desirous of finding good, mature and sincere attitudes at work. He fostered a sense of accountability. Ministry must not become simply an opportunity to develop and promote "one's own ministry." The care of the Churches and the wellbeing of the individual are paramount. Reputation must be earned; to minister is more than to teach. It is important that we communicate everything in a spirit of humility.

Paul alluded to the combined testimony of all the Churches. Networking has its benefits. In this particular case, it was the means by which new blood was introduced into the communities. It prevented the Church of Christ from being too closeted and isolated, and avoided parochialism.

---

[18] 2 Corinthians 8:16,18

CHAPTER SIXTEEN

APOSTOLIC COMPANY

The value of a company of people working together to accomplish the will of God is quickly evident when reading through the New Testament. God owns and gives favor to such a focused unity. The ministry of Christ is a stewardship of God's blessing to the world. God adds the dimension of His presence to such a grouping, starting with a very special combination of men and women, clear in their calling and gifting, genuinely committed together in heart relationships. Their endeavors bring about the extension of God's Kingdom on earth by the accompanying presence of the Holy Spirit.

- **Apostolic**: Sent to accomplish a given task; a sense of commission figures highly.

- **Company**: A community of gifted ministries, harnessing their resources for a common objective.

These words typify the nature and mission of sound leadership.

An apostolic company is: "a strategy for corporate maturity; teams of builders working in harmony, setting Churches on the way to maturity, and creating a people who are able to fulfill the purpose of God for their lives, and are released in their own particular gifting and callings."[1]

God's goals are people oriented. Our task is to be focused on the objective. Jesus said, "I will build my Church,"[2] and we are laborers together with Him in that endeavor. Bryn Jones and his associates practiced one of the strongest emphases on apostolic work in the UK for over twenty-five years. He expressed a deep conviction regarding the nature of the Church when he said:

> "We anticipate the Church enjoying a worldwide restoration. Apostolic companies in every country finding each other, and in the Church finding the means to work together in genuine unity. A sure antidote to competitiveness or politics. This has always been God's purpose and is not an unrealistic dream. A global harvest will require good, healthy relationships existing between leaders of Churches. Whilst diversity, styles and operations may continue, our sense of need of each other ought to outweigh the small-mindedness that has eroded the effectiveness of Christianity and its influence in the world."[3]

Company Defined

"Company" carries a sense of the *companionship* and the *diversity of thinking* that works together to achieve the task. It speaks of four key components:

1. **Relationship** – Jesus called His disciples first and foremost to follow Him ("... follow me and I will make you fishers of men"[4]).

---

[1] Bryn Jones, Briefing paper 15/1/1993, UK

[2] Matthew 16:18

[3] Bryn Jones, *Bible Week Celebration Sermon* (Dales, 1980)

[4] Matthew 4:19

2. **Diversity** – provides for a kaleidoscope of ways and creative developments ("… iron sharpens iron"[5]).

3. **Unity** – not uniformity, but a genuine togetherness that adds strength to the whole, resulting in the task being made lighter.

4. **Accountability** – health checks and counter-balance measures in place, ensuring credibility and mutual respect for each other. Paul encouraged such transparency when challenging Peter (see Galatians). Accountability was also exercised when handling large sums of money. Consider the offering for the persecuted Church that was taken;[6] also Paul's handling of the breach between Philemon and Onesimus.[7] In understanding the nature of a company, three particular aspects need to be considered.

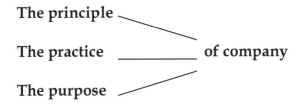

The principle

The practice _____ of company

The purpose

The Principle of Company

To appreciate the principle of apostolic company,[8] the way in which Jesus operated with the disciples needs to be considered, as well as the nature of

---

[5] Proverbs 27:17

[6] 2 Corinthians 8:7-15.

[7] Philemon 8-16.

[8] Jesus was obliged to be content with fishermen and publicans for Apostles, and devotedly thanked His Father for giving them to him. (See A. Bruce's *The Training of the Twelve*, (London, T+T Clarke, 1906) pp. 37-38)

later apostolic companies in the New Testament which emerged after Jesus' resurrection.

Jesus, the Great Apostle, is the cornerstone for all to be measured by. He lived and worked with a group of people whom He had called to follow Him. They were being schooled for future leadership, which involved pioneering the work of God and establishing the Church in a pagan world.

There are three passages that refer to the choosing of people to form the first company.

1.   Matthew 10:1-4

The first apostolic company was composed largely of provincials from Galilee, which itself became a provocation of contempt amongst the Pharisees and the Scribes. The training and honing of their skills took place on the job.

2.   **Mark 3:13-19**

Peter appears as the prominent one in the listings, whilst Judas always features as last.

3.   **Luke 6:12-16 and Acts 1:13**

There is a particular core Jesus seemed to draw aside more frequently than the whole.

The Practice of Company

It is significant that Jesus selected His company a considerable time after His ministry had begun. Some commentators suggest that He started the process about halfway through. This illustrates the critical reasoning behind ministry having a company context. The high profile of Jesus and His healing ministry and His revolutionary message of the Kingdom had brought about huge demands; hence, the need for the assistance of others to work with Him, besides that of his intentional approach of training his disciples in the field of action. The demands placed upon the ministry of Jesus were quite considerable. Jesus knew how to withdraw for a while. He encouraged his own disciples to do likewise.[9]

It was the same for Paul the Apostle in his time: he saw an advantage to having others harnessed to him in the work. Note how he sends people in his place to carry out what he considered needed to be done. They were couriers of his words of encouragement and correction to the Churches when he was tied up (often literally) in other places.

Consider:

- *Onesimus* – he was useful to Paul.

- *Epaphroditus* – a great encouragement to Paul, and like-minded.

- *Priscilla & Aquila* – instrumental in pioneering the work at Corinth.

- *Lydia* – a faithful woman, generous in her support of the work of the ministry.

The Purpose of Company

In the development of any work, project, task, or community, there will always be tension between establishing and expanding.

---

[9] Mark 6: 30-31

Things that come about by the direct influence of ministry need to be established in order for them to be fruitful. The Apostle Paul referred to these demands upon him, especially the "concern for all the Churches".[10] Hence, in every company where there is a harnessing of gifts together, each must play their part in the objective of equipping others.

> "... to prepare God's people for works of service, so that the body of Christ may be built up until we all reach unity in the faith and in the knowledge of the Son of God and become mature, attaining to the whole measure of the fullness of Christ."[11]

> "Convinced of this, I know that I will remain, and I will continue with all of you for your progress and joy in the faith..." [12]

Expanding the Spheres of Influence

The thought of expanding the believers' spheres of influence into greater circles of outreach should take place continually. Consider what Jesus says in directing His own disciples:

> "But you will receive power when the Holy Spirit comes on you; and you will be my witnesses in Jerusalem, and in all Judea and Samaria, and to the ends of the earth." [13]

Jerusalem – The immediate locality was affected with the vibrant message

---

[10] 2 Corinthians 11:28
[11] Ephesians 4:12-13
[12] Philippians 1:25
[13] Acts 1:8

of the Kingdom.

Judea and Samaria – Intermediate: the reach to the regions.

Ends of the Earth – Ultimate: God's intention has always been to reach the whole world.

The Apostle Paul was aware that, in order for the message to reach further afield, he needed the cooperation of God's people in the Churches to work with him in the constant pull to reach out beyond what had already been established.

> "Neither do we go beyond our limits by boasting of work done by others. Our hope is that, as your faith continues to grow, our area of activity among you will greatly expand, so that we can preach the gospel in the regions beyond you. For we do not want to boast about work already done in another man's territory."[14]

It is too easy to remain engrossed in local endeavors and lose a sense of the importance of working together to spread the message and influence of the Kingdom. Stretching to reach outward and invest in others will always require faith. It is mutual; the Church and the leadership need to be harnessed together as a whole, forming a strategic partnership which is urged for by the Apostle Paul.

Spheres of Influence

Each ministry carries with it a particular gifting and its own sphere of influence, whether working alone or in harness together with other ministries. This defines the term "Prophetic Portfolio." Whenever there are projects such as training programs, humanitarian relief, leadership

---

[14] 2 Corinthians 10:15-16

development initiatives and mission, there will often be a company of ministries teamed for a common purpose.

Core Company

When it comes to strategic planning, where a number of key ministries work together, it is helpful to work through details with a core grouping of leaders. Doing so avoids overloading everyone with details; helps to gain a broad spectrum of understanding of what is taking place across the field of the work; creates opportunity to focus; and facilitates a forum at which to arrive at a comprehensive understanding of the situation.

There are some biblical examples of projects in which we see these principles in action:

- Jesus sending disciples ahead of time for the preparation of the Passover. [15]

- The sending of the seventy on short-term missions. [16]

- The commission of a team of ministries to teach the world with the message of the gospel.[17]

The Advantages of Apostolic Company

A successful apostolic company facilitates the **expansion of the work**, adding variety of input and preventing stagnation. In this way, being locked into the local leader's limitations can be avoided. The wider gifting of ministries should input into the Church. Often Churches are held back from developing because of the bottleneck caused by congregations who

---

[15] Matthew 26:17-18.
[16] Luke 10:1-24.
[17] Matthew 28:16-20; Acts 1:8.

are locked into "one man" operations. A properly functioning apostolic group will encourage thinking "outside of the box" and open up horizons of opportunity.

An apostolic company will see strong relationships emerge. Companionship is developed. Jesus did not seek to train an elite squad that only related on the basis of their gifting or achievements. He looked for, and found, a genuine forging of relationships. Friendships are not an optional extra or fringe benefit. They are a vital part of what comprises the Kingdom of God and the Church. In fact, friendships are the ideal context in which to train others and provide a healthy accountability.

Apostolic and prophetic ministries working in conjunction with evangelists, pastors and teachers, require agreed and understood lines of accountability. Church leaders, in particular, are entrusted with a profound responsibility, having a far-reaching effect on the lives and wellbeing of so many. All leadership is healthy leadership when accountability is a reality. The safety factors are enhanced when leaders are open to entreaty: it can often help in spotting early signs of a breakdown of leadership.

The danger of a lack of accountability speaks for itself. Pseudo-accountability, one that seems to exist but is never exercised in practice, is even worse.

> "Keeping leaders accountable is always tricky business... on the one hand leaders are implicitly trusted to protect the common good and make sound decisions... On the other hand leaders must answer to someone should their decisions prove to be detrimental to others."[18]

---

[18] W. Beausay, *The Leadership Genius of Jesus* (Nashville, Nelson, 1997) p.37

A lack of accountability in leadership leads to breakdown, disagreements, misunderstandings and error.

Eroding Biblical Accountability

These are a few of the things that erode genuine accountability amongst leaders:

- Inviting examination, but unwilling to receive criticism or the call for adjustment in practices.

- Undermining of sharp-minded people, who may disagree with certain aspects of practice. This can be done by belittling their criticism in front of others, or by agreeing in public and rubbishing it to colleagues in private.

- Discussing issues in the open with everyone in the room and yet not having full knowledge of all sides of the facts.

- Marginalizing of those who think differently, insisting that they are divisive or not joined in heart with the mainstream.

Relationships - A Key to Accountability

Most people's understanding of an apostolic company is that it is mostly "task oriented." This is not exclusively so with Jesus. As seen in the scriptures, He prizes relationship first.

"You are my friends if you do what I command."[19]

'You are, if you do...' This is not a social club of friends. It is friends

---

[19] John 15:14

on a mission, friends in a context that puts a deeper significance on their togetherness.

A company cannot function successfully outside the bounds of good relationship, built on mutual trust and cooperation. It is not individuals working for the promotion of their own ministry, but individuals working together for a common purpose to achieve a common goal.

> "God, who has called you into fellowship with His Son Jesus
> Christ our Lord, is faithful."[20]

A spirit of cooperation is key; it cannot be legislated, organized or enforced. This is the basis for advancement in the purposes of God. The Apostle Paul exercised this ethic in his ministry when he consulted with James and Peter and the apostles in Jerusalem (Galatians).

The Company - A Flexible Entity

The New Testament never over-structures ministry or Church leadership. There is a great deal of flexibility in the nature and practice of leadership and Church life in the instructions in scripture.

Jesus clearly had a core of team members that remained consistent throughout His ministry. Four people in particular are constantly seen together with Jesus, even from amongst the twelve. Furthermore, the twelve seemed to form a nucleus from among the seventy, and so on.

However, there are two other aspects that seem to shape company ministry:

- Prophetic Engagement

---

[20] 1 Corinthians 1:9

- Projects and Administrative Structure

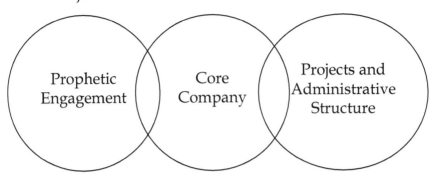

Prophetic Engagement

This means a sense of purpose, a common objective in what is seeking to be realized; having an understanding of what a person's particular role is meant to be in a given endeavor.

> "But I think it is necessary to send back to you Epaphroditus, my brother, fellow-worker and fellow-soldier, who is also your messenger, whom you sent to take care of my needs."[21]

Epaphroditus joined Paul in his ministry for a season only, and the Church at Philippi was instrumental in supporting this. Paul recognized that it was only for a season. He did not abuse the Church's generosity. He respected their trust of him and their loyalty to him. This is something that all too often can be taken for granted. Not all involvement in the wider arena needs to be on a permanent basis.

The Church took great interest in the needs of Paul. The support of his ministry and that of the apostolic company was quite special. It extended their sphere of influence into the regions beyond. It reflected their own sensitivity to God-given ministry and their generosity of heart in their

---

[21] Philippians 2:25

desire to provide practical support.

It was a great boost to Paul, who made full use of such an investment. Every successful activity requires practical options for resource.

The apostle did not "steal" the ministry of Epaphroditus, but maintained good communication with the Church that sent him, and recognized when the time was right to send him back to Philippi. It was not only money that was laid at the apostle's feet, it was also people, whose skills, supportive efforts, and willingness to serve was all that mattered.

The use of the phrase "prophetic engagement," refers to a clear sense of one's mandate, an allocated task needing to be achieved. Everything is in the context of a changing dynamic, particularly the ever-transitory nature of leadership and Church life.

Consider this as it applied to the Church at Philippi. The Philippian Church owed a great debt to Paul for the instrumental way in which he had responded to the Spirit and helped to establish them in the faith. He was unable, even from the birth of the Church, to have a great deal of input, but he never ceased to keep an active interest in their welfare. He often engaged with the Church in counsel, input, correction, correspondence and in the strategic direction of appropriate ministries to assist the Church.

Apostolic ministry such as this could ill-afford to be "busy-bodying" in the affairs of the Church. The existing overseers and servants in ministry were doing a considerable job. Paul was consulted on a regular basis, and the nature of the involvement was reciprocal. This Church provided for the reach of the apostolic ministry by supplying financial support and personnel.

The nature of Paul's authority was consultative. It was nonetheless forceful. Leadership did not operate in isolation from their need of broader input. Local leaders took care of the day-to-day matters and together they fostered a Kingdom dimension in the affairs of the Church.

Projects and Administrative Structure

As mentioned earlier, projects inevitably emerge. This comprises the practical aspect of the ministry, providing tools to further the wellbeing of people who are being exposed to the teaching and preaching of the gospel. The early Church soon developed in this respect, especially with the huge intake of people from all walks of life. Illustrations of this are found in Church history.[22] The commitment of leaders, preachers, evangelists and a vast army of people are vital for the strengthening and growth of the Church.

Jesus was known for His teaching and His kind deeds. The early Church had a radical testimony of doing good to the community. It later became one of the chief reasons for the spread of the gospel and the influence of the early Church.

Plurality and Diversity

It is a mistake to view apostleship as being a rigid or stereotypical ministry. Throughout the early Church there are numerous examples of apostles busy in the work. Their ministries were diverse in terms of gift, calling, measure and focus of activity, and levels of authority.

---

[22] For example, Acts 2:42

It is clear from the examples found in scripture record of some of the most prominent of the early Church's apostles that an apostleship is not a "cookie cutter" or stereotypical in its outworkings. Ministry, gifting, measure and callings are not given out in equal portions, nor does the Holy Spirit repeat Himself.

James, the brother of Jesus, seems to take the senior role in the Jerusalem Church where he appears to have lived. He took charge of the company of apostles and elders on the circumcision issues (Acts 15). He played an important role in guiding the dialogue of the council through probably its greatest challenge, which was the spread of the gospel into the Gentile world. He determined the essentials of the gospel, and adopted a fresh and courageous approach beyond the usual conservatism of the Jews.

Peter occupies most of the accounts of the early Church, as recorded in the book of Acts. The first 12 chapters focus on the activities of Peter as he is sent out with the gospel. His influence was to spread throughout the Jewish Diaspora, over-spilling into the Gentile community. All this was within the divine plan, and yet the congregations in Jerusalem did not immediately cope with what was taking place – they needed some persuading.

> "The apostles and the brothers throughout Judea heard that the Gentiles also had received the Word of God. So when Peter went up to Jerusalem, the circumcised believers criticized him and said, "You went into the house of uncircumcised men and ate with them."[23]

The advance of the Kingdom does not always carry the approval of all the Church. The early signs of the Jerusalem Church showed the believers becoming possessive and proprietary in attitude, and in danger of

---

[23] Acts 11:1-3

exclusivity. They were afraid that the purity of the message would be diluted by the invasion of the Gentiles. The apostle had to set the pace in obedience to the Spirit, helping break the Church out of unreality and conservatism.

Peter's activity appeared to trigger an avalanche of communication along the routes of the Jewish settlements, spilling over into the Gentile community with powerful demonstrations of conversions and Holy Spirit baptisms. This was the case with the early Christian zealots who had been gripped by the cause of the Kingdom and were eager to spread its message further afield.

John, to begin with, worked very closely with Peter, and later he carried significant influence throughout Asia. Tradition has it that he eventually took a senior role within the Church at Ephesus.

Barnabas seemed to be a very determined man and exercised his apostleship rather differently from that of Paul. His particular contribution seemed to be conciliatory in nature; he was useful in bridging relationships amongst the apostles. Consider, for example, his linkage with Saul of Tarsus – later to become known as Paul. He supported the cause of John Mark in the dispute that raged with Paul as to whether he was fit to accompany them on the next missionary trip.[24]

Paul thrived on teamwork. He was responsible for establishing the foundations of practice for the Gentile Church. His ministry highlighted some of the distinctive features of an apostle with great measure, such as:

- A very definite revelation of the gospel to the Gentiles (Galatians).

- Unwillingness to compromise on the essential issues regarding the Jew and the Gentile (Romans).

---

[24] Acts 15:36-40

- Strongly involved in bringing direction to the style of meetings and the behavior of members of the Church (Corinth).

- Committed to the working of the supernatural.

- Instrumental in the establishing of works and the appointing of leaders to govern those works (Acts/Timothy).

- Forthrightness in defending the gospel to the political and social players of his day (Agrippa, Festus, etc in Acts).

- Tenacious in refuting religion that denied the power of God.

- A catalyst for different ministries, helping them to play their part in the spread of the Kingdom (Philippians).

- Forever reaching out to nations beyond his own with the mission of the Kingdom.

Besides these people who made up what could be considered the first rank of apostles, there were numerous others operating throughout the regions. For example:

Andronicus and Junias

> "Greet Andronicus and Junias, my relatives who have been in prison with me. They are outstanding among the apostles, and they were in Christ before I was."[25]

The mention of Andronicus and Junias together, especially in the Greek usage, seems to suggest that they might have been husband and wife. If this was the case, Junias could have been a female apostle. It cannot be taken for granted that every husband and wife in leadership operates quite like Andronicus and Junias did. Certainly, there were a

---

[25] Romans 16:7

good number of apostles besides the "Apostles of the Lamb." However, it is a fine example of two people operating in ministry together, showing mutual respect for each other. The woman was not denied the right to engage in ministry, nor did she gain it on the basis that her husband was in leadership. It seems there was an obvious awareness of the value of the interaction of each other's calling and gifting.

Seldom is such a liberty found in modern Christian circles. Often, women in particular are held back by small-minded thinking in men. Sometimes they are held captive by inadequately interpreted scriptures that serve to bind rather than release their gifting in Christ. Open discussion is needed on the genuineness of a broader spectrum of leadership that provided a greater release to women.

> "The expression 'of note among the apostles' could mean well known to the apostles, but scholarly opinion rejects this interpretation. Junias (masculine) could actually be (feminine) since the text reads Iouvian (acc.), in which case Andronicus and Junias would presumably be man and wife, like Aquila and Priscilla. The circle of apostles would then include women;"[26]

Epaphroditus

Epaphroditus was intrinsically linked to Paul, who was sensitive enough not to abuse or take for granted the good will and generosity of the Church.

> "But I think it is necessary to send back to you Epaphroditus, my brother, fellow-worker and fellow-soldier, who is also

---

[26] A. Richardson, *An Introduction to the Theology of the New Testament* (California, SCM Press, 1958) pp. 320-321

your messenger, whom you sent to take care of my needs."[27]

Epaphroditus is a beautiful picture of someone who is genuinely caring, dedicated and desirous of being a support to Paul. Selfish ambition is not found in this man. He is truly a cup of refreshing and someone to imitate.

The Apostolic Church: God's People

The use of the term "apostolic" carries with it a sense of mission, purpose and responsibility to "accomplish a task for which it has been commissioned." Apostolic ministry does not exist for its own ministry's sake. It must impart a broader sense of the mission and destiny of God's people in the world.

It is a distinctive element of the Church of Christ to effect change in the community and to further the cause of Christ to reach mankind with a message of hope. This broader bequest of Christ to the Church provides a multifaceted ministry to empower and propel the community into a dynamic relationship with the society at large.

> "It was He who gave some to be apostles, some to be prophets, some to be evangelists, and some to be pastors and teachers".[28]

The New Testament clearly defines these ministries as the foundation of healthy Church life; one that truly reflects Christ's purpose. It is bigger than the small-minded approach that so often limits the Church's effectiveness. Today's Church must be clear as to the kind of foundation it

---

[27] Philippians 2:25
[28] Ephesians 4:11

builds on.

> "… built on the foundation of the apostles and prophets, with Christ Jesus himself as the chief cornerstone."[29]

> "By the grace God has given me, I laid a foundation as an expert builder, and someone else is building on it. But each one should be careful how he builds. For no-one can lay any foundation other than the one already laid, which is Jesus Christ."[30]

All ministries must focus on Christ as the center.

Apostolic Communities: God's Order

Paul says to the Corinthian Church:

> "Now you are the body of Christ, and each one of you is a part of it. And in the Church God has appointed first of all apostles, second prophets, third teachers, then workers of miracles, also those having gifts of healing, those able to help others, those with gifts of administration, and those speaking in different kinds of tongues."[31]

> "This is the only place in the New Testament where God specifies an order of function for the various ministries… This is not a pecking order to show status but rather a functioning order to accomplish the task. It is not an attempt to give apostles three stars, prophets two stars and pastors, teachers

---

[29] Ephesians 2:20

[30] 1 Corinthians 3:10-11

[31] 1 Corinthians 12:27-28

one star... If we change the order it does not mean that nothing is built. Rather, what is built will not be as effective..."[32]

The apostles explained the heart of Christ to His followers. They clearly instructed the people in life, much like the Rabbi's in the synagogue. They were highly respected amongst the people as explainers of the Way. One must remember that the early Church did not have the canon of scripture that is available today.

A hallmark of apostolic leadership is having an ability to explain and expound more fully the essential revelation of the gospel of the Kingdom. This goes beyond the mere explanation of concept to translating principles into practice throughout the Church.

Apostolic Allotment of Responsibility: Power Executed

In the rapid development of the Church, the ministries developed a sense of their own particular allotment or charge from God to their ministry.

Peter chiefly concentrated his ministry alongside the scattered Jewish communities, which, by virtue of the activity of the Holy Spirit, brought him into contact with the Gentile Christians.

"When they had testified and proclaimed the Word of the Lord, Peter and John returned to Jerusalem, preaching the gospel in many Samaritan villages."[33]

James seems to remain as an apostolic authority in Jerusalem, whilst Peter travels far more extensively.

---

[32] B. Jones, "Apostles Today - For Tomorrow's Church", *Restoration Magazine*, p. 31
[33] Acts 8:25

John emerges as a highly respected apostle amongst the Churches and, for the best part of his ministry, resided in Jerusalem.

Paul, in his writing to the Galatians, defines this sense of allotment, or charge, that each apostle carried.

> "As for those who seemed to be important – whatever they were makes no difference to me; God does not judge by external appearance – those men added nothing to my message. On the contrary, *they saw that I had been entrusted with the task of preaching the Gospel to the Gentiles, just as Peter had been to the Jews.* For God, who was at work in the ministry of Peter as an apostle to the Jews, was also at work in my ministry as an apostle to the Gentiles. James, Peter and John, those reputed to be pillars, gave Barnabas and me the right hand of fellowship when they recognized the grace given to me. They agreed that we should go to the Gentiles, and they to the Jews. All they asked was that we should continue to remember the poor, the very thing I was eager to do."[34] [emphasis added]

The Church will never need to escape its apostolic nature. This has been firmly established in its head, being Christ Jesus, referred to as "The Great Apostle." The code of the Church's produce is rooted in apostolic teaching. Paul was also instrumental in his time in the writing of scripture and in the securing of the gospel to the Gentiles. He established clear instructions to assist the life of the Church in its process of maturing in Christ. He discipled many communities through his numerous letters and provided answers to their questions.

Apostolic ministry is about building on the right foundations of truth.

---

[34] Galatians 2:6-10

The primary task of apostles in apostolic ministry is to partner with other ministries, to act together as custodians of a revelation of the gospel, and to assist God's people to understand the true nature of the Church as it was meant to be, in line with the Word of God.

The mandate is clear in Ephesians 4. It is to establish God's people in maturity of thinking and in scriptural practices fitting to the Church's call.

Principles of the Apostle Paul's Mandate

Relationships with leaders

It is clear that the Apostle Paul had a valued relationship with Church leaders, ensuring a healthy interaction.

Local and global heart for the Church

Although his care for the Churches continued throughout his ministry, it did not negate his deep and continuing interest in the welfare of God's people as a whole. He continued to extend his reach to nations beyond.

Dynamic role

It seems that in the early communities, the eldership acknowledged the changing role of the apostle. They were not overly dependent upon him, yet they continued to acknowledge the valid contribution he had to make.

Partnership and interconnectivity for the Gospel

The evolving situation of a growing Church meant a decreasing engagement for Paul with everyday Church life, yet he continued his partnership with the Churches. Philippi was one of the first Churches in Macedonia to resource him, supplying money and people. Such links between the apostolic mission and the local development of Church forged a resilient partnership in the gospel.

Strategist

Apostles should not be considered as just visiting ministries. Paul was often included in planning and commenting on the progress or regress of Church situations.

Rooted in the community

Antioch held a special significance for Paul. It was instrumental in his early (ministry) commissioning (see Acts 11). The apostle often returned there for seasons after extensive trips to regions beyond.

Tensions Arising Between Leaders and Churches

The Apostle John, in his epistles, portrays the tensions that existed between the leader of the Church in Ephesus and the apostolic ministry.[35]

The Apostle Paul also faced challenges in his relationships with the Churches. The Asian Churches proved to be quite disheartening. "Everyone in the province of Asia has deserted me," Paul reported in his writings.[36]

In 2 Corinthians Paul was obliged to make a defense, explaining the role of the wider ministry in relation to the local pressures on the leadership and management of the Churches. Working together to pioneer Churches and to import the Church, Paul must establish clear parameters for his own legitimacy of calling and practice. Paul was determined to keep alive a sense of mutual cooperation and appreciation for the Church

---

[35] 3 John
[36] 2 Timothy 1:15

he loved, yet was seldom physically able to reach.

> "Now this is our boast: Our conscience testifies that we have conducted ourselves in the world, and especially in our relations with you, in the holiness and sincerity that are from God. We have done so not according to worldly wisdom but according to God's grace. For we do not write to you anything you cannot read or understand. And I hope that, as you have understood us in part, you will come to understand fully that you can boast of us just as we will boast of you in the day of the Lord Jesus."[37]

The danger with any leadership which fails to handle people with respect is that it will fail to produce a mature Church. Apostolic or local leadership that operates on a bureaucratic basis will stunt the growth of the Church. Paul was intent on establishing a better understanding of leadership, and a better quality of believer. The mistake that people make today is to evaluate "growth" in terms of "body count." God is looking for a people mature in Christ, not just entertained by activities and events.

> "Not that we lord it over your faith, but we work with you for your joy, because it is by faith you stand firm". [38]

It is inevitable that the issue of gaining and maintaining mutual respect for trans-local ministry is to be faced. A good question to ask is, 'What role does an apostle have once the Church is established in its own eldership?'

Once local eldership is clearly established, the role of the apostle needs to change in his working toward that Church, unless the apostle is a

---

[37] 2 Corinthians 1:12-14
[38] 2 Corinthians 1:24

resident ministry and the Church is an integral part of the apostolic base of operation.

A real tension exists, not so much over whether there should be authority in the Church, but rather over what the nature of that authority is, whether elders have sole authority, and whether there is a difference between elders and Ephesians 4 ministries. There are distinct differences existing in any eldership that is truly multiple, that is to say that, there are differences in measure, gifting and specific callings. Some ministries may operate on a broader scale than others. Eldership is from the Greek word *presbuteros*, sometimes translated as "bishop." It describes a function not an office. It does not emphasize a particular gift; it involves the following:

Overseeing: watching over, caring for, and protecting:

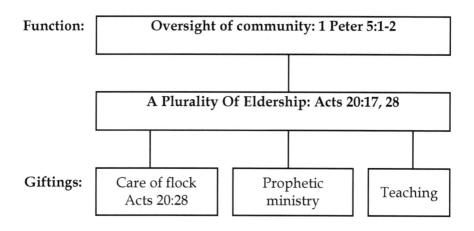

Paul had no doubt concerning his apostleship. It was intrinsically linked to his relationship with, and activity towards, the established Church, as well as to his pioneering work. However much it may have been contested in some Church circles, apostleship was not a theoretical exercise for him. The fruit of his apostleship was tangibly evident in the Christian community.

"Even though I may not be an apostle to others, surely I am to you! For you are the seal of my apostleship in the Lord."[39]

- The understanding of the gospel is what the Apostle Paul sought to protect. His treatise to the Churches in Galatia is a case in point.

- The Nature of the Church: The Apostle John writes three Epistles to emphasise the nature of the Church and how each one should conduct themselves out of respect for one another.

- James, in his Epistle, tackles the need for people to tame their tongues and practice respect for each other.

- Instruction of the Church order in meetings was a crucial matter to the apostles. The way in which the meetings were handled, the administration of the Lord's Supper and the need for wholesome relationships in the Church community. Paul uses such wonderful metaphors to underscore these issues.

Honoring Apostolic Ministry: Some Helpful Observations

The New Testament Church esteemed the apostolic company and recognized their responsibility before God...

"James, Peter and John, those reputed to be pillars..."[40]

They were considered as ministries that brought a sense of stability to an ever-expanding Church and work of God. Ordinary people could appeal to the apostles for direct intervention, as in the case of the Corinthian Church (see 3 John and 2 Corinthians).

---

[39] 1 Corinthians 9:2

[40] Galatians 2:9

Recognizing Emerging Ministries in the Church

Apostles were responsible for recognizing and endorsing bona-fide apostolic ministry. It was not so much their task to create apostles, but it was their responsibility to recognize and acknowledge them as they became evident.

Apostolic ministry was not a badge of office, it was a person entrusted with a task. Every apostle must be able to focus on the particular task entrusted to them.

It is significant that not all those in leadership were referred to as apostles. Consider such people as:

Timothy: Thessalonians 3:2; 2 Corinthians 1:1

Titus: Titus 1:4

Apollos: 1 Corinthians 3:5

Apostleship is not a status that people acquire. Therefore, it does not concur that everyone in ministry will eventually become an "apostle." It is important, however, for the apostolic ministries to help people understand their calling and avoid manufacturing or inventing roles for them in order to keep their allegiance to a cause.

> "The refusal of the title to Titus is all the more pointed when in 2 Corinthians 8:16-24, St. Paul is trying to commend Titus to the Corinthians in every way he can think of, especially see verse 23."[41]

---

[41] A. Richardson, *An Introduction to the Theology of the New Testament* (California, SCM Press, 1958) pp. 319-320

"As for Titus, he is my partner and fellow-worker among you; as for our brothers, they are representatives of the Churches and an honor to Christ."[42]

"Copy Cat" Ministries Must Be Avoided

Not all that called themselves apostles were, in fact, apostles. The college of apostles protected the Church from impostors.

"And I will keep on doing what I am doing in order to cut the ground from under those who want an opportunity to be considered equal with us in the things they boast about."[43]

The early Church was troubled by self-appointed hopefuls. Apostolic ministry, whilst having a particular task and zeal, does not operate unmindful of others.

"I went in response to a revelation and set before them the gospel that I preach among the Gentiles. But I did this privately to those who seemed to be leaders, for fear that I was running or had run my race in vain."[44]

In this respect, there existed a communal bond that acknowledged a spiritual authority that already existed and a moral responsibility, rather than a hierarchical leadership. Apostles did not hold control, but they certainly commanded respect and were anointed with an authority that was not to be handled lightly.

---

[42] 2 Corinthians 8:23
[43] 2 Corinthians 11:12
[44] Galatians 2:2

Relational and not Structural Functioning

It has been noted that the Apostle Paul flourished in the context of companionship. Furthermore, he promoted an understanding of the value of Church community. Whenever Paul wrote to the Church, his appeal was always broader than the existing leadership. He saw the value in keeping the connection with the heart of the community. He avoided promoting an elitist view of leaders. Although there were times that he would spend with leadership, the bulk of his reference and his appeals were direct to the people.

Strauch, in his book *Biblical Eldership*, makes some very helpful points on this.

> "Disorder and sin in the Church in Corinth had to be dealt with but Paul calls on no one person or group to resolve the problem. Was there no one to call upon? Of course there was! Paul could have called upon the dedicated Stephanus, 1 Corinthians 16:15-18; Gaius, in whose home the Church met, Romans 16:23; Erastus the city treasurer; Crispus, a converted chief ruler of the synagogue, Acts 18:8; or a number of other gifted men and prophets, 1 Corinthians 1:5-7." [45]

There is nothing hollow about the Church and its apostolic conventions. It can only add to the establishment of the people and the strengthening of leaders who have a demanding task, but it will only be as effective as the genuine development of heart for each other. The moment that over-structure takes place, the true benefit of apostolic Churches is thwarted.

---

[45] A. Strauch, *Biblical Eldership: Restoring the Eldership to its Rightful Place in Church*, (Colorado Springs, Lewis & Roth, 1994) p.102.

CHAPTER SEVENTEEN

APOSTOLIC MINISTRY IN THE NEW TESTAMENT

Having looked at the major features of leadership in general, this chapter will focus more particularly on the individual gifting, particularly of the apostolic and prophetic ministries.

Good leadership in the New Testament Church was vital to the success of the Kingdom and to the security of the people. If leadership is unclear as to the nature of the Church, it certainly will be distorted in its practice. The New Testament concept of leadership is to be considered a partnership with the Holy Spirit and is marked by its ability to handle the Word of God correctly.

> "The organization of the ecclesia must conform to the essential nature of the ecclesia, and not to that of preceding or contemporary institutions." [1]

The nature of the Church is that of the family of God, with God as the great Father. The Church is not a cell group or a house group; it is the home of all God's people – the gathered Church.

---

[1] R. Newton Flew, *Jesus and his Church*, (New York, The Abingdon Press, 1938) p. 187

The Title "Apostle"

The Greek word for "apostle" is *apostolos,* which is derived from *apostellō.* It denotes a sending of a person for a given task. In the Old Testament Septuagint (the seventy) version of the Bible, the word is used frequently.

> "The Septuagint version uses the word some 700 times.... The translators rightly realized that the Hebrew verb does not describe the sending, so much as its essential purpose, the authorization of the messenger."[2]

Although the term "apostle" held some significance with the early Jewish Christians, it was not a word familiar to the Greek-speaking Churches. Richardson refers to the term in classical Greek:

> "It was chiefly seen to refer to naval and overseas expeditions and was not commonly used for messenger.... Its adoption does not seem to arise from ordinary, current usage."[3]

According to the Mishna,[4] the word "apostle" carries a slightly different emphasis. "He who is sent by a man, is as he who sent him."[5]

> "This entrusting of full powers to another to act in the name of the person who has sent him is common, both to the idea of the late Jewish Apostolate and to those sent forth by Jesus."[6]

> "He who receives you receives me, and he who receives me

[2] C. Brown (ed), *The New International Dictionary of New Testament Theology, Vol. I* (Grand Rapids, Zondervan, 1975) p. 127

[3] A. Richardson, *An Introduction to the Theology of the New Testament* (California, SCM Press, 1958) p. 323

[4] MISHNA: The Mishna is the section of the Talmud consisting of the collection of oral laws that were edited AD200.

[5] Danby, *The Mishna*, (Oxford, Oxford University Press, 1933) p. 24.

[6] See R. Newton Flew, *Jesus and his Church*, (New York, The Abingdon Press, 1938) pp. 109-110

receives the one who sent me."[7]

The term "apostle" is used throughout the New Testament approximately 131 times.[8] There are numerous instances recording the existence and activity of apostles and prophets. Any reference to the term "apostle" in the pre-resurrection stage seems to confine its usage to that of a specific task or mission, and, in that sense, apostleship is for a certain time span or mission.

> "Jesus went up on a mountainside and called to him those he wanted, and they came to him. He appointed twelve – designating them apostles – that they might be with him and that he might send them out to preach and to have authority to drive out demons."[9]

> "Calling the Twelve to him, he sent them out two by two and gave them authority over evil spirits... The apostles gathered round Jesus and reported to him all they had done and taught." [10]

Certainly, after the Ascension, an entire book is named after the work of the apostles, and it introduces a greater understanding of apostleship. Yet it is not until Paul expounds on his own apostleship that the role and function of the apostle can be seen more clearly.

Hort and Murray conclude that the term "apostles" runs throughout the book of Acts. They draw attention to what they see as a definite change that has taken place in the role of the post-Pentecostal apostles, away from the temporary and short-term mission meaning which was

---

[7] Matthew 10:40

[8] C. Brown (ed), *The New International Dictionary of New Testament Theology, Vol. I* (Grand Rapids, Zondervan, 1975) p. 128

[9] Mark 3:13-15

[10] Mark 6:7, 30

used in the gospels.

> "Their original mission, from which apparently preceded the title 'apostle' given them by our Lord, was strictly confined to Judea (Matthew 10:5), not to go into any way of the Gentiles, and enter not into any city of the Samaritans: but go rather to the lost sheep of the house of Israel."[11]

Gradually, however, the commission of Christ was realized. They must expand beyond the boundaries of the Jewish nation, yet they were never to ignore their own kinsfolk. They gave them the first opportunity to respond to the gospel of the Kingdom.

> "But you will receive power when the Holy Spirit comes on you; and you will be my witnesses in Jerusalem, and in all Judea and Samaria, and to the ends of the earth."[12]

The apostles were not seen as "visiting ministries." They were the guardians of truth passed down to the Church by the Great Apostle and High Priest, Jesus Christ Himself.

Regarding belonging to the community of God's people, "[t]he entrance into the society of the Church was through baptism."[13] According to Rackham, in his commentary on Acts, the apostle is the principal authority.[14]

> "Membership means fellowship with the apostles... the Church is apostolic because it cleaves to the apostles."[15]

The first ministries, prior to the setting in of elders in the Churches,

---

[11] R. J. A. Hort and J. O. F. Murray, *The Christian Ecclesia* (London, Macmillan, 1914) p. 35.
[12] Acts 1:8
[13] R. J. A. Hort and J. O. F. Murray, *The Christian Ecclesia*, p. 32
[14] R. B. Rackham, *Acts of the Apostles*, (London, Methuen and Co. Ltd., 1911) p. 33.
[15] Ibid p.34.

were in fact "apostolic." This was soon to change; the Apostle Paul felt the need "to set in order things those left undone" (Acts 14:23), and sent ministries to the Churches recently founded. He sent instructions to establish Churches with their own eldership.

The first apostles were in a unique position, in that they were establishing foundations for the whole of Christendom. It would be grossly amiss for all apostolic ministries to class themselves in the same league. It is improper to believe that apostles today have the same degree of uniqueness as the "Apostles of the Lamb."

> "The twelve share the same call and share a common commission. They share the commission of being the foundation stones of the New Jerusalem. Even though Paul and numerous other apostles share in the apostolic calling, they do not share in the commission of the Twelve. What is entailed in being one of the twelve foundation stones is not clearly stated, neither does it imply the Twelve were the only foundational apostles, but it does at least mean, that in some sense their commission was unique. That the Twelve received a unique commission does not make them a special class of apostles. All apostles after them share the same calling, but no apostle after them shares their distinct commission. The calling continues, though the commissions differ." [16]

Authenticity of Apostolic Ministry

Who gives the apostle their credentials?

---

[16] M. D. Peters, *Apostles Then and Now* (USA, Occasional Paper, 1997)

These were the very questions that Jesus had to deal with in His own ministry. His endorsement did not come from the religious leadership of the day.[17]

Apostolic ministry must find its birth and authorization from God and not from human origin. Jesus put great emphasis on the results of His ministry; it bore the hallmark of supernatural activity.[18] The Apostle Paul also made it clear that he respected his contemporaries, but that his confidence was solely rooted in a divine commissioning.[19]

> "For it is not the one who commends himself who is approved, but the one whom the Lord commends."[20]

The Apostolic Patterns of Jesus

Jesus Christ lived and ministered for such a short time, yet His apostolic mandate and approach was so incredibly effective. His leadership was principled and His approach to people teaches the Church today how to harness the untapped potential in others. His exercise of apostolic ministry is helpful in showing us today how to develop a culture that will equip others to be effective. He gave Himself unreservedly to a relatively few uncelebrated men and women. They became effective in learning to overcome their failures and to move passionately and creatively in demonstrating to the world the joy and the power of knowing and serving God.

---

[17] Luke 20:1-8
[18] Luke 7:22
[19] 2 Corinthians 10:8-18
[20] 2 Corinthians 10:18

Characteristics Of Christ's Apostolic Ministry

A Clear Sense of Purpose

Jesus made this apparent in His own devotion and obedience to the Father. He was focused with a sense of purpose, a task to complete and a people to equip.[21]

A Discipling of Others

Apostolic ministry prioritizes the need to train,[22] make disciples, and impart the burden and purpose of the Lord to others. This is evident not so much in the training of specific skills, but in the development of a meaningful relationship with God, and the expression of Christ-likeness in their ministry. Jesus was committed to imparting God's Word into their hearts and beginning a process that would produce godly character.[23]

> "Discipling men and women is the priority around which our lives should be orientated." [24]

He had a keen sense of responsibility to work specifically with the people entrusted to Him[25]; to those He felt a deep joining with.

---

[21] John 17:6

[22] John 17:7-8

[23] John 17:6-8

[24] R. E. Coleman, *The Master Plan of Discipleship* (New York, FH Revell Co, 1987) p.10

[25] John 17:12

A Compassionate Involvement [26] *(A People Person)*

Jesus was not just task-orientated; He was "people involved." People felt that He took a genuine interest in their welfare. In spite of the demands upon Him, He still had time to engage with people.

> "I have made you known to them, and will continue to make you known in order that the love you have for me may be in them and that I myself may be in them." [27]

A Person Accustomed to Prayer

Jesus modeled a kind of prayer that would help shape, unlock and protect those entrusted to Him;[28] prayer that carried with it a sense of guardianship in the Spirit[29] for the welfare of God's people and His purpose on the earth.[30]

A Culture of Nurturing and Respect

Jesus invented the idea of equipping His people.[31] He was truly apostolic in that He became a catalyst to release people into their own calling. The most marked way in which Jesus developed the disciples was to create a culture of nurturing and respect. Jesus kept His disciples in touch with the realities of life. He did not keep them cocooned and detached from the world. He encouraged open dialogue and made room for times of reflection and questioning. He teased out of others their inner thoughts in an atmosphere that was safe.

Apostolic ministry must foster a healthy environment for the exchange

---

[26] John 17:19

[27] John 17:26

[28] John17:9

[29] John 17:15

[30] John 17:11

[31] Ephesians 4:11

of thought and discussion. If it ceases to do so, it becomes counterproductive, restrictive and legalistic.

> "A learning enquiry based and reflective culture is one where ideas and information come through unhampered by people who are worried or fearful... Empowered individuals feel that what they do has meaning and significance. They have discretion and obligations and live in a culture of respect where they can actually do things without having to check through five levels of hierarchy..."[32]

Jesus was a visionary; constantly reaching beyond limitations and small-mindedness; always aware that the future requires a people equipped to face it – a people who, in their own gifting and in their perception, learn to become adequate for the task and so able to shape it.

The Place of Accountability

Accountability factors are built into the apostolic role model of Christ, and it is vital in all equipping ministries. Jesus reflects this when speaking to His Father.[33]

- Accountability of practice

  "I have brought you glory on earth by completing the work you gave me to do." [34]

- Accountability of message

---

[32] W. G. Bennis and B. Goldsmith, *Learning to Lead*, (London, Perseus Books, 1997) p. 17.
[33] John 17
[34] John 17:4

"For I gave them the words you gave me and they accepted them. They knew with certainty that I came from you, and they believed that you sent me." [35]

• Accountability of the use of resources

"While I was with them, I protected them and kept them safe by that name you gave me. None has been lost except the one doomed to destruction so that Scripture would be fulfilled." [36]

Paul had this same attitude. He understood that there was no room for a credibility gap. It is exacting, yet essential, that we see the importance of the responsibility of stewardship.

"For we are taking pains to do what is right, not only in the eyes of the Lord but also in the eyes of men." [37]

The Modus Operandi of an Apostle

"The Son of Man has come not to be served but to serve...[38]"

Jesus schooled emerging apostolic ministries by the way in which He treated them.

The greatest lesson to be learned must be to discover that true dignity is not found in the eloquence of our words, but in heart expression; in deeds of kindness and respect to others. The apostles must never become too busy to bend and tackle the seemingly small issues or menial tasks.

"Sometimes when I consider what tremendous consequence

---

[35] John 17:8
[36] John 17:12
[37] 2 Corinthians 8:21
[38] Matthew 20:28

comes from little things… I am tempted to think that there are no little things." [39]

The disciples were being schooled for their own emerging apostolic ministry. They could not grasp that the key principle that Jesus operated on was "serving." He did so full of grace and with all humility.

"… so he got up from the meal, took off his outer clothing, and wrapped a towel round his waist. After that, he poured water into a basin and began to wash his disciples' feet, drying them with the towel that was wrapped round him." [40]

Again, this was not just a political maneuvering; it was the driving principle of His ministry. A fundamental requisite for all apostolic and Ephesians 4 ministers is to grasp that they are, above all else, servants. People will soon measure their grasp of this.

"The only measure of what you believe is what you do. If you want to know what people believe, don't read what they write, don't ask them what they believe, just observe what they do." [41]

All ministries, by their very nature, are serving. Apostles are not around to be served; they exist to serve the Lord and His purpose. It is only by this approach that the real resource of God's community will be unlocked. [42]

---

[39] B Barton, *Great-Quotes.com*. Retrieved December 8, 2010, from Great-Quotes.com [www.great-quotes.com/quote/13749]

[40] John 13:4-5

[41] A Montagu *Famous Quotes and Authors.com*. Retrieved December 8, 2010 from [www.famousquotesandauthors.com/keywords/measure_quotes_5.html]

[42] Ephesians 4:11-12

A Corporate Entity

Jesus, having established His ministry, did not operate in isolation. Rather, He developed a meaningful companionship and encouraged dialogue and the sharing of life together with those who were soon to become apostles.

The snapshot of apostolic ministry in Ephesians 4 is also one of an apostolic company and not lone rangers. The advantages of such an operation are:

- Expression of diversity of gifting when it comes to strategic thinking and planning, avoiding sameness.

- It provokes initiative, rather than the stifling of new ideas.

- It avoids lock-up, promoting a greater sense of participation.

People today long to see a true expression of unity of purpose without the common pitfall of uniformity of appearances. We are all His workmanship – created for good works.[43] The word in the Greek for "workmanship" is also the word for "poem" – a poem being a synergy of words, well constructed, flowing in harmony and producing a melodic sound.

The apostolic spirit of Christ will always encourage the valuing of diversity, promoting a fuller expression of His purposes on the earth, and this, coupled with singleness of heart to that purpose, will be our strength.[44]

"The essence of synergy is to value differences – to respect

---

[43] Ephesians 2:10
[44] 1 Corinthians 12:4-7

them, to build on strengths, to compensate for weaknesses." [45]

This is essentially a sound pattern of Christ and believers do well to measure what is apostolic by the example that Christ has set.

---

[45] S. Covey, *The 7 Habits of Highly Effective People Personal Workbook* (New York, Simon and Schuster, 1989) p. 62.

CHAPTER EIGHTEEN

PROPHETIC MINISTRY

Elements of the Prophetic Spirit

There are specific elements that are keenly associated with the activity of the Holy Spirit and they form part of the inner motivations of the prophet.

Conscious Empowerment

The prophet knows when the Spirit of the Lord is dealing with him in a specific way, for example Ezekiel respects the hand of the Lord upon him. Often it is experiential not theoretical. A sharpening of the senses takes place and a keen awareness of the Holy Spirit's presence becomes that much more real.

> "The hand of the LORD was upon me, and he brought me out
> by the Spirit of the LORD and set me in the middle of a valley;
> it was full of bones."[1]

Specific Insights

The Holy Spirit often interprets events and scriptures in a way that the human mind would not consider. Peter discovered this when he was

---

[1] Ezekiel 37:1

relaxing on the rooftop and awaiting his meal. The Holy Spirit spoke to him in a way that his natural inclination would not have seen.

"He became hungry and wanted something to eat, and while the meal was being prepared, he fell into a trance. He saw heaven opened and something like a large sheet being let down to earth by its four corners. It contained all kinds of four-footed animals, as well as reptiles of the earth and birds of the air. Then a voice told him, 'Get up, Peter. Kill and eat.'

"'Surely not, Lord!' Peter replied. 'I have never eaten anything impure or unclean.'

"The voice spoke to him a second time, 'Do not call anything impure that God has made clean.'

"This happened three times, and immediately the sheet was taken back to heaven.

"While Peter was wondering about the meaning of the vision, the men sent by Cornelius found out where Simon's house was and stopped at the gate."[2]

Sense of Earnestness

Soberness, the fear of God, is a very real stimulus when God speaks to a person, even if the word of prophecy or the Spirit's direction is very positive. This brings to the prophet and the prophecy a sense of authority; coupled with the fear of the Lord and accountability to the leadership, this has a very real, sobering effect. The commissioning of Jeremiah is a very good example of this.

---

[2] Acts 10:10-17

The Commissioning of Jeremiah – Jeremiah Ch. 1

There are three elements of the prophetic spirit: the **focus** of the prophet; the **substance** of the Word; and the **passion** of the delivery. These actually empower the prophet to have an appropriate respect for God, and the task entrusted to him/her.

Focus was primary; this can be seen by the repetition of the Lord's questioning of the prophet. For example, the question, "What do you see, Jeremiah?" in verse 11, and again in verse 13, forces Jeremiah to engage with the Lord on the issue, becoming totally clear that he was seeing what God was seeing.

The **substance** or weight of the Word of God was emphasized in verse 7, verse 8, and again in verse 17. The warning was given to Jeremiah not to be afraid of the people or their reaction to the word he would deliver.

Given these challenges, it was of the utmost importance that Jeremiah's **passion** would sustain his ability to deliver the word in the tone prescribed by God, in order to achieve the desired result. He must do so without lacking in confidence or being apologetic for what he is saying.

The messenger becomes aware of the critical nature of God's stirrings.

Focus

This speaks of the ability to highlight or underline, bringing the issues at stake into clear view. For example, compare the use of a macro versus wide-angle camera lens. One captures the whole panoramic view of the horizon, yet the other is able to focus right down to a particular blade of grass.

"Then Peter stood up with the Eleven, raised his voice and addressed the crowd: 'Fellow Jews and all of you who live in

Jerusalem, let me explain this to you; listen carefully to what I say.'"[3]

During a prophetic move of the Spirit which swept across the UK in the early 1970's, it was very noticeable how acute the Holy Spirit's prophetic utterances were in Church life. Especially so in public meetings, where people were enquiring after God and seeking to know what He had to say to the Church. There would frequently be a time rich in prophetic words, which followed those times of enquiry. These meetings were often referred to as "Body meetings" or "Body Ministry." Evidently, the Spirit was bringing a specific focus to the Church. Often directional words, they changed lives, building a commitment in the life of His people.

Conversely, it soon became a "Vogue" happening and, unfortunately, knock-offs began to surface. People would come forward with "prophetic words" in meetings, often unclear, speaking in vague pleasantries or harshly condemning the congregation. It tended to leave people wondering, confused or understandably fearful of some of the manifestations of the Spirit.[4]

Substance

A sense of the weight and substance of the message is important. Such phrases as, "The burden of the Lord..." (OT) or, "This is what the Lord says..." or, "He that has ears to hear, let him hear..." all reflect on the importance of what is being said. It is not superficial, but sets a tone for, and is a vital part of, the total message that God is communicating.

Stephen was substantial in his prophetic perspective on the purposes of God throughout the ages. It was a weighty critique of the current New

---

[3] Acts 2:14
[4] See Acts 7

Testament Church situation, in the context of the ages past.

Passion

Zeal is a vital element to the prophetic. Prophets are borne along by the Spirit. They speak as the Spirit moves them. They are radical and often quite forthright.

It's important to note that the New Testament establishes a turning point in prophetic ministry. John the Baptist was the last of the old order of prophets.

> "I tell you the truth: Among those born of women there has not risen anyone greater than John the Baptist; yet he who is least in the Kingdom of Heaven is greater than he. From the days of John the Baptist until now, the Kingdom of Heaven has been forcefully advancing, and forceful men lay hold of it. For all the prophets and the Law prophesied until John. And if you are willing to accept it, he is the Elijah who was to come. He who has ears, let him hear." [5]

> "The Law and the prophets were proclaimed until John. Since that time, the good news of the Kingdom of God is being preached, and everyone is forcing his way into it." [6]

Something profound happened on the day of Pentecost. It was a hallmark of the Spirit's empowering of people. A multiplication of prophetic utterances took place. Whole Church communities were released in a new understanding and declaration of God's purposes.

In the 1970s, using the word "passion" in Church language was frowned upon. Emotions were considered to be of the devil. The Spirit was

---

[5] Matthew 11:11-15
[6] Luke 16:16

portrayed as anything but passionate. Thankfully, this was to change. When the Spirit of God stirs in the prophetic word, there is a sense in which to remain silent and unmoved would be more unbearable.

> "For we cannot help speaking about what we have seen and heard."[7]

The prophetic ministry was rooted in a prophetic burden. This kind of propensity was to shape the thinking and direction of the Gospel of the Kingdom.

God uses the interactive to grab people's attention, and His people should not be surprised by it.

> "Suddenly a sound like the blowing of a violent wind came from heaven and filled the whole house where they were sitting."[8]

The Holy Spirit and the Prophetic

It is important to establish the crucial place that the Holy Spirit has in the whole interactive realm of the prophetic. It is impossible for a true prophet to accurately operate in the calling of a prophet without the development of a deep and intimate relationship with the Spirit of God.

An understanding of the nature of the Spirit is key. Fellowship with the Holy Spirit is a very real blessing and benefit of the new covenant. Through it, God is able to teach, provoke and inspire His people in His purpose.

---

[7] Acts 4:20
[8] Acts 2:2

God Himself is prophetic – that is, He is a communicator of His divine life and purpose to man.

"...For the testimony of Jesus is the spirit of prophecy."[9]

The Holy Spirit has a prophetic nature, which can be seen by His activity in the world and the Church.

"Concerning this salvation, the prophets, who spoke of the grace that was to come to you, searched intently and with the greatest care, trying to find out the time and circumstances to which the Spirit of Christ in them was pointing when he predicted the sufferings of Christ and the glories that would follow."[10]

The Chief Initiator of the Prophetic is The Holy Spirit

On numerous occasions throughout the Old and New Testaments, the Holy Spirit is the causative factor, or key promoter, of the prophetic. Frequently, the activity of the Spirit is seen as having provoked a prophetic event, demonstration or declaration. For example:

"Then the Lord came down in the cloud and spoke with him, and he took of the Spirit that was on him and put the Spirit on the seventy elders. When the Spirit rested on them, they prophesied, but they did not do so again."[11]

"… you will meet a procession of prophets coming down from the high place with lyres, tambourines, flutes and harps being

---

[9] Revelation 19:10
[10] 1 Peter 1:10-11
[11] Numbers 11:25-26

played before them, and they will be prophesying. The Spirit of the Lord will come upon you in power, and you will prophesy with them; and you will be changed into a different person."[12]

It is the human desire to "control" that often hinders the work of the Holy Spirit. In fact, much activity in the Spirit's name can be more of a soulish engagement. In these biblical references, another dynamic was at work. God was in control, and His workings superseded anything that could have been contrived or controlled by mortal man.

The Era of the Spirit is in Essence the Prophetic

The New Testament introduces the reader to new beginnings and a new era. After 400 years of prophetic silence (referred to as the "inter-testamental period"), the birth of the Messiah and the coming of the Messianic Age produce an outbreak of prophecy.

Gabriel to Zechariah – Luke 1:13

Elizabeth – Luke 1:25

Gabriel to Mary – Luke 1:30-37

Elizabeth – Luke 1:41-45

Mary – Luke 1:46-55

Zechariah – Luke 1:67-79

Angels to Shepherds – Luke 2:8-14

Simeon – Luke 2:25-32

---

[12] 1 Samuel 10:5-6

Moreover, the Spirit specifically initiates these prophecies (see Luke 1:41, 1:67, Luke 2:27).

John the Baptist exercised his prophetic ministry *consistently* full of the Holy Spirit (Luke 1:15). This is in contrast to the prophets in the Old Testament who were *occasionally* filled with the Spirit. Jesus started His ministry in a prophetic fashion, *full* of the Spirit. There was nothing dry or lacking in inspiration or passion when Jesus communicated the Word of God. The result was that He imparted of Himself into people and removed the veil from their eyes.[13]

When the Church age dawned on the day of Pentecost, the era of the Spirit is seen to be the era of the prophetic. Now every believer can be filled with the Spirit and every believer can prophesy.[14]

The Characteristics of the Prophet

1. A Person of the Spirit

There is nothing mystical about such a person. It is a pity that human nature tends to over-emphasize the prophets and distort their role. We have all seen how the imagination can run wild regarding prophecy. Failure to correctly understand this concept will hinder believers from being comfortable with the ministry of the prophet. Over-intensity will frighten individuals away from seeing Christ in the Prophet.

To contemplate this, consider that Christ is the finest example of a prophet. Isaiah referred to Him as a servant, and lists in chapter 42 a

---

[13] Luke 4:1, 14, 18-21
[14] Acts 2:17-18

number of endearing qualities of such a prophet. The chief distinctive is found in verse 1, concerning the activity of the Holy Spirit in His life:

> "Here is my servant, whom I uphold,
>
> my chosen one in whom I delight;
>
> I will put my Spirit on him
>
> and he will bring justice to the nations."[15]

Many prophets in the Bible carried a particular emphasis or unique burden in their ministry. But the common thread in them all is the activity of the Holy Spirit, shaping them and directing them in the divine objective.

> "For prophecy never had its origin in the will of man, but men spoke from God as they were carried along by the Holy Spirit."[16]

Consider the following examples:

Elisha

There was no doubt that Elisha knew the call of God on his life to be a prophet. He was closely mentored by Elijah, the great cornerstone prophet. Yet he was keen to encounter for himself a very real experience of the power and the presence of the Holy Spirit.

> "When they had crossed, Elijah said to Elisha, 'Tell me, what can I do for you before I am taken from you?'
>
> "'Let me inherit a double portion of your Spirit,' Elisha replied."[17]

---

[15] Isaiah 42:1
[16] 2 Peter 1:21
[17] 2 Kings 2:9

Elisha was quite different from Elijah in the outworking of his prophetic ministry. There is room for such diversity in the will of God. The Holy Spirit led Elisha to move in the miraculous and in powerful displays of God's heart to the community.

Ezekiel

> "The hand of the Lord was upon me, and he brought me out by the Spirit of the Lord and set me in the middle of a valley; it was full of bones."[18]

The Spirit initiated this in Ezekiel, broadening his vision and deepening his understanding of what God was doing in his time.

> "The Spirit then lifted me up and took me away, and I went in bitterness and in the anger of my spirit, with the strong hand of the Lord upon me."[19]

There are times when the Holy Spirit overwhelms a person, transporting them to deeper levels of understanding and filling them with deep feelings of empathy with what God is about to accomplish at a given moment.

John the Baptist

> "His father Zechariah was filled with the Holy Spirit and prophesied…"[20]

A great injustice takes place when believers underestimate the crucial role of the Spirit in the life of the prophet and, indeed, in the whole outworking of the prophetic. New Testament believers do not have a monopoly on understanding the activity of the Holy Spirit. The Holy Spirit was at work through a whole line of prophets that preceded Christ.

---

[18] Ezekiel 37:1
[19] Ezekiel 3:14; see also 8:3 and 11:24
[20] Luke 1:67

Remember the prophet Joel who was so eloquently quoted by Peter in the Acts of the Apostles:

> "I will pour out my Spirit upon all flesh, and your sons and your daughters shall prophesy, your old men shall dream dreams, your young men shall see visions."[21]

There is something beautiful about prophetic realities such as these. No one is excluded, whatever their background or gender. It is the desire of God that we see a great synergy of people, working together with the Holy Spirit and all released in the Holy Spirit in prophetic witness.

Illustration

Several years ago, I attended a young prophets' weekend, and arrived as the meeting was already in progress. No one was seated; young people were pressing into God's presence with passion. The Holy Spirit fell on the gathering and a great release was taking place. The Spirit fell on young men and women and they began to prophesy in earnest. It was so powerful that even today those same people will testify to the enduring changes that took place that weekend. They were filled with a real passion for God, stirred in worship and keen to open up to the Spirit's leading. They became deeply sensitized to the Spirit and quick to respond to His voice. A greater appreciation of one another and a mutual respect was a result.

Clearly, the Holy Spirit is able to affect human personality and invest in people great insight, understanding and creative ways of seeing. This is, in fact, what took place at Pentecost. Eyes were opened to see the true nature of God's redemptive acts in the world.

---

[21] Joel 2:28; Acts 2:17-21

2. Sensitivity to the Spirit

It should not be a surprise that the very nature of the Holy Spirit is prophetic. The Spirit of Christ is the Spirit of prophecy. Everyone who develops the gift of prophecy, or who seeks to fulfill the ministry of the prophet, must become sensitive to the stirrings and prompting of the Spirit.

> "In the last days, God says, I will pour out my Spirit on all people. Your sons and daughters will prophesy, your young men will see visions; your old men will dream dreams. Even on My servants, both men and women, I will pour out My Spirit in those days, and they will prophesy."[22]

3. Ability to Confront and Challenge

The prophet must have the ability to call people to attention, to bring focus, a clear sense of God's purpose and the need for a practical response. Boldness is a key requirement for this task. Prophesying calls for the courage to say it as God says it is. This was true for Samuel of old and it certainly proves a necessity for the prophetic declaration of Peter:

> "'Therefore let all Israel be assured of this: God has made this Jesus, whom you crucified, both Lord and Christ.'
>
> "When the people heard this, they were cut to the heart and said to Peter and the other apostles, 'Brothers, what shall we do?'
>
> "Peter replied, 'Repent and be baptized, every one of you, in the name of Jesus Christ for the forgiveness of your sins. And

---

[22] Acts 2:17,18

you will receive the gift of the Holy Spirit. The promise is for you and your children and for all who are far off – for all whom the Lord our God will call.'

"With many other words he warned them; and he pleaded with them, 'Save yourselves from this corrupt generation.' Those who accepted his message were baptized, and about three thousand were added to their number that day."[23]

Prophetic utterance must not be restricted by people's reactions to it. The apostles were not hindered by a fear of the consequences. Whenever confrontation was inevitable, they did not hold back. They feared God rather than man. The fear of God is just as vital today for the proper exercising of the prophetic gift.

4. A Grasp of Current Affairs

There is not any prophet mentioned in the Bible who lacked an understanding of the state of the nation or the politics of the hour.

"Now, brothers, I know that you acted in ignorance, as did your leaders. But this is how God fulfilled what he had foretold through all the prophets, saying that his Christ would suffer. Repent, then, and turn to God, so that your sins may be wiped out, that times of refreshing may come from the Lord, and that he may send the Christ, who has been appointed for you – even Jesus. He must remain in heaven until the time comes for God to restore everything, as he promised long ago through his holy prophets. For Moses said, 'The Lord your God will raise up for you a prophet like

---

[23] Acts 2:36-41

me from among your own people; you must listen to everything he tells you. Anyone who does not listen to him will be completely cut off from among his people.'

"Indeed, all the prophets from Samuel on, as many as have spoken, have foretold these days. And you are heirs of the prophets and of the covenant God made with your fathers. He said to Abraham, 'Through your offspring all peoples on earth will be blessed.' When God raised up his servant, he sent him first to you to bless you by turning each of you from your wicked ways."[24]

Too often, a limited understanding of the prophetic limits prophesying to Church gatherings and meetings. Relegating prophetic ministry solely to words of prophecy severely undervalues its potential to have dramatic life-changing consequences. Prophetic ministry encompasses not only prophecy but also preaching, prayer, acts of service, evangelism and pastoral care. In truth, it affects every aspect of the believer's life and work.

Prophets are made keenly aware of the world around them. They will know the state of the Church within the world; they perceive the moral condition of the nation; they have genuine concern for the plight of the poor and the place given to righteousness and justice.

5. The Precipitator of Decisions

When Agabus spoke, he actually provoked wisdom in the apostles to apply themselves to find a solution to the situation at hand.[25]

The prophetic vision that Peter received from the Holy Spirit

---

[24] Acts 3:17-26
[25] Acts 11:27-30

precipitated a decision and an action on his part. True prophetic ministry is not only enlightening, stimulating and edifying, it is also very practical and often times specific. In a creative way, Agabus illustrates the equipping nature of the prophetic ministry to the Church by challenging the Church to prepare for years of famine ahead, leading to practical action by the Church.

6. A Seer

A prophet must be a seer – able to discern the current situation and what needs to take place to allow progress. They must have a basic grasp of the pattern of the workings of God and His intentions for the times.

God is able to forewarn His people of events about to take place (both crises and opportunities) to help them to be more effective. The prophecy must be clear and not overly ambiguous. It should never leave people puzzled as to what is meant by what has been said.

The prophetic cannot tolerate unreality. Christ shows this in His statement to the Church in the book of Revelation when He said, "you have a reputation of being alive, but you are dead.[26]" His keen eyes were able to bring into focus the real issues at stake and so deliver His people from religiosity, duplicity and frivolity. One of the greatest drawbacks of organized religion of all times is when it silences or marginalizes the prophetic voice.

7. Dramatic and Demonstrative

Agabus is the finest New Testament example of the way in which

---

[26] Revelation 3:1

prophecy comes not just with statements, but also with demonstrations that underscore what God is actually saying to his people. Jesus was similar in the way in which He dealt with those who followed and listened to Him. For example, the little child that He used to emphasize the point about entering into the Kingdom of God.[27] In a similar way, He referred to the image on the coin, "Whose portrait is this?"[28]

Perhaps the most significant demonstration is the breaking of bread, when Jesus took bread and wine.[29] These elements were symbolizing His profound work of redemption. All of these things were clear, demonstrative and illustrative.

An Example of a New Testament Prophet – Agabus

Agabus is referred to in the book of Acts on two occasions.

> "One of them, named Agabus, stood up and through the Spirit predicted that a severe famine would spread over the entire Roman world. (This happened during the reign of Claudius.) The disciples, each according to his ability, decided to provide help for the brothers living in Judea. This they did, sending their gift to the elders by Barnabas and Saul."[30]

The Church was going through considerable persecution and at the same time experiencing revival. Agabus appeared on the scene, bringing to the Church a forewarning of hazard that was about to affect them.

> "After we had been there a number of days, a prophet named

[27] Mark 10:15

[28] Matthew 22:20

[29] Matthew 26:26-29

[30] Acts 11:28-30

Agabus came down from Judea. Coming over to us, he took Paul's belt, tied his own hands and feet with it and said, 'The Holy Spirit says, "In this way the Jews of Jerusalem will bind the owner of this belt and will hand him over to the Gentiles."'

"When we heard this, we and the people there pleaded with Paul not to go up to Jerusalem."[31]

On this occasion Agabus travelled from Jerusalem to Antioch. He clearly had access to the leadership team of the Church and was well respected by them. It seems that he was not a prophet in isolation. He was a man of relationship and that is clearly reflected in the way he is able to associate with Paul and Barnabus, as well as with the brothers in Jerusalem.

In the UK revival in the 1960s, there was a man in the north of England who was known as a prophet. The people were afraid of him. He would turn up unannounced out of seeming isolation and prophesy in the meetings. His voice was like thunder and quite strange. This, sadly, is what made him seem so authentic. It was later discovered that he lived the life of a recluse, had a broken marriage and left disheveled relationships in his wake. He was not accountable to anyone. He was a loner. This is not God's normal requisite for prophetic ministry. It is a grave mistake to restrict any understanding of the prophetic and prophecy into stereotyped images with a "King James accent", rather than studying biblical examples.

The characteristics of Agabus:

- He was known and respected by existing apostles and prophets. He was not an obscure individual, operating independently.

---

[31] Acts 21:10-12

- He worked clearly in conjunction with, and not in isolation from, other Prophets – a team effort to a common purpose.

- He spoke with clarity and authority, and was clearly recognized as being anointed by and sent from God.

- He was a trans-local, itinerant minister. He had a door of acceptance into the different Churches, yet he was considered to be one of the founding members of the Church at Ephesus.

- His prophecies were very practical, inspiring and unambiguous. The style of the prophecies was distinctly graphic, demonstrative and illustrated by drama.

All these elements are clear in Acts 21 where we see an enacting of a prediction over the life of Paul. It came not only to inform him, but also to warn him of the cost of proceeding to Jerusalem. It commanded the attention of the people and gripped their hearts. It carried a sense of the authority of God and the substance of God's heart into a given situation.

The New Testament order of a prophet operated within a team. The team was committed to common objectives with the apostles. Apostles and prophets are referred to in the scriptures as the foundations of the Church, not as the bricks of the building. Harnessed together, apostolic and prophetic ministries can be powerfully effective.

Further Examples of Prophetic Style – The Legacy of the Prophets

Let us look at the various styles characteristic of some of the prophets:

Christ

- *A coin out of the fish's mouth (Matthew 17:27)* - The powerful use of the imagination.

- *A coin bearing Caesar's image (Matthew 22:20)* - The exercise of wisdom in the context of a crisis concerning the affairs of God.

- *A little child put before the people (Matthew 18: 2-4)* - Making use of object lessons and drama to emphasize a critical point and make people take note.

- *The cleansing of the temple (Matthew 21:12-13)* - The discerning element of the prophetic, protecting God's people from compromise and its evil effects.

- *The foot washing (John 13:3-10)* - The ability to impact the individual with truth.

- *The explaining of the new covenant: bread and wine (Luke 22:19-20)* - The use of the symbolic to encourage participation of people with the Divine.

Ezekiel

- *Told to pack his case in front of the people as a sign (Ezekiel 12:3)* - His life becomes the illustration of God's intent.

- *The breaking of the sticks and their blossoming (Ezekiel 7:10)* - The supernatural element of God's intervening brings a sobering awareness into the public proceedings.

Jeremiah

- *Jeremiah was always personally affected by what he had to communicate (Jeremiah 27:1-2)* - He had the ability to draw upon common objects to illustrate spiritual truths.

- *The potter's house (Jeremiah 18:1-10)* - The prophet is taught to observe a very practical illustration of a potter at work to illustrate the divine shaping operation.

- *The almond tree (Jeremiah 1:11)* - Once again, a common sight is used to illustrate a profound statement of the times and seasons under God.

Elijah

- *The sacrifices and the pouring of water on Mount Carmel (1 Kings 18:19-38)* - The provocation of God's powerful presence made manifest.

- *The touching of the mantle. (1 Kings 19:19)* - There is a tremendous effect on the lives of those who are repositioned by prophetic intervention.

- *The call of Elisha (2 Kings 2:8-13)* - He was demonstrative and confrontational.

- "Now Elijah the Tishbite, from Tishbe in Gilead, said to Ahab, 'As the LORD, the God of Israel, lives, whom I serve, there will be neither dew nor rain in the next few years except at my word.'" (1 Kings 17:1).

Peter

The illustration of the clean and the unclean (Acts 10:9) - God prepared Peter, prompting him by the Holy Spirit not to hesitate to visit with Cornelius. The prophet today has to remain teachable and reachable by the Holy Spirit's inspiring as he or she takes on new initiatives and strategies for the advance of the purposes of God.

Agabus

The announcement of famine, the separation of Paul and Barnabas and the binding up of the belt (Acts 11:28, 21:10-11) - Forewarnings have been very crucial in preparing the Church in times of crisis.

The Book of Revelation

Revelation 1:10, 3:22 - The demonstrative way in which God unveils the Christ to John the Apostle in order to address the Churches going through persecutions is full of illustration.

Nathan – A Story Teller

"The LORD sent Nathan to David. When he came to him, he said, 'There were two men in a certain town, one rich and the other poor...'" (2 Samuel 12:1) - This story is a typical prophetic tool for illustration, used to catch the imagination. It was not dissimilar to the method that Jesus used in His time.

Gad - A Strategist

> "Before David got up the next morning, the Word of the LORD had come to Gad the prophet, David's seer..." (2 Samuel 24:11) - Similarly, Jesus conditioned the first apostles on the strategy of the Spirit in Acts 1:8: "But you will receive power when the Holy Spirit comes on you; and you will be my witnesses in Jerusalem, and in all Judea and Samaria, and to the ends of the earth." God is a God of strategy.

Elisha – Remedial Miracles in the Community

- Elisha's example counteracts the notion that to be a prophet is to always be confrontational. Some of the most effective prophets in their time have been deeply compassionate and caring.

- The combination of prophet and shepherd is compatible and we see it clearly in the life of Christ. John the caring apostle also has a sharp prophetic gifting as can be seen by his writings.

Women also played a key role in the activity of prophesying and in the function of prophets.

Miriam

> She carried a significant influence amongst God's people (Exodus 15:21) - She was considered to play an important part in prophetic worship and in the leading of the women in celebration before God.

Deborah

Judges 4:4-10 - Deborah was renowned for her wisdom in counsel and for the discerning nature of her judgment. Her authority was evident to all and she had earned the respect of the people.

Huldah

- "Hilkiah the priest, Ahikam, Acbor, Shaphan and Asaiah went to speak to the Prophetess Huldah, who was the wife of Shallum son of Tikvah, the son of Harhas, keeper of the wardrobe. She lived in Jerusalem, in the Second District." (2 Kings 22:14)

- *2 Chronicles 34:24* - Her contemporaries were Jeremiah and Zephaniah, and she was sought out more than they were. She was the one that the priests and the king consulted to confirm the validity of the scriptures that they had discovered. She gave authorization and confirmed that the discovery was authentic. It resulted in bringing about a revival in the land.

Anna

We find her responding with fervor and prophetic insight at the birth of Christ and His presentation in the temple (Luke 2:36-38) - She was a committed believer of the Messianic promises of God.

Gamaliel – A Secular Prophet

- "But a Pharisee named Gamaliel, a teacher of the law, who was honored by all the people, stood up in the Sanhedrin and ordered that the men be put outside for a little while." (Acts 5:34)

- This man was greatly respected by his peers. He was clearly used by God to speak of what was happening in his time in terms of the moving of the Spirit.

- There is no reference to the conversion of this Pharisee, yet he proved to be a man of great influence in his time. He was considered to be an interpreter of the Law of Moses.

Encountering Prejudice in Ministry

"They replied, 'Are you from Galilee, too? Look into it, and you will find that a prophet does not come out of Galilee.'"[32]

Many misconceptions flourished about prophets in the time of Christ. This is indicated by the remarks recorded in John's gospel. The exasperation felt by the religious hierarchy, which became obvious when under pressure, certainly revealed bigotry, a type of verbal assassination, and an attempt to undermine the validity of the prophetic nature of Christ. The remark made was couched in provincial terms, as if to say, "What does such a 'country boy' know about these things?"

Thank God He never needs to have human approval before choosing to launch His plan, place and choice of personnel! The greatest sadness is not the bigotry of one person, but the apparent blind acceptance by other of their statements without any further enquiry into their validity. It seems that before credibility could be gained, the carnal, natural, religious-minded men had dismissed any sign of promise and branded Jesus as

---

[32] John 7:52

being deceived and a deceiver.

This is not a new phenomenon; it was the same problem that confronted some of the greatest prophets, such as Elijah when addressed by Ahab in 1 Kings 18. Clearly Ahab, and those who had been influenced by him, held a negative view of Elijah. Ahab's greeting to him said more about the condition of Ahab's own wicked heart than about Elijah's ministry:

> "When he saw Elijah, he said to him, 'Is that you, you troubler
> of Israel?'"[33]

Jesus was to encounter this attitude time and time again throughout His ministry, as illustrated in Luke 7:

> "For John the Baptist came neither eating bread nor drinking
> wine, and you say, 'He has a demon.' The Son of Man came
> eating and drinking, and you say, 'Here is a glutton and a
> drunkard, a friend of tax collectors and "sinners".'"[34]

God has never restricted His work to the elite in society. His message and His redemption breaks through all barriers and man-made restrictions: social, political and cultural.

The Subtle Shapers of Public Opinion

In the media craze of the twenty-first century, and with the electronic telepathy of the internet, believers need to be all the more sure of the things that are allowed to influence their understanding. The subtle influences that shape the notions held of one another can rob the blessing

---

[33] 1 Kings 18:17
[34] Luke 7:33-34

and deposit of God. Paul the Apostle determined that he would not relate to people on such a carnal level:

> "So from now on we regard no one from a worldly point of view. Though we once regarded Christ in this way, we do so no longer."[35]

Victims of Prejudice

When it comes to explaining the nature of the prophetic ministry, it is important to take into account the occupational hazard that those such as Jeremiah were warned of. He discovered early in his ministry that he would be subject to criticism, misunderstanding and the mixed motives in the hearts of those that would hear him. He was warned by God never to be threatened or intimidated by such behavior.

> "... 'Do not be afraid of them, for I am with you and will rescue you,' declares the LORD."[36]

> "Get yourself ready! Stand up and say to them whatever I command you. Do not be terrified by them, or I will terrify you before them."[37]

The true victim of prejudice is the perpetrator of it and those who choose to listen to such bigotry.

Substantial prophetic ministry should be of stature and able to impart a faith response in the recipient. The opposite is true of so-called prophecies that are empty and notably subjective. Prophets must be able to deliver

---

[35] 2 Corinthians 5:16

[36] Jeremiah 1:7

[37] Jeremiah 1: 17

their word to kings and to priests. True "prophetic ministry" is not afraid of being scrutinized because all who deliver utterances in God's name must be accountable and therefore responsible for the word that is delivered.

If a person prophesies that the end of the world will take place on a specific date, and that day comes and goes and everything continues as before, then, obviously, that was a false prophecy. Therefore, the same strict assessment should be placed on books, even if (or perhaps especially if) they are considered to be "best-sellers" or sensational and attractive. The question to any discerning believer remains: "What effect does such harmful prophecy have on the Church?"

Too many people have swallowed the spurious and believed the lie. It is time for humility, honesty and a greater degree of reality. There is enough ignorance in the Church concerning prophetic ministry. There is so much propaganda that would deny the existence or inhibit the proper use of prophetic gifting. The Church too easily does injustice to this vital element in teaching and preaching ministries. The scriptures carry a warning to us all not to despise the prophetic.

Honoring the Prophet

In most cases, although prophetic callings, ministries and giftings have often been misunderstood, people in general realize that they carry a sense of awe and fear of God.

It is nothing new that the prophetic word is often immersed in controversy. There is so much to learn about honoring true prophetic ministry.

- It is time to acknowledge the validity of prophetic gifting and calling (1 Thessalonians 5:20).

- Make room for times of prophetic utterance in the gathering of God's people (1 Corinthians 14:4-5).

- Consider and weigh what is being spoken in prophetic ministry (1 Corinthians 14:29).

- Evaluate what steps need to be taken to safeguard the Church from abuse.

- Provide education about the prophetic ministry.

Further Study

Compare the differences that exist between prophetic ministry (Ephesians 4:11-12) and the gift of prophecy (1 Corinthians 12).

CHAPTER NINETEEN

PASTORS – CARING MINISTRY

In many evangelical circles of the Church, the conventional image of pastors is of one elevated to the platform, responsible for the meetings and for the overall wellbeing of the Church community. Consequently, the pastor becomes isolated from the people because he is put on a pedestal. He has soon become the professional teacher, preacher and coordinator of Church life.

The meetings become the priority to him and his chief concern is to satisfy a congregation of listeners. Too frequently, such an elitist approach leads to the pastor being "out of touch" with the day-to-day pressures of ordinary people. These challenges are amplified in the so-called "mega Churches". The pastor becomes the CEO, "the boss" or "the president", with no proper development of true companionship or meaningful sharing of ministry at a team level. In fact, additional ministries are viewed as "staff", who can be hired and fired, and in some cases are required to sign legal contracts and confidentiality agreements.

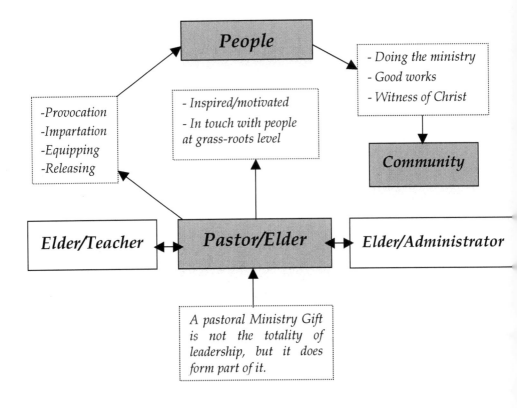

Often, a pastorally gifted ministry with a calling to be part of an eldership in a locality can be viewed as a ministry 'first amongst equals'. Furthermore, an Ephesians 4:11 gifting of pastoral ministry that has not been entrenched[1] can have a far-reaching influence, beyond one single local congregation.

David Hansen refers to the subtle difference between a pastor who loves the dynamic of people and people related events, as opposed to one who has a deep love for people themselves.

---

[1] Exclusively locked into the local

"The two are very different. Love of the experience of people is a form of self-gratification; love of people requires compassion. The word is 'splencha' from which we get 'spleen', which means compassion."[2]

The nurturing pastor/teacher giftings are welded together in the original language and thus we can infer that they are one and the same gift. "Filled with compassion, Jesus reached out His hand and touched the man. 'I am willing,' He said. "Be clean!"[3]

The pastoral ministry is a very special calling, in that it engages people and facilitates an understanding of God in the most practical areas of life. Charles Simpson discusses this topic at length:

"The Bible is a book about God and how He has revealed Himself through the lives of people. God is constantly working faith in human experiences. God does not allow truth to remain abstract or isolated from the every day realities of ordinary people. His care constantly confronts us with truth…"[4]

Four Crucial Areas for Leadership in The Church

The Church is not always pastored (shepherded) well by leadership; one reason for this is that humanistic management techniques have become the order and the sample for modern day pastors at the expense of clear biblical procedure.

---

[2] D. Hansen, *The Art of Pastoring: Ministry Without All the Answers* (Downers Grove, InterVarsity Press, 1994) p. 37

[3] Mark 1:41

[4] C. Simpson, *The Challenge to Care* (Eastbourne, Kingsway, 1988) p. 3

There are requirements and boundaries set for all pastoral leadership in the Church. They are not restrictive, they are liberating. If taken seriously, these principles will restore a proper sense of pastoral leadership in our communities and lessen the amount of "management style".

1   Keeping the objective in view

Leadership in the Church has as its primary function the building up of people into maturity – equipping, enabling and encouraging them in their faith and in active involvement in good works. Programs and planning should take into account the constituency of the Church in terms of age groups, the various ethnicities and the wider community in which the local Church is based.

2   Devoted to the Church

> "Keep watch over yourselves and all the flock of which the Holy Spirit has made you overseers. Be shepherds of the Church of God, which He bought with His own blood."[5]

God's people are very precious to Him. He purchased them with His own blood. People are to be treated with a sacrificial commitment; at any cost we must serve God's people.

> "To the elders among you, I appeal as a fellow elder, a witness of Christ's sufferings and one who also will share in the glory to be revealed: Be shepherds of God's flock that is under your care, serving as overseers – not because you must, but because you are willing, as God wants you to be; not

---

[5] Acts 20:28

greedy for money, but eager to serve."[6]

3   Avoiding a hierarchical approach

Leaders, and pastors in particular, must unlock the ministries in the people and not keep everything locked into themselves. Paul clearly established in his epistles the normal expression of a Spirit-filled Church as one of a people who are actively engaged in the work of the ministry and are playing their part.

> "Now to each one the manifestation of the Spirit is given for the common good… so that there should be no division in the body, but that its parts should have equal concern for each other."[7]

> "Paul the great Church planter taught that there is a wide diversity of gifts and services among the brethren but no sacred clergy."[8]

Referring to the way many Churches operate, Girard states:

> "No one expects much of the lower, or laity caste, except attendance, tithe and testimony. And everyone expects too much of the upper, or clergy caste, including the clergy themselves."[9]

4   Creating and maintaining a dedicated leadership team

---

[6] 1 Peter 5:1-2

[7] 1 Corinthians 12:7, 25

[8] A. Strauch, *Biblical Eldership* (Colorado Springs, Lewis & Roth, 1995) p. 257

[9] R. C. Girard, *Brethren Hang Together* (Grand Rapids, Zondervan, 1949) p. 123

"Paul and Timothy, servants of Christ Jesus, to all the saints in Christ Jesus at Philippi, together with the overseers and deacons."[10]

Throughout the New Testament, an interchangeable term is used to explain the view of leadership that exists in the Church – overseers and elders.

"The reason I left you in Crete was that you might straighten out what was left unfinished and appoint elders in every town, as I directed you. An elder must be blameless, the husband of but one wife, a man whose children believe and are not open to the charge of being wild and disobedient. Since an overseer is entrusted with God's work, he must be blameless – not overbearing, not quick-tempered, not given to drunkenness, not violent, not pursuing dishonest gain."[11]

Leading According to Biblical Patterns

"The word 'leader' does not appear in the gospels. Could it be that leadership has more to do with learning to follow or serve rather than learning to command, supervise or manage? Is it more concerned with right attitudes more than on certain skills? Many of the insights we need are embedded in the images, which Jesus used to describe His followers."[12]

Jesus, in reference to Peter, makes our first introduction to the term pastor/shepherd in the New Testament. The context is very important; it

---

[10] Philippians 1:1

[11] Titus 1:5-7

[12] D. W. Bennett, *Metaphors of Ministry: Biblical Images for Leaders and Followers*, (Grand Rapids, Baker Book House, 1996) p. 11

is in line with his commissioning:

> "When they had finished eating, Jesus said to Simon Peter, "Simon son of John, do you truly love me more than these?" "Yes, Lord," he said, "You know that I love You." Jesus said, "Feed my lambs." Again Jesus said, "Simon son of John, do you truly love me?" He answered, "Yes, Lord, You know that I love You." Jesus said, "Take care of my sheep." The third time He said to him, "Simon son of John, do you love me?" Peter was hurt because Jesus asked him the third time; "Do you love me?" He said, "Lord, You know all things; You know that I love You." Jesus said, "Feed my sheep".[13]

Patterns of New Testament Leadership:

1. Devoted to Christ

2. Motivated by the love of Christ

3. Functional servanthood – not status driven

4. Able to engage the minds of people

5. Imparting an informed faith

6. Open to correction

7. People oriented

8. Team involvement – fostering a sense of society

---

[13] John 21:15-17

1. Devoted to Christ

The first priority for leadership is to be devoted to Christ. All ministries in the Church must find validation, based not on a job description, but rather on a deep and affectionate bonding to Christ. The commission given to Peter was based on a clear foundation of his love for Jesus. This was to be the real motivation of his gift and calling.

2. Motivated by the love of Christ

Paul, the Apostle, was clear that his ministry was constrained by the love of Christ.[14] Exercising influence in the Church must be seen to be more than a hobby or pastime. It is a calling to hard work and sacrifice for Christ and His body. Leadership was only viewed in the context of the people, not as being above the people, therefore any attempt to exalt leaders on a pedestal was not allowed. It is all too easy for leadership to become isolated from and elevated above the people, yet it leads to distancing which, in itself, is harmful.

3. Functional servanthood

Servanthood is what embodies leadership in the Kingdom of God. It is never to be considered as lacking in dignity, given the nature of the One whose house the leaders serve in.

> "But you are not to be called 'Rabbi,' for you have only one Master and you are all brothers. And do not call anyone on earth 'father,' for you have one Father, and He is in heaven. Nor are you to be called 'teacher', for you have one teacher,

---

[14] 2 Corinthians 5:14

the Christ. The greatest among you will be your servant. For whoever exalts himself will be humbled, and whoever humbles himself will be exalted. [15]

The example of servanthood in pastoral leadership is clearly seen in looking at how Christ gave of Himself and invested time to instruct those He cared for. Jesus placed importance on the kind of influence He had on them, not to what position He held over them. This was particularly emphasized when He took the towel and the basin in order to wash the disciples' feet.[16] It certainly was not a public relations stunt, as will be discussed later.

4. Able to engage the minds of the people

The essential goal for Jesus was to influence the thinking process of those under His care. He did so by teaching them on a whole spectrum of life-related issues. He was determined to broaden their thinking, and provoke them to respond to things that He said; i.e. "Who do people say that I am...? What do you say?"[17]

5. Imparting an informed faith

Jesus' aim was to deposit in His disciples an intelligent faith and a confidence in God. He was not committed to making people comfortable, nor indeed did He seek to answer all their doctrinal questions. It was necessary to lead them to a place of faith. He was not spending all His time and energy addressing their souls or their intellect, except as a means

---

[15] Matthew 23: 8-12
[16] John 13:5;13:14
[17] Luke 9:18

to the end of faith. This can be seen by the way he does not answer the disciples' questions on Israel in Acts 1.

6. Open to correction

Jesus was the model for the disciples' humility in leadership, teaching them to receive correction when necessary. He showed them how they should think of themselves once in positions of influence. Jesus, instead of bringing to them teaching on management techniques, taught them how to become humble leaders. This factor is focused upon in epistles such as Philippians.

7. People oriented

Jesus showed that ministry was not task oriented, but people oriented. It was not just about efficiency in getting the job done. It was about possessing the right motivation in order to obtain the desired result. The best example of this can be found in John 17 in the way Jesus expresses His heart to His Father in prayer.

8. Fostering a sense of society

The context of all ministry gifting in the Church, inclusive of pastoral ministry, was one of cooperation and teamwork.

> "It was He who gave some to be apostles, some to be prophets, some to be evangelists, and some to be pastors and teachers, to prepare God's people for works of service, so that the body of Christ may be built up until we all reach unity in the faith and in the knowledge of the Son of God and become

mature, attaining to the whole measure of the fullness of Christ. Then we will no longer be infants, tossed back and forth by the waves, and blown here and there by every wind of teaching and by the cunning and craftiness of men in their deceitful scheming. Instead, speaking the truth in love, we will in all things grow up into Him who is the Head, that is, Christ. From Him the whole body, joined and held together by every supporting ligament, grows and builds itself up in love, as each part does its work." [18]

Pastoral ministry is:

- Meant to be a provocation to others, so that they might be schooled in the Word of God and develop into mature people.

- About assisting others to find their own ministry and calling in life. It is not meant to become the focal point of all ministries.

- About caring, in all aspects of life, for the overall wellbeing of the community of God's people.

- About feeding the flock, so they are well nourished in the Word of God.

The Challenges for Leadership in Relationship-Based Groups

Church groupings that emphasize the importance of relationship and covenant encounter some of the most challenging situations.

---

[18] Ephesians 4:11-16

- Because relationship is important in this context, it calls for a greater degree of time, effort and involvement in engaging with people's lives.

- People's expectations are lifted and they come to expect more from relationships and less from programs, meetings and offerings.

- When relationships break down, as they are prone to do, the effect is far more devastating on all parties concerned.

Pitfalls Needing to be Addressed

- Eldership (leadership) that spends most of its time in planning programs and too little time in oversight of people.

- Elders who are more interested in the development of their own ministry than in the equipping and releasing other people, resulting in people who are unfulfilled or stifled.

- In the delegation of "people care" to house group leadership, eldership often find that the people talk more to their house group leaders than they do to them, resulting in the eldership being out of touch.

- Unavailability of elders who do not seem to have enough time. Some may well be preoccupied with day jobs and overloaded when it comes to their time or energy capacity for the people.

- Elders who see themselves as overseers of the programs rather than overseers of the people. There is a great need to take an interest in the development of people themselves.

- Eldership and leadership teams that are comprised of people who are too similar result in a lack of diversity and challenge among them. This leads to a tendency to make close-minded in decisions, which then creates Churches that become very narrow in their focus and cease to be an accurate representation of the fullness of the Body of Christ.

In an informal review that was undertaken by senior charismatic leaders (including myself), who were practitioners engaged with several new Churches that had mushroomed across the UK in the mid seventies (these Churches were largely meeting in homes and led by non – traditional ministers), there were some very important issues that surfaced.

Among these issues was the fact that people are looking to develop healthy relationships and not just meet for direction and purpose. Also it is not only the ministry gifting, it is the person who is the gift to the Church. He gave gifted *people* to the Church, as elaborated in chapter 4 of Ephesians.

Priorities for Leadership Teams

- They must always operate on the basis of the unity already secured and established in Christ. A lack of unity at eldership level will result in a deterioration of the health of the Church and seriously affect its growth potential, or even its chances for survival.

- A corporate leadership team is best if it includes more than just "elders", and certainly a healthy mix of men and women would add a good dimension to the decision-making machinery.

Too many elders think that they have the monopoly on Church direction. Sadly, too few men have overcome their problems of women in leadership capacity. The term "leadership" is used here to prevent people from having too narrow a definition of oversight. An ineffective leadership is often locked into an elite group, with insufficient exchange on a broader spectrum. It is clear from the story of Mary and Martha that Jesus prized the inclusive approach to men and women.[19] He often enjoyed the company of both genders and provoked discussion on spiritual truths with both.

Adjustments Called for at the Helm of the Church

- Leaders are meant to be custodians and not "control freaks" of God's people. A greater degree of stewardship needs to be practiced, as opposed to ownership.

- Leadership must resolve its insecurities as soon as possible, as the greatest "lock-up" in the advance of the Church is an insecure leadership.

In decades of working with leadership in the Church both in the UK and abroad, I have found that this issue has proved the most crucial/critical to the growth of a healthy Church. There are many ways in which an insecure leadership degenerates into "control freakishness." Here are some very real telltale signs:

- No one is allowed to take initiative without it first being checked out by the leadership.

---

[19] Luke 10: 38-42

- People are only allowed to voice an opinion if it confirms and does not contradict the declared intention of the leader.

- The inability to endorse emerging/changing leadership during their particular season of oversight into a Church or group of Churches.

- Voicing strong disapproval of people who leave the organization, Church, or group, and labeling them as being disloyal to the "God-appointed leadership."

- No accountability in the handling of money for themselves, whilst putting strict accountability on others who are in some way connected to the use of money.

Hallmarks of a Healthy Leadership

1. A leadership that regularly prays together and seeks God's counsel for direction and exposition of His Word to the people.

2. A decisive leadership that is also able to engage with the people and be in grass roots conversations.

3. A leadership that is not secretive but develops openness at all levels of responsibility, so that people can understand where the thinking is at and feel considered and part of the process.

4. A secure leadership that acknowledges problems as well as successes and is not afraid to receive wisdom into a situation from good people in the Church.

5. Large doses of humility should be a daily intake of the leadership, so that pride does not take hold. They must recognize that God's

"best" is not locked into the eldership, so as not to show ignorance of God's gifted people and resources.

6. Leadership must serve the people in the fear of God, and be able and happy to make others look good – quick to identify the gifting of others and their callings in God.

7. A serving oriented, hard working, and diligent leadership, but one that does not have to do everything themselves; instead, they encourage participation and release others to fulfill responsibilities in their own way.

8. This leadership is not controlling or micromanaging people's lives, but is full of faith to release the people, to learn and grow, even from their own mistakes.

Errors to Avoid

Finally, here are some errors for leaders to avoid:

1. Never use the pulpit to belittle others.

2. Shun using words to lock people up in an unhealthy kind of loyalty.

3. Never pull down another in order to pull yourself up in the eyes of others.

4. Never stoop to the discrediting of people who do not fit into your box.

5. Accept the fact that we do not have a monopoly on truth or revelation.

6. Avoid competitiveness at all costs.

7. Allow people to leave the local congregation without suggesting that they have fallen from grace.

CHAPTER TWENTY

ELDERSHIP:
A SEASONED AND MATURE LEADERSHIP

If the whole aim of leadership is to mature God's people, then it is essential that leadership itself is a model of maturity. At the very outset of the discipling process with Jesus, He sought to lead the first apostles into relationship with God and school them in the responsibilities of community, by developing a mature approach to the scriptures.

The very nature of the term 'eldership' suggests a level of maturity in leadership; the elder is no novice. There are certain qualities that stand out in this respect. Let us consider two of them:

1 Quality of Character and Conduct

Essentially, Christ is the model of good leadership. He encapsulates the role of apostle, prophet, pastor and teacher. His character and his maturity exemplify the qualities of leadership that are required.

Fundamentally, New Testament leadership, at whatever level of gifting and calling, demands wisdom and stature, and not just charisma. Again, this quality is best seen in Jesus himself:

"And Jesus grew in wisdom and stature, and in favor with God and men."[1]

Furthermore, a good leader must have the ability to relate to God spiritually and to engage with people in a practical, approachable way. The leader must develop both spiritual and relational intimacy; to neglect either one will have grave consequences.

2 The Corporate Nature of Decision Making

"Then the apostles and elders, with the whole Church, decided to choose some of their own men and send them to Antioch with Paul and Barnabas. They chose Judas (called Barsabbas) and Silas, two men who were leaders among the brothers."[2]

This is a very interesting way to make a decision and it may form a good model of decision making for the Church today. The ruling body of the early Church was a plurality of elders, not all of whom (in the case of the Jerusalem or Antioch assemblies) were made up of local ministers.

Crucially, the corporate nature of eldership has proved to be a safeguard for ministries and Churches. It fosters unity and solidarity in leadership and prevents isolation and division. Indeed, the fact that the disciples were sent out in pairs on a mission illustrates the importance of companionship and counsel in leadership.

---

[1] Luke 2:52
[2] Acts 15:22

Relational Leadership in the Kingdom of God

Leadership is a relational word. One cannot be a leader theoretically; it requires practical responsibility. The fact that leadership in the New Testament placed its focus on relationship with Christ is of huge significance. It was not an over-structured hierarchy that had no allowance for flexibility as the work expanded. If it had been hierarchical, it would have worked the Church into a "Jewishness" - an inflexible wineskin, a structure lacking fluidity. As it was, the Holy Spirit needed to burst the Jewish wineskin of hierarchy, and so the Church was given a relational, apostolic leadership.

The Apostolic Nature of the Church & the Fivefold Ministries

One of the most illustrative passages on the apostolic nature of the Church is found in Ephesians 4. We cannot read Ephesians without seeing that the Apostle Paul is more concerned about 'connected living', than he is about a theoretical correctness.[3] This sense of connectedness can be seen to have two dimensions: being connected to God and being connected to each other.

His involvement with the Church in Ephesus was a very personal one and went back many years; Ephesians is a letter that is wrapped up in relationship. Indeed, he was writing to a community he knew from its very beginning, some of whose members he had baptised himself.

This is the context in which he makes mention of the Ascension gifts of Christ to his Church. These gifts are not a list of abstract titles, they relate

---

[3] Refer also to Acts 19 for a grasp of just how much the apostle Paul values the Church.

to the personal and the real - the various strengths and qualities entrusted to real people to add to the wellbeing of the Church of Christ as a whole.

Apostles, Prophets, Evangelists, Pastors & Teachers

When Jesus ascended (Ephesians) he gave gifted ministries to the Church as gifts of his ascension: Apostles, Prophets, Evangelists Pastors and Teachers. These ascension gifts of Christ mark the filling full of the victorious ministry of Christ. The ascended Christ secured the basis of the wellbeing of the Church by the giving to the Church of these ascension gifts, for the spiritual development in the equipping, repairing of the Church community.[4]

Collaboration with the ascended Christ is the least believers can do. The emphasis is on the fact that it was Christ who, in his victorious ascension, saw fit to strengthen the Church by the provision of the five-fold ministries. Collaboration calls for the Church, to this day, to respect the wisdom of this provision of Christ. Furthermore, it is incumbent on us that we continue to recognise the validity of these ministries and work with them in the edifying of the Church.

These ministries are the Apostles, Prophets, Evangelists, Pastors/Teachers.

The fact that these giftings are so different is important. One of the notable benefits of such diverse ministries at work in the Church is the cross-pollination of the gifting and graces.

As James Fredericks famously stated: 'Much of the vitality in a

---

[4] A medical term 'repairing' is used here to mean the setting of the joints of the body of Christ back in place for the work of the ministry.

friendship lies in the honouring of differences, not simply in the enjoyment of similarities.'[5]

From the very outset of the ministry of John the Baptist, through to the ministry of the great Apostle Jesus Christ, the Kingdom rule of God was the primary message. This was no less the case in the Church that was established after the coming of the Holy Spirit at Pentecost to those first Apostolic communities. The Kingdom of God and the Local Church ought to be the focus of all sound apostolic endeavour.

There is no particular order of priority given to the spiritual gifts in Romans 12. Yet in 1 Corinthians 12:28 there is a definite ranking of Church leadership positions as follows:

First	-	Apostles
Second	-	Prophets
Third	-	Pastor/Teachers

Finally, there are those with gifts of healing, miracles etc. (there is no order of priority within this last grouping).

Apostles

A large number of evangelical Christians grew believing that there were only twelve apostles, yet there are at least sixteen people referred to as apostles in the New Testament. Paul saw himself in his own words as an apostle born out of time. Barnabas is also named as an apostle and Epaphroditus in Philippians 2:25.

What do we mean by an apostle? First and foremost, they were

---

[5] J. Fredericks, 2013

Christ's provision for the equipping of the Church. Furthermore, an apostle ought to be considered as someone possessing a good dimension of wisdom. A wise master-builder is the term that the Apostle Paul used in 1 Corinthians 3:10.

> 'By the grace God has given me, I laid a foundation as a wise builder, and someone else is building on it. But each one should build with care.'

We have derived the word 'architect' from this word. Apostles ought to be the pioneers of communities who are characterized by their missional outlook. Apostolic ministries are primarily concerned with the wellbeing of Churches, setting them into good order when and where required.

Peter was a fisherman. He drew in nets with 3,000 fish for the Lord at Pentecost. John was mending nets when Jesus called him. In John's writings He seems to fill in the gaps that the other New Testament writers have left, so enabling us to grasp some of the most sublime truths about the redemption Christ has given us. There are things in John's Gospel that simply do not appear anywhere else (not to mention the book of Revelation!). Paul was a manufacturer and an 'architect' of tents. In his subsequent ministry he becomes a craftsman of the Word of God and an architect giving shape to and forming the Church.

Such ministries had a broader perspective of Church. They carried a considerable responsibility in forming the truth on which the Church was founded.

Yet the ministry of the apostle is still crucial to the Church today. The term "apostolic ministry" would not have been used fifty years ago, and is only seldom used today. The term itself has often been considered taboo. However, its popularity is on the increase, particularly in Charismatic and Pentecostal Churches. In truth, there have always been ministries in the

Church that are, by nature, 'apostolic', but it is only more recently that they have been labeled as such.

Prophets

These were the seers in the Old Testament; they saw the need and purpose of God. They were the men God used in relation to that need and God would open the eyes of the soul, for the prophet to see. The prophet would often seek out God's direction for the people and, in times of trouble, Israel would turn to the prophet for guidance.

Nathan is a great example of such a man. God showed him the detail regarding David's life and actions. God revealed to Nathan His displeasure with David and Nathan arrested the heart of David with this personal revelation; a revelation that saw David adjust his ways.

The ministry of the prophet in the Church (like that of the apostle) comes with a strategic gifting. As in the Old Testament, the prophet of the New seeks God's guidance and direction for the people. For example, the prophet Agabus was used, along with others, in helping the apostolic community to strategize concerning the future.

Teachers

Teachers nurtured the people in the growth of their understanding of God's Word. In this way the teachers saw the people being shaped into the temple of God. Like the ministries of the apostles and prophets, the ministry of the teacher was to be held in high esteem. They were entrusted as stewards of the revelation of God's Word, yet they needed to be held accountable by other ministries for the integrity of their teaching.

Elders and Deacons

Acts 20:28 refers to the elders as 'Shepherds' of the Church - the overseers of the flock. In the passage Paul is departing from Ephesus and knows he will not likely see them again. He secured the future of the Church there by entrusting the care of the flock to its elders.

Not all elders are pastors. Some were apostles, prophets, and teachers. Peter, for example, was considered to be an elder in his apostolic ministry. When the challenge concerning the tradition of circumcision arose between the Jewish and Gentile believers, it was the apostles and elders who came together to discuss the problem.[6] They sent out the prophets Silas and Judas to help deal with the situation, so we know that prophets were also in the eldership.

In truth eldership in general terms embraces all the ministries, and this is demonstrated throughout the New Testament. For example:

- In Philippians 1:1 apostles, prophets, elders are included as part of the oversight.
- Acts 20 suggests that the other ministries are part of the eldership.
- In Acts 13, prophets and teachers comprised part of the Church oversight as they sent Paul and Barnabas out.

The role of the deacon is quite different to that of the elder. Nowhere in the New Testament do the deacons govern the Church. Overseers'-elders govern the Church. The deacons were chosen to meet a need and would govern the task given to them. When the task was completed, and they were no longer needed they were released from their duty.

---

[6] Acts 15

This dynamic is clearly demonstrated in Acts 6, in which deacons were chosen to meet a particular need – handing out the food. The situation developed from a complaint regarding how the food was being distributed unevenly and the Hellenist widows were missing out as a result (yes there were complaints even in the early Church!) This was a source of tension between the Hebrews and the Hellenists and it was clear action needed to be taken. The apostles could not stop teaching God's Word in order to serve food, so instead seven men 'of good repute'[7], deacons, were recruited to see to it that the food was distributed more fairly. In verse 6, the apostles laid hands on them. The beginning and the end of the process was handled with their oversight.

So we can see how it started with a particular area of need: they needed people to do the job of seeing to the widow's needs. The apostles decided the deacons were needed to meet this need. Because of the sensitivity of this particular job the deacons had to be of good repute and acceptable to the crowd. And so we can see how deacons function: meeting needs within the Church as and when they arrive by the direction of the eldership.

The Meaning of Eldership

Most translations of the Bible do maintain the integrity of the text when it comes to establishing the primary function of eldership, which is to rule. But it is to rule in a way that requires diligence, care and skillfulness in the life of the leader rather than ruling in a domineering, controlling or stifling way. A wise elder is one who helps people to mature and not one who locks people into himself.

---

[7] Acts 6:13

Eldership is translated as:

King James	-	The rule over
Amplified	-	Spiritual leaders
NASB	-	Leaders
NIV	-	Leaders
Revised Version	-	Rule over

There are two Greek words used interchangeably in the New Testament that are crucial when it comes to understanding the nature of eldership. They are:

Episkopos - "This group of words is formed from the root *skep-* with the prefix *epi* and denotes the activity of looking at or paying attention to a person or thing. *Skipeo* (Goal, *skopos*) suggests the continuing recurring character of such action, while *episkeptomai* suggests an act that is complete in itself. The verbs can mean to observe, review (Xen., Anab., 2,3,2), superintend (Plato, Rep., 6, 506 B), watch over, scrutinize (Xen., Mem,. I 6,4) and also inspect, examine (Xen., Mem., 3,2,10)."[8]

Presbuteros - "is found in the New Testament in three senses, in the Synoptic Gospels, and at the beginning and end of Acts the same is used of the lay members of the Sanhedrin. In the central portion of Acts, the Pastoral Epistles, Jas. 5:14, and the salutations in 2 and 3 John, the Christian Elder is meant. The

---

[8] C. Brown, *The New International Dictionary of New Testament Theology*, (Grand Rapids, Zondervan, 1986) p. 188

expression *presbyteroi* in the same context to describe the men who exercised leadership in the Christian Church at Jerusalem on the Jewish synagogue pattern (Acts 11:30; cf. 21:18). On the analogy of the Sanhedrin this presupposes a *gerousia*, council of Elders, in which the leading role is played by the *apostoloi* (apostles). Both are mentioned together in Acts 15:2,4,6,22 f. and 16:4. By adopting this term, Luke enabled the continuity between the Old Covenant and the New to find expression in the structure of the Church. He uses the term in describing the Pauline Churches (cf. the travel narrative, Acts 14:23, and the mention of Elders from Ephesus, Acts 20:17). By the time of the composition of Acts it is clear that the Pauline Churches of Asia Minor had adopted the 'Presbyterian' system of government."[9]

The Nature of Eldership

Shepherding entails an element of rulership; bringing the government of God to bear in the issues of the Church. The shepherd brings **decision** where there is **indecision; resolution** where there is **irresolution; clarity** where there is **confusion; order** where there is **disorder; conclusion** to **longstanding issues.**

An elder is not an elder if he is not 'eldering'. If the man of the house is weak and does not discipline his children it is not long before his children call the tune. When elders stop ruling, the Church will call the tune. This is the biggest failing in the Church across the country today: elders are not eldering. This is when Satan takes advantage. It is to the benefit of all for

---

[9] Ibid

the elders to rule well.

However, when the father who has not disciplined his children suddenly takes action, it could be that the child who has been used to calling the tune will leave home. When we try to bring order to the Church, some will leave. Be prepared to lose half of the Church community or more. Yet we must bring order to the house, we must embrace this.

In Titus 3:10 Paul writes: "Reject a factious man after a first and second warning." Here, Paul is asserting the need to rule in a decisive way. If there is a troublesome individual, Paul says, warn him. And if he continues, warn him again. If he still continues, then you reject him.

This is not harsh. Difficult individuals must repent or be put out by the judgment rule of the eldership. Either that or we will lose the whole Church. Rule must take place, with righteous judgment.

Yet the elders are not only rulers but also overseers, watching over the Church. They must, for example, observe how the people respond to the Word when it is taught. When the people are hungry for God they need to be given more. If they are puzzled, the Word needs to be explained to them in a more digestible form.

Furthermore they must 'guard the flock of God, of which He has made you overseers'.[10] Elders are not to simply oversee the meetings, but also people's lives. They must be actively concerned with seeing the people flourish in their walk with God.

Quite simply, elders are leaders. It was Jesus who said, 'the sheep hear my voice. A stranger they will not follow'.[11] A leader should lead by

---

[10] Acts 20:28
[11] John 10:5

example. Paul's exhortation to the Church was for them to remember his own character and practice in life and ministry. His life was a clear example and the embodiment of what He taught. 'The elder must be apt to teach.' The people will give an account to God of your eldership, of how the flock was handled, the people entrusted to you by Christ.

A Clear Commission

In the New Testament, leaders chosen to take responsibility for God's people had to meet certain requirements. The first apostles were "well-groomed" in terms of their own commissioning. They needed to be clear regarding several things that would fit them for the cause of apostolic leadership.

You would not invite yourself into the role of apostle. It was not a "take it or leave it" position, or something that you could do as a hobby or a "fill-in". The earliest disciples were called out of successful careers into their primary calling – to serve the Master Himself. Their commission was first and foremost to follow Jesus – "Follow me and I will make you…"

Throughout their time with Him, Jesus' main focus was on His own relationship with the Father. This can be seen in:

- How He sought instruction;[12]

- His dependence on daily prayer and reflection;[13]

- His readiness to do what was required of Him from Heaven.[14]

Jesus led the disciples by example. He taught them to avoid becoming

---

[12] John 17:8

[13] Mark 6:46; Luke 9:28

[14] John 5:19

preoccupied with the task at hand, but instead to focus wholly on their relationship with God. This required spiritual discipline and Jesus instructed them to:

- Withdraw into the quiet;[15]

- Wait upon God in prayer;

- Relate to others in the community.

He stressed that their leadership would only be effective if they were willing to be led by Him: "Apart from me you can do nothing…"[16] And it was by Christ's authority that their commission was blessed: "As the Father has sent me, so I send you…"[17]

The Apostle Paul saw the importance of this and was determined to establish that his commissioning came from God and not from other men. The task of all leadership is to recognize those whom God has commissioned.

There can be many different kinds of apostles, depending on the nature of the commissioning. In 2 Corinthians 10:13-15, Paul seems to suggest that the nature of a person's calling to leadership is unique to them and may be quite different to that of another. Not all leaders are meant to have the same roles or act in the same way. Paul's remarks in this respect show how important it is to understand the different measures of gift or calling that exist in our ministry as leaders. He writes:

> "We, however, will not boast beyond proper limits, but will confine our boasting to the field God has assigned to us, a field that reaches even to you. We are not going too far in our

---

[15] Mark 6:30-32

[16] John 15:5

[17] John 20:21

boasting, as would be the case if we had not come to you, for we did get as far as you with the gospel of Christ. Neither do we go beyond our limits by boasting of work done by others. Our hope is that, as your faith continues to grow, our area of activity among you will greatly expand."[18]

To be truly effective, apostles must be able to communicate clearly, and without apology, what their particular commissioning is about. Yet it is shortsighted to put individuals into boxes, to label them simply as 'leaders', and not allow for the development of their unique gifting and measures.

We must recognize that 'commissions' change, as do the seasons of their fulfillment. Peter's early ministry was wholly concentrated on the Jewish Diaspora. Later he found himself commissioned by the Spirit to pave the way for the gospel to go to the Gentiles also. The Holy Spirit was clearly in the driving seat with Peter, monitoring the momentum of the gospel in its spread to the whole world and directing him in his ministry.

Apostles, Prophets and Elders – A Strategic Partnership

We see in the New Testament that apostolic and prophetic ministries had a role of strategic oversight regarding the work of the Kingdom and the spread of the gospel. These ministries helped to establish the Church on a sound theological basis. Yet they were also very much active in the local Church, such as at Ephesus in the book of Acts.

Judas and Silas were such men who were considered prophets and

---

[18] 2 Corinthians 10:13-15

who travelled far afield, but also carried government within the Church.[11] Judas and Silas were senior elders: chief among the brethren. The same word used to describe "leading" or "chief" is used in Hebrews:

> "Remember your leaders, who spoke the Word of God to you. Consider the outcome of their way of life and imitate their faith. Obey your leaders and submit to their authority. They keep watch over you as men who must give an account. Obey them so that their work will be a joy, not a burden, for that would be of no advantage to you. Greet all your leaders and all God's people. Those from Italy send you their greetings..."[19]

The partnership between elders and apostles is of critical importance. It will only function if all parties work with respect for one another and an openness and flexibility to adjust to changing circumstances.

Consider Peter's approach in speaking with elders – he saw himself as "a partner in the purpose":

> "To the elders among you, I appeal as a fellow elder, a witness of Christ's sufferings and one who also will share in the glory to be revealed."[20]

The term 'partner' suggests mutual respect and cooperation. In addressing the Church Paul also appealed to the local Church to honor and respect the other ministries that came amongst them from time to time.

> "So if you consider me a partner, welcome him as you would

---

[19] Acts 15:22

[20] 1 Peter 5:1

welcome me."[21]

Paul shows this same respect in the way he speaks to the Churches. Writing to the Church at Corinth, where he had been required to intervene quite strongly, Paul speaks, not in a domineering way, but in a way that promotes a corporate and mutual respect. Paul never commanded the Churches, except the ones he had founded, as a 'master - builder' himself, but he visited counseled and strategized with others. Every decision comes out of consultation, not dictation.

"As God's fellow workers we urge you not to receive God's grace in vain."[22]

The key emphasis here is upon the sense of shared responsibility in the endeavor of establishing the Church and preaching the gospel.

So does every Church require apostles and prophets besides the pastors and deacons? Quite simply: YES. Apostles and prophets pioneered the Church. The Church came to exist because of Paul's apostolic ministry.

The Nature of the Church – Questions that Arise

1. Why should the Church not be institutionalized?

2. What is the nature of the Church and its relation to the apostolic and prophetic ministries?

3. What are the practical effects of such a community in a local, trans-local, or international setting? What are the benefits? What are the demands?

---

[21] Philemon 1:17

[22] 2 Corinthians 6:1. See also Acts 16:4, 40 and Titus 2:7-8

4.   What should the role of eldership be in the 21st century Church?

How to Distinguish a Healthy Church

In today's world, leading Churches and engaging in the nurturing of faith and the maturing of the saints is not an easy task. In fact, society has grown increasingly sophisticated and hostile to the spiritual life. People seem starved of time and simply lack the inclination to seriously pursue spiritual formation. The role of the oversight of the Church is a demanding one and the equipping of Church leaders for the task does not come easy.

Nevertheless, the Church remains a vital part of society. In every sense it is there for the public benefit. In the metaphorical language of biblical literature, each believer in Christ is considered to be as salt, light and leaven to the world with which they interact on a day-to-day basis. Contrary to what some may think, this interaction with the demanding affairs of real life ought to result in the development of a robust and attractive Church.

The ascension gift ministries flowing together in cooperation with the Holy Spirit and each other produce some of the clear hallmarks of a healthy Church. In the context of community, there are several such hallmarks that should distinguish a healthy Church community in our world. These hallmarks assist us in our attempts to work towards a healthy Church expression in today's world. They are:

Compassion for People

Compassion is crucial for all of us. It is not so much found in what we do, but is an automatic expression of who we are. A life lived without compassion is a life denuded of its true calling and its humanity.

The Spirit calls us higher into a true expression of Christ in us: compassionate and caring. This is what was evidenced in the apostolic community that we have read about. Yet we live in a world filled with a sentiment that is quite opposed to the work of the Spirit in us, where compassion is rejected. The Church is to be an example, in this context, of a compassionate community.

Companionship - A Shared Life

The people ought to have a deep sense of being joined together. A healthy Church is to be a wholesome community of believers. People need to know a sense of security. If people are perceived as just a number, attendees at an event, then they will be unfulfilled and underdeveloped in their spiritual life. Congregations are of course important yet community puts the greater emphasis on the expression of the Kingdom of God both within the local Church and beyond.

There is something deeply profound that takes place in an authentic community. Its members are not just attached to one another, they are deeply joined.

They have shared life together with all that that implies. There is no room for competitiveness or selfishness. The Spirit is liberating and deepening, and the Spirit brings a sense of meaningfulness.

It is not about becoming attached; it is far more profound than that.

Consider the graces that Paul refers to in the opening of Ephesians 4; all of which accentuate our humanity. This is the primary concern of the apostolic heart. He highlights four graces that we must be encouraged to flesh out in our relationships.[23] These are humility, gentleness, patience and tolerance or forbearance in love.

The duality of revelation wrapped up in relationship is the apostolic exhortation. Spirituality to be real, must not escape humanity but rather enrich it. Jesus said the way to the Father is not through a methodology, it is through a relationship.

The Love of God is Visibly Expressed in the Church

A clear expression of this level of relationship in the Church is found in Luke's description of a community of Christians in Acts 2:42-47. What is striking here is their genuine commitment to one another. This was no small achievement, as the natural tendency of the people would have been to be preoccupied with their own survival. Yet their spirituality expressed itself in a generosity of heart and a mutual appreciation of their common humanity which transcended selfishness and distrust. Their relationships with one another brought about a sense of 'belonging'; it felt like it was good to come home to the family.

In verse 45 we read that they sold their excess property (though not their own homes), giving the proceeds to those who needed it. Such tangible expressions of love remain as an inspiration to all of us who follow in their footsteps. We are reminded that we are the Church and we are a living community. If we are not measuring up, we each must examine ourselves and ask the question, "Is my heart a caring heart – do I

---

[23] Ephesians 4:2

look for ways to express God's love to others? Am I being what I expect of the Church?"

One should also consider whether or not, there is a clear sense of his Holy Spirit at work in provoking a serving heart in the core activities of the Church. Or as the case may often be, the congregation as a whole rely on the same few people to keep the community operational. The danger for smaller Churches in particular is that the Church leaders end up being the only ones who will rearrange the furniture, tidy the facility and host events.

Tangible expressions of the grace of God at work are worth considering:

These elements were modeled for the early Church by the servanthood nature of its leadership and Jesus exemplified the same, by his own life and ministry. He was a person in authority, yet a true servant. One who was not obsessed with status, nor diminished by having such a serving outlook in life. Jesus washed his disciple's feet and said, "I your Lord and Master, do this". This was the first time Jesus called himself 'Lord and Master' because He emphasized His authority by serving their needs.

When the river of the Spirit washes over us, soaks us, so that we are wet through and through (anointed), our lives are changed. We can no longer live for ourselves, nor can we do things simply out of a sense of duty. We are debtors to mercy and grace, and we become devoted, willing servants of the purposes of the Kingdom of God. This is truly regal: that we should stoop and consider working for the betterment of one another.

The Church does not exist just for the benefit of itself; it is there to affect the wider community. The Church is always in a context and the Church must always seek to affect its context. The message we proclaim must itself find its outworking in the local, regional, national and international. It is the incarnational, living, active aspect of the Kingdom that is important, rather than the theory.

This was at the heart of the burden of apostolic ministry. It sought, in line with the ascension of Christ, to establish groups of believers with a keen sense of the Kingdom agenda of God for their generation. Hence throughout Ephesians and in other scriptures the Church is referred to as the body of Christ with its many members.

Acts 2:42-47 gives an eloquent summary of the kind of community that the Holy Spirit nurtures in line with the sovereignty of Christ and the outworking of the Kingdom of God. The people were gripped by the importance of the Kingdom; its fire had caught their hearts, unlocking in each of them an expression of devotion to the apostolic teaching and a generosity of heart to each other and to the work of God.

Their commitment to the cause of Christ and his Lordship was consistent. It was quite clearly sustained by the outworking and dealings of the Holy Spirit in their lives.

Admittedly, when it comes to commitment there are those who behave as if they are nomadic Christians, with no real sense of loyalty or responsibility in the Church community. These people are not so concerned about being 'joined' to the Church; they simply attend its meetings. They are often more interested in what the Church can do for them than they are in what they can do for the good of the Church community as a whole.

Some Church gatherings foster this kind of culture, often lacking deeper and more meaningful relationships and failing to lead people to a place of maturity. There is a lack of a sense of family.

In such instances, the leadership is often wrongfully taught to keep a distance from the flock, and to preserve their sense of being one step removed from the parishioner, so to speak.

The Global Church

Yet a Church's commitment is not just to the local, but also to the global. The local Church is also part of the universal; we are members of one large family, joined together as the body of Christ. This is a wonderful accomplishment of the grace of God at work on an international scale. Yet, this does not diminish the Church's design as a grass roots movement, which relates on a local level.

This has practical benefits for the believer in Christ. A healthy apostolic expression of Church consists of people who are able to share a common experience, a subculture, a day-to-day living of life with a local expression and testimony. This is a people with a vision to reach the nations near or far and with a passion for the spread of the Kingdom by the aid of the Holy Spirit.

Such times are to be prized, when the Holy Spirit is at work strengthening the Church and enlarging the mind of its leaders so that they do not become trapped in a small, parochial mindset but buy into the Kingdom vision beyond the local.

Generous Giving

In his epistles John makes clear how important hospitality and generosity within the Church community is for the spread of the gospel. It was this spirit of generosity that He appealed to when He instructed the Church to play its part in the spread of the influence of the message. In particular He instructed the believers to support in tangible ways the messengers, and ministries who, for the sake of the Kingdom, travelled far and wide to spread the good news.[24]

> "...If we believe that God has given everything, then giving will be our way of living."[25]

We are called upon to use our own wherewithal and resources for the common good of others and especially the household of faith. 'Do good to all men especially the household of faith'.

What motivates our giving to God and to each other? We ought not to give with a sense of compulsion, as this contaminates the gift itself. Legalism should not be the reason for our giving and nor should we be influenced by the expectations of others.

This is most shockingly illustrated in the story of Ananias and Sapphira, as seen in Acts 5:5. They claimed to be giving more than they were in order to impress and gain recognition in the community, yet their

---

[24] 3 John 1
[25] M. Volf, *Free of Charge* (Grand Rapids, Zondervan, 2006) p. 89

selfishness was punished most severely and their deceit lives on in infamy. Clearly it would have been better for Ananias and Sapphira not to give at all than to give with these motives.

At the same time, we must not hold back in the sharing of our lives and our substance in the Church. The Church should be marked by a generosity that is in stark contrast to the selfishness of the world. As Eugene Peterson writes:

> "One of the supreme ironies of [the age] is that the society that has talked and written most about the fulfillment of the self shows the least evidence of it. People obsessed with the cultivation of the self, the good life, the abundant life, have little to show for it but a cult of selfishness."[26]

Coordinated, generous giving without ulterior motives and super glue attached is vital to the life of the Church. It is essential that Church members have a heart to give of themselves for the community and are able to fully trust their giving to the financial oversight of the eldership.

Passion in the Church

For many of my earlier years as a Christian I found from firsthand experience, that Evangelical Churches downgraded feeling, saying, "we walk by Faith, not by sight!" and, " We must detach ourselves from emotions for they will cause us to be diminished in our Christian development". This sort of Stoic, stiff upper lip was the order of the day.

There is a sense in which emotions must find expression without causing people to be too subjective in their Christian walk. Yet, clearly, we

---

[26] E, Peterson, *Leap Over the Wall* (Harper Collins, 1997) p. 110

see on several occasions in the Gospels that Jesus was able to express his emotions. His humanity had texture to it, and was a part of who He really was. It endeared him to his followers, they could identify with the genuineness of his testimony. If we are encouraged never to have feelings we would be less than real. What a sad state of affairs we would find ourselves in: frustrated and boring.

Thank God for our emotions: where would we be without joy? It is the means of our true strength and the texture of a healthy human soul.

Yet, there are extremes out there in the Church community. There are often immature Christians who create problems for the Church with their excessive desire for experiences, without ever seeking the guidance of the Word. They are ever in search of a novel experience and new ways to tap into the things of God, as if God can be manipulated by our schemes and methodologies to give out rewards. These people are often deluded, professing to have an inside track on other believers, a sort of elite bunch with a special kind of anointing. They eventually become like floating debris on the tides of trends and fashions.

Conviction of the Holy Spirit

The community is launched into a lifelong relationship with the Holy Spirit and with each other. And one of the chief characteristics of the Holy Spirit is his work of convicting. He brings judgments that result in a change of belief. Indeed, there is nothing clouded or uncertain about the direction of the Holy Spirit. This was certainly the case in Peter's sermon earlier on and even more so in the story of Ananias and Sapphira.

In contrast, we would tend to err on the side of ambiguity and play the power of clear conviction down. We are too often afraid of upsetting one another and we can fail to confront wrongful behavior and attitudes. For this reason, we need to embrace the Spirit of wisdom, boldness and courage.

Furthermore, we need to cultivate a respect for the Spirit. Ephesians 4:30 reads:

> 'And do not grieve the Holy Spirit of God, with whom you were sealed for the day of redemption'.

How our belief is reflected in our behaviour is crucial to the integrity of the person of the Holy Spirit. Our conduct towards each other and our confession is indicative of our respect of God's presence within us and toward each other.

Clearly the recognition, and understanding of and the cooperation with the voice and direction of the Holy Spirit is crucial to every believer and furthermore to every Church community.

A Deep Sense of the Fear of God in the Gathering

Fear in this respect, is closer to the word 'reverence'. A sober respect for the things of God is a wholesome and a healthy disposition to have.

God's presence is not only to bless and to heal but is also to bring the judgment fire – the wrath of God on unrighteousness. The fear of God in the gathering keeps the Church blessed and pure. We cannot help but ask the question: do we walk in the holy fear of the Lord?

We looked earlier at the story of Ananias and Sapphira in Acts 5. In verses 5 and 11 Luke describes a 'great fear' coming upon the Church and all who heard of what happened. What if God did this today to all who pretend that they are what they are not? Ananias was unrighteous in heart.

Have we bypassed the judgment of God?

One of the evidences of respect for God is a hunger for his Word - to be taught of the Lord. This hunger can conquer our short attention spans and cause us to not only hear the Word but to be transformed by the Holy Spirit's application of it into our daily living.

The Tangible Presence of God

The presence of God heavily resting on the gathering, the Glory of God filling the house inspires a sense of awe, respect, concentration and response. These are crucial indicators of whether or not the gathered Church give due respect to the Lord.

It is a telling thing to be in a meeting that is meant to invite God's presence yet is marked by his absence.

The manifest presence of God makes all the difference in a meeting.

Meetings can run like clockwork, streamlined and well choreographed, with beautiful singing and good preaching, yet all the while, in the heart there is something missing.

That 'something missing', is often the tangible presence/fear/glory of God. Nothing can fill the absence of God's presence. Things can go wrong in a meeting - a guitar can go out of tune with the piano, a preacher can lose his notes - but the presence of God will make up for every deficiency.

Visible Evidences of the Life of God in the Gathering

This is not just the evidence of the nine gifts described in 1 Corinthians

12:8-10, but also of helpers, cheerful givers, administrators, and so on.[27] Each person must take their place of responsibility within the community in order to serve God's purpose for their lives.

1. God's life gives flow to worship:

Bright chorus sessions are not necessarily worship, nor is worship just an introduction to a meeting. We receive the Word from God but God receives Worship from us. He wants us to worship Him in Spirit and in truth.

God *needs* us to respond to Him as He responds to us. He loves us and we love Him back in response. The worshipping of God is the responsive aspect of His Spirit working in us. Sometimes we express this worship in a chorus, at other times our Spirit just wants to say things to God that we can't express and we just cry. Sometimes we sing in tongues – bringing blessing to our souls as God receives our worship.

Oftentimes attempts are made to make too many things happen in the gathered Church. Sundays may provide a window in on the life of the Church, but is hardly the place to try to accommodate every person's desire to reach the microphone.

2. New Birth:

Another aspect of the visible flow of life is that people will be born again simply by entering into the presence of real worship or because they have been caught by the testimony of a Christian. The Holy Spirit may deeply touch a person's heart in these seemingly ordinary elements of a Church

---

[27] See Romans 12

meeting as well as in the spectacular.

3. Clear Expression of Giving of Finances:

Once again, a Church's giving provides a good pulse check of its spiritual wellbeing. The chief characteristic of Christians ought to be generosity in all respects, and in the giving of finances particularly.

      i)   Tithe – giving back what is owed.

      ii)   Offering – giving begins here out of what is left.

      iii)   Creative Giving – to one another as the need arises.

Obedience isn't the only important quality in this matter. There must also be faith: a condition of the heart regarding the giving of finance to the work of the Lord. We must believe God in our giving.

Concluding Remarks

The Church is about heart and soul dynamics. Such an authentic community as this is the product of the Spirit that is engaging the Church and strengthening its members. The person and the work of the Spirit is transformational: the Holy Spirit brings about a dynamic that enriches the heart and energizes the devotion of the people. There is no limit to the possibilities available for a community baptized in and motivated by the Holy Spirit.

There are so many elements to the enhancing of leadership, which remain intimately involved with the person of the Holy Spirit. Particular among these is the discernment of the true heart and nature of issues and problems within the flock of God whom they oversee. This discernment is more crucial than ever in today's society: a society that has come loose of its moral moorings on issues of sexuality and the like.

The Church is a community finding itself increasingly marginalized in a supposedly 'pluralistic' society. Discernment and wisdom are the attributes that we need to engage in helping the community of believers to know where to draw the line, without itself becoming judgmental.

One thing is certain: we are not left alone. We have everything we need to make us Godly and fit for purpose as we continue to play our part in influencing the way people think, live and, not least, view God.

EPILOGUE

A CHURCH IN HIDING – IS ANYBODY THERE?

There are very real dilemmas that face the Christian community in its attempt to be relevant and the problems that have plagued the Church for centuries are no less real for it today. Consider the challenges presented by a so-called 'politically correct' world. Our modern society often seeks to tame the more extreme prejudices that flare up in the Church from time to time, often resulting in the suppressing of legitimate expressions, moral concerns and sound spiritual principles. In truth, the Church that is truly able to follow the ethics of Jesus would soon discover that it is no more tolerated in society than he was.

The Church can (and often does) react to this by seeking to popularize the Christian community. It is an old mistake to believe that somehow the Church must become glossy and glittery in order to attract outsiders, all to satisfy our desire for popularity. Sometimes there is a cringe-factor; when Christians do take the chance to speak up or produce programmes for televising, one cringes at what is often passed off as a good witness.

Surely, the Church does need to make full use of technology, music and arts - without question it should. Indeed, a person in our society would struggle to know what the Church is; its lack of visibility in the wider community is partly to blame. But it must never sell its soul in the process of trying to promote itself.

At the other end of the spectrum, the Church can react by curling up into its cozy meetings and withdrawing from active engagement with the wider community of which it is a part. Yet this clearly contradicts the prayer of Jesus recorded in John 17:

> 'I pray, not that you take them out of the world, but that you keep them in the world...'

The Church has to take its rightful place within the wider community and its individual members need to be equipped for the real world. The world is poorer for the lack of Christians who truly engage with it.

It is no farce to raise this matter because there are those who teach that engagement with the world is to be discouraged. This only serves to highlight the need for more sound teaching and a better grasp of what the Bible means by 'worldliness'. I have often stated in leadership forums about the disproportionate time we give to planning meetings for the converted, in contrast with the amount of time we give to training people to play an important part in the real world.

No longer should there be the question – 'where is the Church?' The Church has to become more accessible to the outside world because, in reality, it is the most attractive community that there is. In the words of Brennan Manning in his book *The Signature of Jesus*:

> "The greatest need for our time is for the Church to become what it has seldom been: the body of Christ with its face to the world, loving others, regardless of religion or culture, pouring itself out in a life of service, offering hope to a frightened world, and presenting itself as a real alternative to the existing arrangement."[1]

---

[1] B. Manning, *The Signature of Jesus* (Colorado Springs, Multnomah Books, 2004) pp. 9-10

Index

elder 48, 52, 85, 116, 133, 163, 199, 210, 218, 235, 245, 260, 262, 264, 270-2, 277-8, 284-9, 291-2

eldership 207, 209-10, 214, 219, 260, 263, 270-1, 274, 277-8, 284-9, 294, 301

Elijah 233, 238-9, 249, 254

Elisha 238-9, 249, 251

empowerment 5, 8, 73, 83, 89, 95-6, 99, 101, 103, 114-5, 117, 119, 122, 127, 129, 133, 169, 177, 203, 223, 229, 231, 233

Ephesians 11, 73, 76, 90-1, 94, 174, 190, 203-4, 207, 210, 222, 225-6, 257, 260, 269, 271, 279-80, 296, 298, 303

eschatology 45, 68, 75, 91, 167

Eucharist, the (see: communion)

evangelical 13, 259, 281, 301

evangelism 97, 113, 149, 157, 193, 198, 203, 243, 268, 280

Ezekiel 16-7, 66, 77, 92-3, 229, 239, 248

faith 13, 15, 19, 24-7, 31, 52, 57, 65, 67, 73, 79, 81, 89, 99, 106-7, 112, 119, 129, 130, 134, 148, 161, 165, 171, 178-9, 190-1, 197, 209, 255, 261-2, 265, 267-8, 274, 291-2, 294, 300-1, 306

faithful 18, 26-7, 35-6, 40, 43, 45, 47, 49, 62, 66, 78, 101, 189, 195

family 12-3, 19, 23-4, 28, 48-9, 141, 162, 173, 175, 215, 296, 299, 303

fatherhood 13, 19, 23, 25, 27-8, 31, 45-46, 61, 98, 102, 104, 106, 127, 130, 135, 150, 187, 215, 221, 223, 239, 243, 266, 268, 288-90, 293, 296

fellowship 11-4, 21, 23, 32, 37-8, 83-5, 90, 109-10, 112, 129, 195, 206, 218, 234

finance 48, 197, 301, 306

forgiveness 16-8, 38, 66, 76, 241

Galatians 11-2, 14, 27, 85, 103-4, 121, 179, 181, 187, 195, 200, 206, 211, 213

generosity 135, 141, 181, 189, 196, 202, 296, 298, 300-1, 303, 306

Genesis 19-28, 49, 51, 119

gentiles 27, 64, 75, 78-9, 84, 86-9, 100, 118, 140, 142, 153-4, 156, 161, 164-5, 171, 173, 180, 182, 199-200, 205-6, 213, 218, 246, 284, 291

gifting 100, 151, 181-2, 185-6, 191-3, 199, 202, 210, 215, 223, 226, 251, 256-7, 260-1, 268, 271, 274, 277, 280, 283, 291

gifts 13, 21, 35, 37, 40, 72, 76, 85, 88, 90, 101, 115, 119, 135, 141, 145, 174, 176-7, 181-2, 190, 198, 204, 210, 241-2, 245, 257, 260-1, 263, 266, 271, 279-1, 290, 294, 300, 304

giving 30, 33, 35, 43, 51, 53, 130, 187, 280, 282, 296-7, 300-1, 303, 306 godliness 46, 136, 221, 307

Gospel, the 68-9, 80-1, 86-7, 96, 100, 102-3, 111, 115, 121, 127, 137-40, 142, 150, 153-9, 161-4, 169-71, 173, 175-6, 178, 180, 182-3, 191-2, 198-201, 205-8, 211, 213, 218, 234, 253, 282, 291, 293, 300

government 85, 120, 125, 155, 176, 178, 201, 284, 287, 292

grace 13, 15, 20, 25, 36-8, 40, 47, 56, 61, 69-70, 72, 76, 140, 162, 165-6, 204, 206, 209, 225, 235, 275, 282, 293, 297-9, 303

healing 66, 79, 81, 97, 100, 116-7, 129-30, 155, 189, 204, 281, 303

heaven 68, 81-3, 91, 93, 95, 106, 115, 125-6, 130, 134, 142, 230, 233-4, 242, 266, 289, 293

Hebrew 10, 14, 16, 49, 121, 137, 148, 216

Hebrews, Epistle to the 17-8, 30, 38, 40, 43, 45, 70-1, 73, 93, 121, 137, 285, 292

Hellenist 137, 285

Holy Spirit, the 8, 57, 77, 81, 83-4, 86, 93, 95-7, 99-106, 108, 114-8, 120, 122-4, 126-9, 131, 133, 135, 139-41, 145-55, 157-9, 162, 167, 169-70, 180-1, 185, 190, 199-200, 205, 215, 218, 229-30, 232, 234-43, 246, 250-1, 262, 279, 281, 291, 294, 297-300, 302-6

hope 8, 21, 26, 30, 45, 49, 57-8, 60, 64, 66-7, 74, 78, 80, 82, 92, 96, 100-1, 108, 122, 130, 165-6, 177, 191, 203, 209, 291, 309

hospitality 173, 300

humanity 68, 72, 76, 120, 142, 295-6, 302-3

humility 130, 183, 225, 256, 268, 273, 296

integrity 135, 161, 163-4, 176, 283, 285, 303

Isaiah 16, 57, 61, 66, 68, 75, 77, 79, 87, 94, 139, 179, 237, 238

Israel 10, 16-8, 25, 28, 31-6, 39-41, 43-54, 56-7, 60, 62, 64-7, 69- 71, 76-9, 81-3, 86, 88-9, 92, 94, 111, 127, 218, 241, 249, 254, 268, 283

Israelites 30-3, 36-7, 41, 49, 60-1

James 157, 179, 195, 199, 205-6, 211

James, Epistle of 13, 27, 211

Jesus 8, 11-3, 17, 22, 25-7, 34-7, 41-2, 57-9, 66-9, 71-3, 76-84, 87, 88-91, 93-110, 112, 115-22, 124-8, 130, 132-41, 145, 147-8, 152, 155, 158, 161, 164-71, 173, 175-9, 183, 185-90, 192-5, 198-9, 201-6, 209, 213, 215-27, 235-9, 241-5, 248, 250-5, 260-72, 277-82, 288-309, 312, 315

Jewish 15, 20, 58, 65, 77, 79, 85-7, 96-7, 118, 121, 138, 141-2, 156, 166, 171, 180-2, 199-200, 205, 216, 218, 279, 284, 287, 291

John, Epistles of 173, 178, 211, 300

John, Gospel of 12, 26-7, 31, 35-7, 68-9, 76, 90, 93, 102, 106-8, 115-6, 127, 133, 138, 147, 168, 175, 194, 221-5, 248, 253, 267-8, 282, 288-90, 309

John, the Apostle 134, 200, 205-6, 208, 211, 250-1, 282, 300

Kingdom of God, the 25, 35, 49, 51-7, 66-71, 75-84, 92-3, 101-4, 108, 110, 114, 117, 119, 121-2, 124-7, 130-5, 139-40, 142, 162, 166-7, 179-80, 185, 189, 191, 193, 198-201, 205, 215, 218, 233-4, 245, 266, 279, 281, 291, 295, 298-300, 303

Kings, 1 & 2 45, 47, 54-6, 60, 238, 249, 252, 254

Lamb of God 42, 72-3, 76, 93, 95, 202, 219

law 13, 16, 30, 33, 35-6, 41, 45, 49, 52, 57-8, 61-2, 70-1, 75-6, 81, 86-7, 104, 118, 156, 182, 233, 252-3

leadership 5, 8, 40, 47, 50, 51, 53, 85, 123, 136, 137, 141, 147, 149, 157-8, 170, 176, 179, 182, 185, 188, 191, 193-5, 197-8, 201-2, 205, 208-9, 212-5, 220, 230, 246, 260-74, 277-9, 281, 287, 289-90, 293, 297, 299, 303, 306, 309

legalism 76, 182, 223, 300

Leviticus 35-9, 47, 49, 70

love 11, 12, 16, 25, 28, 36, 46, 49, 62, 76, 84, 94-5, 108, 132, 175, 177, 222, 260-1, 265-6, 269, 296-7, 303, 305

Luke, Gospel of 37, 77-8, 81, 98, 110-1, 113, 119, 132, 179, 188, 192, 220, 233, 236-7, 239, 248, 252, 254, 267, 272, 278, 289

Luke, the Apostle 77, 122-4, 128, 130-1, 137, 138, 142, 161, 168, 287, 296, 303

Mark, Gospel of 36, 41, 57, 68, 75-6, 114, 188-9, 217, 245, 261, 289-90

Mark, the Apostle 182, 200

Matthew, Gospel of 25, 27, 41-3, 49, 66, 68-9, 71, 78-81, 93-4, 106, 108, 110, 113, 136, 138, 179, 186, 188, 192, 217-8, 224, 233, 245, 248, 267

Messiah 51, 57-8, 66-7, 77, 89, 100, 236

ministry 12, 69, 82, 91, 95, 103, 119, 137, 142, 145, 147-8, 151, 160, 164, 176-7, 179, 182-3, 185, 188-91, 195-200, 202-13, 215, 219-22, 225-6, 229, 232-4, 237-9, 241, 243-4, 246, 253-7, 259-61, 263-4, 266, 268-71, 280-4, 289-91, 293, 297-8, 303

mission 69, 77, 79, 84, 97, 99, 102, 106, 108-9, 115, 124, 152, 157, 162, 174, 185, 192, 195, 201, 203, 207, 217-8, 278

money 135, 187, 197, 207, 263, 273

Psalms 57-8, 79-80, 92-3, 125, 134, 179, 317

Printed in Great Britain
by Amazon